AMERICA DISCOVERS COLUMBUS

CLAUDIA L. BUSHMAN

AMERICA DISCOVERS COLUMBUS

How An Italian Explorer Became

An American Hero

UNIVERSITY PRESS OF NEW ENGLAND

Hanover and London

University Press of New England, Hanover, NH 03755
© 1992 by Claudia L. Bushman
Printed in the United States of America 5 4 3 2 1
CIP data appear at the end of the book

Frontispiece: The invented Christopher Columbus, etched by Leopold Flameng, in the heroic style of Washington Irving. Critic Néstor Ponce de León complained in his book, *The Columbus Gallery*, 1893, that "a mere glance shows that this tall commanding man with the plumed cap, cuirass and cloak with loose sleeves, his hand on the hilt of the sword, is some condottiere of the 16th or 17th centuries." Picture from Marquis August de Belloy, *The Life of Columbus*, 1885.

FOR RICHARD L. BUSHMAN

unus erat mundus,
duo sint ait iste; fuere

The world was one, let it be two, said he, and it was so.

Posterity is sometimes more just to the memory of great
men than contemporaries were to their persons. But
even this consolation, if it be one, has been wanting
to the discoverer of our hemisphere.

Joel Barlow, *The Columbiad,* 1807

CONTENTS

This book on the commemoration of Columbus grew out of my work on another commemoration—that of the ratification of the United States Constitution. I was director of the Delaware Heritage Commission, a state agency that planned and coordinated commemorative activities during the years that marked the two hundredth anniversary of the creation of the Constitution of the United States. Delaware's claim as "The First State" is based on being the first to ratify that important document, making 7 December 1787 a particularly important date in the state's history.

Commemorating the Constitution meant conjuring up ways to bring that valued, but distant, document into the consciousness of the citizenry. With the help of the national commission, the state, and many agencies and individuals, our commission instigated every program we could think of, replaying historical events, awarding scholarships, granting matching funds for programs and building restorations, creating and disseminating posters, publishing out-of-print materials, producing films and concerts. We recreated the tavern where the Constitution of the United States was first ratified and sponsored the Great Bicentennial Ladybug Launch, to bring the state insect into the celebration.

As a historian, I enjoyed researching the events of the past and recreating them for commemorative purposes. We transported our delegates to the Annapolis Convention and replayed the election riots, as well as drafting current state legislators to reratify the Constitution. We inaugurated President Washington. Besides that, we researched commemorations of the past and recreated those.

During this last activity, I began to take seriously the ephemera of past celebrations: the programs with their toasts, odes, and banquets;

the parades with their banners and floats; the orations with their rhetoric and selected information. These documents spoke about the time
of celebration as well as about the event being celebrated. I came to
realize that there is not only a history of the event, but a history of
noting the historical event.

These manifestations of homage to an historical event turn out to
be more powerful in shaping the conscious memories of the public
than was the event itself. The public reads the newspaper and attends
celebrations rather than study the history. The people who plan the
celebrations have custody of the popular image of the historical event.
Their packaging of the activity becomes the conscious reality. Their
activities pass into history just as the significant events they have commemorated did.

Before leaving Delaware, I was involved in preliminary plans for
commemorating the five hundredth anniversary of the first landfall of
Christopher Columbus, the first major quincentenary to be noted in
the United States. I spent some time on committees there, thinking up
programs to dramatize the event. After I moved to New York, I discovered that the subject was retaining my interest. I would find myself
near Columbia University, a few blocks from Columbus Avenue, and
regularly frequenting Columbus Circle. There was no escape from the
mariner.

One day I wondered how people in the past had noted anniversaries
of the first landfall. I spent a few hours at the New-York Historical
Society and discovered that the story was better than I had expected.
Columbus was virtually ignored in the early colonies. But the time
arrived when his legacy became useful to the revolutionary nation,
whereupon he was reconstructed for American purposes and adopted
into the American pantheon of heroes. His voyage into the hearts and
minds of patriotic Americans does not seem to have been contrived
by promoters; he was wholeheartedly adopted because of a series of
circumstances in the nation's history. Tracing the developments of his
appropriation as an American symbol has been an absorbing pleasure.

The illustrations that are so much a part of the Columbus legend
have been collected from many sources. I have primarily looked for
pictures created or used in the United States in the eighteenth and
nineteenth centuries. Some of these came from the artists' imaginations; others were adapted for this country from European models or
used in contemporary books available here. The aim has been to select
images that indicate some of the ways Columbus was presented to the
American public. I have appreciated the help of curators at all the
institutions credited. Many more American Columbian images could
be added to these.

Although descriptions of the admiral were written by those who knew him, no visual likeness remains. Owners of many European portraits of Columbus have claimed that their pictures were painted from life, but those claims were largely dismissed in 1892 when the paintings were submitted to rigorous scrutiny. Images of Columbus vary widely, and some critics deplore the license that artists have used to depart from the conventional tall, grave Italian with the prematurely grey hair. Even so, there are generally enough clues to make him recognizable.

I began this project in all innocence, ignorant of the vast body of material that has been written on Columbus. Everyone has had something to say on the subject, and new sources have continually turned up. Even limited to works in English, mostly published in the United States, and primarily in the eighteenth and early nineteenth centuries, the materials available could float three small ships. The bulk of these sources plus the relative obscurity of many of them required that this book be suggestive rather than comprehensive. I have tried to trace the trends rather than consider all the sources.

I have received considerable help and encouragement on this project. Greatest thanks go to Richard Bushman who has supported this project emotionally and financially, as well as serving as a resident advisor on the eighteenth century. I would also like to recognize the help in various ways of Nancy Roelker, Joanna Bowen Gillespie, Justene Mataleno, David D. Hall, Sarah Goldstein, Jean Bingham, Anne Paolucci, Dennis Laurie, Irene Q. Brown, Leo Lemay, and Laurel Thatcher Ulrich.

In researching this book, it has been a pleasure to browse alongside so many first-rate minds, through rare and forgotten tomes, in libraries where such volumes are guarded and protected. I feel fortunate to have read books and discovered information unknown to other living people. I have used the resources of the New-York Historical Society, the New York Public Library, Butler and Avery libraries at Columbia University, and occasionally the Library of Congress. I also want to acknowledge the support of generous grants made to me by the American Antiquarian Society and the Huntington Library. I am very grateful to these admirable institutions for maintaining and sharing their rich collections of materials and for their helpful staffs and pleasant working places.

Along the way, someone asked me what contemporary person Columbus is comparable to. I was stumped in coming up with anyone who combined the imagination, the practical skill, the good fortune, and the force of will to equal the old admiral. My best answer is to compare Columbus to the man who conceived the atomic bomb, designed it and worked out the bugs, loaded it on an airplane, climbed into the cockpit, flew across the ocean, and dropped it. The analogy is far from perfect, for the bomb was developed and deployed by many hands and moved along by people who knew exactly what they were doing. Still, the combination of the imaginative and the practical, the ability to take a small action with vast and immeasurable consequences for good and ill, seems apt to me. And, after all, Columbus was headed for Japan, or Cipangu at least.

Columbus, the accidental voyageur to our land, has been with us in song and story for many years. He is among the richest of American symbols, involked for widely varying purposes. We reinvent him every time we need another symbol. We are now reinventing him for the twenty-first century.

New York, N.Y.   C. L. B.
May 1991

CHAPTER ONE

The Admiral at Five Hundred

Ring out, my soul,
And celebrate fulfillment, O my spirit!
For on this morning, on the grey horizon,
There loomed an island fringed with leafing palms
Which in the growing light
Were interspersed with many flowering trees
Of gold and scarlet blossom,
And all surrounded by a sparkling beach
On which the gentle breakers splash and gurgle.

Fostor Provost, *Columbus Dream and Act* 1986

The voyages of Christopher Columbus changed the face of the earth, bringing together the New World and the Old World, for good or ill, in a connection never to be broken. Columbus began a new era in history. He is considered to be the founder of the America that exists today, even though he never set foot on the North American continent. Honored for his navigational achievements, Columbus and his personal story, with its theme of dogged perseverance, has been incorporated into the myth of the nation.

Yet, commemoration of Columbus in America was a late eighteenth-century phenomenon. Like the mythical New World itself, the idea of Columbus lay fallow for a long time, covered over with clouds, waiting to be discovered. Additional voyages, conquests, settlements, and the growth of little colonies on the eastern seaboard of North America all passed into history before much notice was taken there of the bold Genoese explorer or the poetic form of his name, which should have identified the world he claimed. What Americans have thought about Columbus and how he became an American hero, beginning some three hundred years after the first landfall and continuing through the nineteenth century when he was firmly established as a presence in the American imagination, make up the subject of this book.

The questions guiding the work have been about what people knew of the Columbus that sailed into national consciousness, what they said about him, what he symbolized, and how his myth has grown. Since the subject is the American discovery of Columbus, most of the sources considered were written in English and were available to people living in this country. Columbus as he was understood in America is at some distance from the actual explorer, and perceptions and myths are as important here as facts. Much written material, the histories, the poetry, the published orations, the books for children, and the accounts

Constance Del Vecchio Maltese painted Columbus in 1989 as the first in a series of sixteen portraits of explorers. Discovering that no one had painted a likeness from life, she used the description by his son Ferdinand—"He was a fine figure of a man, blond, blue eyed, and turned completely grey in his mid-thirties"—as the basis for choosing a model. Her Columbus is a "young, virile, strong-jawed Ligurian who could relate to twentieth century imagery." By permission of the artist.

of celebrations and descriptions of monuments, was shaped by the patriotic and revolutionary spirit of the emerging United States. Columbus was created as a historical and symbolic personage along with the new nation.

What could Americans have known about Columbus historically? He himself wrote an account of his first voyage, and his son Ferdinand wrote his father's biography. Bartolomé de Las Casas, a friend and priest who lived in the New World colonies with Columbus, wrote an account of his experiences. Documentation existed, but only gradually were materials translated into English and transported across the seas. While the earliest documents were slowly being made available, brief English accounts began to tell his story, emphasizing his role in the spread of Christianity. Somewhat later indigenous American publications began to describe the feats of the admiral, but they characterized Columbus as a foreign explorer, not as the European who laid the groundwork for the colonies. Chapter 2 traces his development from one among a number of Spanish explorers to his recognition as a peculiarly American figure.

The North American colonists considered Great Britain their home and Britannia their mother. This relationship changed as tensions between England and her colonies led to war. The colonists needed a tradition that bypassed Great Britain, and they needed a name that would bind them into a group. These elements they found in the story of Columbus and in the poetic form of his name, Columbia. Chapter 3 tells how the Revolution changed the colonies from New Albion, suggesting a junior status or subjugation, to Columbia, suggesting equality.

Poets found in Columbus a metaphor for the new nation. In his tale of adventure, in the heroism of a man in pursuit of a vision shared by no one else, Columbus gave courage to generations of outsiders. He served as the courier leading America into her place in the Grand Design of western culture and world history. He was also the tragic, mistreated visionary whose actions brought sorrow to pristine lands. As told in chapter 4, both views have been part of the American poetic record since the eighteenth century.

In 1792, after the new nation was established, the three hundredth anniversary of the landfall was commemorated. The leaders of the events were learned, antiquarian, and verbal New Yorkers and Bostonians who recognized the occasion with orations, monuments, odes, and parades. Although we commemorate other holidays by giving presents, sending cards, eating traditional foods, or setting off fireworks, the original Columbian ceremonies, as described in chapter 5, are still with us.

Samuel F. B. Morse, noted American artist and inventor, painted this portrait of Columbus in 1828 on a commission by the Common Council for the City of New York. He was paid $90.50 for this portrait based on a 1650 copy of a 1592 painting. A thoughtful Columbus holding a compass turns from Europe and gazes into space. Courtesy Collection of the City of New York, City Hall, Governor's Room; photograph courtesy of the Art Commission of the City of New York.

The Columbian legend has dwelt most securely in the literature written for schools. This moral and adventurous model led directly to the detailed biography by Washington Irving, which firmly installed the admiral on the American scene as a heroic presence. This famous account and the books leading up to it are described in chapter 6.

The heritage of the Irving biography was seen in extravagant representations of the mariner in literature, art, and history. Yet, even as he was praised, an ambivalent note was sounded. Most historians honored Columbus while they questioned sources and debated fine points, but the dark side was never totally out of sight. Chapter 7 describes the lofty artistic and literary images that were created and the devastating criticisms leveled.

In 1892, Columbus was honored as the noble discoverer and founder of a New World, the harbinger of progress. The Columbian Exposition in Chicago celebrated success in his name. Chicago itself, the world's newest cultural capital, seemed an achievement in the spirit of the explorer. New York City staged five days of celebration, and other cities dedicated monuments and organized parades. State and national holidays for Columbus Day followed. Veneration for Columbus reached its apogee in the celebrations described in chapter 8.

Together, these chapters tell an interesting story that reveals the world of the early nation in a new way. But this story is only one of the many possible stories that could be told. Some of the facts about Columbus continue to be debated, while some pieces gradually fall into place, yielding many possibilities for discussion. The true story continues to take shape. Even more interesting is the secondary Columbian record, which includes commentary, perceptions, and interpretations, rich and various, always producing something new and unexpected. This material suggests many other stories that should be told. One story would be about how Columbus should have failed, and how he probably did.

The Failure

> The idea of a chance discovery of the American continent not only cancels Columbus' personal purposes and opinions as inoperative, but also turns him into a docile and blind instrument, no longer of some assumed designs of historical progress.
>
> Edmundo O'Gorman, *The Invention of America*, 1961

Columbus was a great seaman who made a magnificent error. He did not know where he was going, and he had no reliable guidance. By the time of his first voyage, people knew that the world was round, but they had not yet set off westward into the unknown. Columbus persuaded himself that the distance between the Azores and Japan was only one-quarter of the actual mileage. This faulty image of the world prevented him from succeeding according to his plan, for his imagined earth had a circumference of just three-quarters the size of the real one. Something was across the waters, but he was wrong about what and where it was. If the New World had not been in his way, Columbus would have perished, for his ships could never have carried supplies far enough to reach the Indies. Everyone would have starved, or Columbus would have been tossed overboard so that his crews could return home. Because of his mistaken conceptions about the globe, when he arrived at the New World, he did not know where he was. He could not reconcile the new place with his expectations, but he could not accept that where he had gotten to was different than the place he had intended to go.

Columbus envisioned the New World from within his European framework. He claimed already inhabited lands for Spain, enacting European rituals. New World gold would enrich his sovereigns, and he promised them too much. In spite of his amazing results, he could not produce the riches he was eager to display. He severely punished the native population in his attempt to produce the gold and to bring the two worlds into line. Columbus, who aimed above all to please his sovereigns, alienated them. Trying to bring honor to Europe by despoiling the new land, he managed only his own disgrace. He lost the honors of the Old World as the privileges the monarchs had promised him were withdrawn.

But he never felt at home in the New World he explored. His experiences cut him off from his homeland without making a place for him in the New World. He was the first alienated American—lost and never found. Though driven to search the west, he never truly left Europe. He could not understand his mistreatment when he felt that he had behaved honorably. Often portrayed as a visionary, Columbus remained stuck fast to the past.

Columbus treasured his mistreatment. After his sovereigns, somewhat inadvertently, replaced him as the leader of his colony and brought him home from his third voyage in chains, he always carried his fetters with him and ordered them buried with him as a bitter reminder. He wore out his final years plying Ferdinand with petition after petition, demanding the punishment of his oppressors and the restitution of all the privileges bestowed upon him by the capitulation of 1492. He felt himself, a great servant of God, betrayed by enemies on all sides. Columbus died a disappointed man, once again sure that he was right and everyone else wrong.

A leader with his drama and vision should have inspired his men to follow him anywhere; they were used to taking orders and should have worshipped him. But they did not. His voyages were rife with mutinous conflict. He kept his own counsels, misleading others, sacrificing them to his cause. He was as stubborn as he was single-minded, a frightening man, driven by his demons.

He spent his life following a vision real only to him. He sailed on where others would have turned back; he sacrificed everything to his cause. In doing so, he wrested success from likely failure, and he made the impossible easy for those who came after him. His solemnity and ceremony imbued a significant event with martial pomp and religious music, suitable myth and color. His stubborn loneliness led him to actions that changed the world.

Perhaps it is unfair to require that all men who make major contributions to society be kindly and generous, that all men who accomplish heroic deeds be heroes themselves. The need to make a great

This severe and monumental sculpture is typical of the effigies of Columbus rising in middle-sized cities across the nation. Egidio Giaroli sculpted this statue, which is located in Wilmington, Delaware, in 1956. The work was commissioned jointly by the Wilmington Sons of Italy and Knights of Columbus. The cross stresses the religious nature of the mariner rather than his navigational contributions. Courtesy Columbus Day Committee.

man out of the person who accomplished a great deed generated much of our Columbian literature. The excessive praise made him worthy of his achievements and compensated for his mistreatment and suffering. He is at the center of every account, the good, wise, noble man badly treated by others. The very wonder and richness of the Columbus stories rests in the mystique of the humble man who could maneuver the crown, discover a world, and found a nation, and, in the end, be portrayed as a victim.

The Myth

Columbus helped create a great myth which was both story and justification of his actions, and which provided metaphors, images, and a logic around which explanations were generated and the actions of many others justified. . . . Part of the myth Columbus created was the image of great odds against a few puny men—unknown distances, elemental forces, and unpredictable hazards. . . . He set out in three small vessels to travel thousands of miles over unknown waters. He sailed in the dark. And he arrived.

James Oliver Robertson, *American Myth, American Reality*, 1980

According to the mythic story, Columbus discovered America. The land was pure, new, empty, pristine, virtually uninhabited. The few people who lived there were considered primitive and uncivilized, just waiting to be improved by western culture and religion. Europeans had been led to this fresh new world by God to establish freedom and Christianity. A humble, visionary man had overcome the prejudices of wise men and the hazards of nature, following his own star to a magnificent destiny. Because of his example, we can all sail uncharted seas, bound by our dreams rather than by the experience of others.[1]

It is the nature of critical inquiry to overthrow accepted assumptions of the past, and such has been done to the myths of Columbus. These New World myths had provided a basis for understanding the world. But we are now uncomfortable with these old assumptions, and we have turned them on their heads. Now we know that Columbus was not the first to come here and was actually more the despoiler than the discoverer, for he laid waste a country full of people living harmoniously in a highly developed culture. We lack confidence in grand solo ventures, being more comfortable with tolerance of others' views and with cooperation. We distrust divine explanations and heroes in general.

The native Americans and slavery always posed a problem in Columbian mythmaking. Since the natives were depicted originally as children of nature living in a good and golden age, it followed that their corruption occurred as a result of exposure to European civilization. The journeys of Columbus, the visionary, on the other hand, had to be part of a master plan and therefore good. To solve this difficulty, Columbus was provided with a crew of rank materialists and potential criminals who needed only the sight of innocence to unleash their limitless greed and ravening depravity. That Columbus himself was benevolent, there could be no doubt, for if God's plan was good, if the doctrine of progress was to be believed, then the instrument by which man's progress was to be worked out in the New World must also be good. In trade for this preservation of his reputation were the leadership abilities of Columbus: In order to demonstrate his essential goodness, he could have only limited power and influence over his wicked underlings. As a leader of men and a colonizer, he had to be an underachiever.

None of this explicative seems relevant any longer. Today people doubt that a plan of progress exists, or that the role of Columbus in history was inevitable and therefore good. Today's thinkers are willing to entertain the idea that the voyages of Columbus were a big mistake. He should have stayed home and left the original Americas in peace. Even this thought, however, is not a new idea. Whether or not America was a mistake was debated in the eighteenth century. The Abbé Raynal, a French cleric and man of letters who wrote a history of the New World, sponsored a contest where money prizes were awarded for essays discussing the subject.[2] Yet the old mythic story is still told, while new myths are being created.

In the century since the Columbian Exposition, the mariner's reputation has suffered. In 1892, Columbus symbolized progress. In 1992, he symbolizes American failure. The Admiral of the Ocean Sea who gave a new world to Castile and Leon, long revered as the discoverer of America and as the person whose gift to the civilized world was second only to that of Jesus Christ, has been thrust from his position of honor. He has been found guilty of disregarding the rights of the native population of the new lands he visited and of instituting policies that led to the decimation of indigenous populations. He set in motion the relentless torrent of greedy Europeans who despoiled the pristine land, filling it with adventurers and outcasts from tired civilizations. Though still honored and praised by certain ethnic groups, he has fallen from his high position. Racial guilt and environmental devastation justify the opposition of protest groups.

In the past, the statement "Columbus discovered America" was a truism. Now that "truth" is no longer acceptable. Instead of discussing the "discovery"—for no man can claim to discover a land already inhabited—we carefully speak of the "encounter," the "enterprise," and the "exchange," guarded words that emphasize the business nature of

Columbus in the New World, by Edwin Austin Abbey, 1906, shows an armored mariner claiming the sandy new land while participating in religious services. The bright designs of the banners and priests' robes are equaled by the flying cranes in the background. Courtesy Yale University Art Gallery, Edwin Austin Abbey Memorial Collection.

the voyages, the greed of the explorers, and the "gift" to the New World of degenerate European culture, values, vices, and germs. These are the concerns of contemporary people. Potentially enthusiastic celebrations for America's first major quincentary are thus tempered with concern for groups wronged and with sorrow that the first relations between Europe and the American continents were lacking in sensitivity and tolerance.

In the past, Columbus was traditionally distanced from other wicked Spanish conquerors. Such protection tends now to be denied him. Times are such that discussion of his virtues will be subordinated to exposés of his avarice and cruelty.

Hans Koning is one of the more outspoken critics of Columbus. His revisionist history rejects the grade school vision of the mariner. He condemns Columbus for his profit motives in launching the Enterprise of the Indies. Koning is willing to grant Columbus the originality and fierce ambition needed to set that western course, but that is all. Koning sees Columbus as cruel both in small ways and on a continental scale, the man who began the "bloody trail of conquest across the Americas." For Koning, the virtues traditionally associated with Columbus and the European world were actually vices. His persistence, his relentless seeking, his capacity to *stop at nothing* were frightening examples of the corruption of unshaped power.[3] Columbus rolled destructively over the rights of others.

Modern writers have increased the subtlety of their portrayals but have not arrived at a consensus in their opinions of Columbus. Is the superb sailor, the tireless and practical man depicted by Samuel Eliot Morison in his extended biography, *Admiral of the Ocean Sea: A Life of Christopher Columbus*,[4] the same man Björn Landstrom depicts in his *Columbus, the Story of Don Christobal Colon?* The latter paints an irreverent portrait of a man with many unheroic attributes. Essentially pious and a visionary prophet, this greedy man nurtured his grievances and became a "sniveling old fogy."[5]

Alfred W. Crosby considers all of the classic Columbian biographies, with their ethnocentric biases and folk-tale qualities, obsolete. He calls these past history books, including those well researched and true to their sources, bardic history. These works deal with heros rather than with the realities of economics, archaeology, and biology. He asserts that larger forces and not individuals direct the true course of history. Crosby considers Columbus less a villain than the "advanced scout of catastrophe for Amerindians." He sees the old history as a hybrid of revolution, nationalism, and romance, optimistic and bland.[6]

Whatever their differences, writers continue to find something to say about the mariner. In general, the negative story is told by those who know the most about the historical record. The positive version comes from the religious and the patriotic, who find a hopeful metaphor for virtuous striving. The Columbus material is wondrously supple, allowing itself to be interpreted and adapted for widely varying circumstances.

Telling the Story

There be three ships
Down on the Quay
Waiting to sail
The Western Sea;
Three lonely ships
Will leave this shore
And we shall see them
Nevermore.

Three ships upon
A hopeless quest
To break the spell
That binds the West,
Three lonely ships
Will leave this shore
And we shall see them
Nevermore.

Louis MacNeice, *Christopher Columbus: A Radio Play*, 1944

Two dramatic accounts of the Columbian story, both written from an Italian Catholic perspective, illustrate how the story can be adapted to individual concerns. In the 1940s, John J. Mazza wrote a colorful folk-tale script for the San Francisco Columbus Day pageant. To reflect the interests of the Italian community, Columbus Day, and also the patriotism of World War II, his *The Discovery of America* had to work within some stringent requirements. In 1942, the United States Army was in possession of the Pacific shoreline, preventing Columbus' traditional landing at Acquatic Park in a replica of the *Santa Maria*. All festivities were moved inland, and Mazza, as Columbus, feared he would have to make a dry landing from a truck. He thus wrote a new script to avoid an ignominious landfall. Isabella could not learn many lines since she was chosen by popular vote just before the celebration. Members of the Independent Order of Red Men, a fraternal group who usually provided natives in full costume, were preoccupied and could not learn parts. So Columbus (Mazza) did most of the talking.

When the Indians emerged from their teepees to greet the sailors from the "ship with wings," the chief told the Spaniards, "If you come in peace, you are welcome to our land and to trade with our people." Columbus replied that he brought "the teachings of the lowly Fisherman of Galilee." As Columbus and the chief sealed their friendship over the Pipe of Peace, an Indian Princess sang a suitable selection. Recommended were "The Indian Love Call" or "The Waters of Minnetonka." When Columbus returned to Spain, he was gracefully greeted by Isabella and granted many honors. The Indian Princess, now known as the "Nightingale of San Salvador," had been persuaded to accompany Columbus to the Old World for a repeat performance. This time she performed an operatic aria, which Columbus said was now "so popular in my native city of Genoa."

Then Columbus waxed prophetic, envisioning American national history to the present time. He saw in vision the independence of the nation and a great father as leader. He saw the Civil War and the freeing of the slaves. He saw two great worldwide conflicts and countless soldiers going out to "save civilization from destruction by over-

This oversized engraving of a royal Columbus, with rich dress, sword, and curled hair, illustrates the mythical elevation of the simple mariner. His arms and a document with his name are displayed on the table. This image was engraved by Rafael Esteve from a painting by Antonio Calliano (Pr. Box 582/20). This item is reproduced by permission of The Huntington Library, San Marino, California.

coming and destroying the forces of evil." As Boy Scouts brought in the flag, all stood, and the "Nightingale of San Salvador" sang the national anthem. This colorful play performed in the 1940s was probably a very moving event in those dim days of international war. More important for this discussion, the play shows how the Columbian theme could prove adequate to any demand.[7]

Mazza's happy, patriotic play with its hopeful ending can be contrasted to *Christopher Columbus: A Play*, by Joseph Chiari, published in 1979. Chiari's play portrays a driven, suffering Columbus and is extended to deal with American slavery. Chiari shows Columbus as silent, obstinate, and blind to anything but the exploration of new worlds. Obsessed by his dreams, he ignored the evil he carried with him. He failed to realize the corrosive, self-abasing aspect of slavery, which left scars on the nation and on Christianity.[8]

After the death of Columbus in the play, three black men come to Beatriz Enriquez, the mother of one of his sons, to demand his body as "the founder of the slave-trade, the first germ-carrier from the Old World." They come in the name of four centuries of black people who "have been torn from the arms of Africa, to have their backs and hearts broken in the sugar plantations and on the galley ships of white men." When Beatriz protests that Columbus "brought Christ to America," they counter that "he brought Hell with it!" When she protests that he could not have anticipated the way his discoveries would be used, they bitterly declare that such discoverers thought they were God's envoys, or "worse still, His substitutes."

The black men assert that discoverers thought they could "exploit the sweat of men, spill their blood and infest the world, as long as they discover [a new land], even if the whole world were to die as a result of their discovery." Only by offering the body of Columbus to bereaved, sorrowing Mother Africa can four centuries of agony and suffering be placated and the ghost of slavery exorcised. Columbus, from death, speaks to his daughter America, saying that it is time to heal old conflicts and to share the fruits of wealth. "Peace in Harlem, peace in Africa, so that my bones may, at last, rest in peace," either in the Carribbean Islands or in Africa, "if these much-injured African children want to take them there!" In this play, the same Columbian material is used to tell a much darker tale. The stirring, anachronistic drama begins with a monastery choir at Evensong and ends with a few bars of Joan Baez singing "all my trials will soon be over."[9]

Such stories layer fiction over perceived fact, borrowing the reputation of the mariner to serve other causes.

The Facts

> The more one studies the life of Columbus the more one feels sure that, after the greatness of his discovery was really known, the accounts of the time were overlaid by what modern criticism calls myths, which had grown up in the enthusiasm of those who honored him, and which form no part of real history.
>
> Edward Everett Hale, *The Life of Christopher Columbus*, 1891

With this group of stories about Columbus, a factual account should be included, although one sets off into unknown waters to attempt such a summary. Most facts about Columbus have been challenged, and the best-known stories are judged apocryphal. The facts of one historian are subject to the disapproval of another, therefore, this account is only tentatively offered.

Columbus was probably born in Genoa in 1451, of poor but respectable parents. He may well have been forty-one years old when he sighted the New World. His father was probably a woolcomber, and the boy apparently followed the family trade, learning to read and write later in life.[10]

He spent some years in Portugal, where the ships of Prince Henry were being sent down the African coast. Perestrello, a navigator, had been given the governorship of the island of Porto Santo in the Madeiras. Columbus married his daughter.

Columbus read the exploration accounts of Marco Polo and may have corresponded with Toscanelli, a Florentine physician and amateur geographer, about western lands. He may have gotten information from ancient predictions, from old salts, from strange items and bodies washed ashore, from the plans of a mysterious dying pilot, and from stories of his mother-in-law. In 1475, he sailed to Chios, a Genoese colony in the Levant. He returned to Genoa and joined a fleet that was attacked by French and Portuguese ships-of-war. After a fierce battle in which his ship was set aflame, Columbus seized an oar and made his way to land and to Lisbon. He may later have sailed to Iceland, where he heard something about Norse voyages.

He was making maps with his brother Bartholomew in Lisbon in 1477. He concluded that, since the Portuguese had found new lands by sailing south, he might find land by sailing west. Columbus proposed to King John II of Portugal in 1484 that he provide ships for a western voyage. King John secretly and unsuccessfully sent out a ship to test this route, and Columbus, then a widower with a young son, left Portugal.

In 1485, Columbus, with his five-year-old son Diego, sailed to Palos

in Andalusia to offer his Enterprise of the Indies to the monarchs of
Spain. On the journey from Palos to Huelva, he called at the Franciscan
friary of La Rábida. A monk there, Antonio de Marchena, was intrigued
with his tale and sent him to the Duke of Medina Sidonia at Seville
and then to the Duke of Medina-Celi, who gave him a letter to the
court at Cordova.

While in Cordova, he entered into an alliance with Beatriz Enríquez
de Harana, the orphan of a peasant family. Beatriz bore a son, Ferdinand, on 15 August 1488.

The monarchs Ferdinand and Isabella commanded Talavera to con-
vene a commission to consider the proposal made by Columbus. The
latter was summoned to Salamanca in the autumn of 1486 to meet with
its members. The University of Salamanca was not involved. In 1490,
after five years, the commission advised against the plan.

Columbus left Seville in 1491 for La Rábida. There, Juan Perez, another friendly monk who was interested in the proposal, wrote to
Isabella, who summoned Columbus to court. Granada's surrender to
Spain had made new interests possible, but Columbus' demand for
recognition as a viceroy and for one-tenth of the income from any new
lands alarmed the crown. Columbus then set off for France. Persuaded
that she might be losing an opportunity, Isabella recalled Columbus
and backed his venture. He assumed one-eighth of the cost and was
promised titles and profits; he pledged to use his profits to rescue the
Holy Sepulchre from the Moslems. Aragon advanced the remainder
of the costs. The town of Palos was ordered to fit out two vessels, and
Columbus undertook the management of the third.

The little fleet embarked from Palos on 3 August 1492, running down
to the Canary Islands and proceeding westerly with the trade winds.
Columbus traveled two hundred miles farther than the longitude at
which he expected to encounter Cipangu, or Japan, then changed
course southwest. On 12 October 1492, he landed on a low, sandy island,
which he named San Salvador.

For ten days the three ships sailed among the minor islands of the
archipelago. Without orders, Martin Alonzo Pinzón sailed his ship
Pinta to look, unsuccessfully, for gold. Columbus found Haiti, which
he named Hispaniola, and accidentally wrecked his ship on the northern side. He decided to establish a colony, La Navidad, there with a
few men and used the ship's timbers to build a fort.

Columbus and the rest of the men embarked for Spain on 4 January
1493, and reached Palos on 15 March after an absence of seven months.
His return was greeted with wonder, and the monarchs invited him
to sit in their presence and describe his adventures.

Boris Plenkovich painted this dramatic image of Christopher Columbus landing in San Salvador. The explosion in the skies reflects the importance of the historic moment. Courtesy Library of Congress.

On 25 September, a second voyage of seventeen vessels with twelve hundred people embarked from Cádiz. Land was sighted on 3 November. La Navidad had been destroyed, and a new town, Isabella, was laid out to its east. Expeditions for gold were immediately launched. The natives resisted efforts to mine gold, and the Spaniards suffered from illness. Twelve ships were sent back to Spain for supplies. Columbus explored the vicinity, finding Jamaica and Cuba, which he decided must be part of the Asian mainland. He required his men to sign a paper to that effect.

Columbus returned to his colony and discovered that some men had sailed for Spain, spreading word there of unrest and mismanagement. When supply ships arrived, Columbus sent them back with gold samples and a cargo of natives to be converted to Christianity and sold as slaves. In March of 1495, Columbus led an expedition into the interior of Hispaniola to subdue the native populations; the natives were harshly treated from then on.

Columbus returned to Spain in March of 1496 to defend his record as governor. The sovereigns treated him well but delayed his third voyage. Columbus finally sailed from San Lucar on 30 May 1498 with six ships. He found Trinidad and the northern coast of South America, including the Orinoco River. These fresh waters almost persuaded him that he had found a terrestrial paradise. When he finally reached Hispaniola, ruled in his absence by his brother Bartholomew, he found that the new town of Santo Domingo had been established. He was also faced with a revolt of some Spaniards, headed by Roldán. While Columbus was dealing with this uprising, his monarchs dispatched a commissioner to Hispaniola to review the situation and relieve him of authority if necessary. On arrival, Francisco de Bobadilla assumed control of the Crown's property, arrested Columbus and his brother, and sent them back to Spain in chains.

The sovereigns were shocked by the sight of the manacled admiral and hastened to make amends, offering Columbus whatever he wanted except new power in the islands, which they wished to see pacified. He proposed a new voyage and sailed from Cádiz on 9 May 1502, on an exploring voyage, reaching Santo Domingo, Hispaniola, with a leaky ship on 29 June. He had been told to stay away from the harbor there and was denied entrance by his enemies Bobadilla and Roldán, who were poised for a journey to Spain. A heavy storm broke. Columbus was able to ride out the furious storm, but the fleet with Bobadilla and Roldán and much of the gold they had gathered was lost and the enemies drowned. Columbus, ill and perhaps delirious, explored the coast of Central America, never realizing how close he was to the Pacific Ocean. Leaving the promising site of new discoveries, the fleet retreated to search for gold. Troubles with his ships and with the natives led to the beaching of two ships at Jamaica, an area near his explorations. His crew spent a miserable year there—mutinous, hungry, and under attack. Columbus was eventually relieved by Ovando, Bobadilla's successor and then governor at Hispaniola, and cared for until he embarked for Spain on 12 September 1504.

He reached San Lucar on 7 November, very ill. Isabella had died, and the repeated letters from Columbus to the king demanding his rights and honors were little attended to. He died on 20 May 1506.

Such was the life of Christopher Columbus, a life of successful exploration and unfortunate consequences. That the world should know of his triumph was second in his mind only to making landfall itself. As he returned from his first voyage, his ship encountered a storm of such violence that the men feared they would all be lost. At this point occurred an incident so revelatory of Columbus that it must be mentioned. The account is quoted from William Robertson's eighteenth-century *History of America.*

Columbus had to endure feelings of distress peculiar to himself. He dreaded that all knowledge of the amazing discoveries which he had made was now to perish; mankind were to be deprived of every benefit that might have been derived from the happy success of his schemes, and his own name would descend to posterity as that of a rash deluded adventurer, instead of being transmitted with the honour due to the author and conductor of the most noble enterprise that had ever been undertaken. These reflections extinguished all sense of his own personal danger.[11]

And so, with the wind blowing and the ship tossing, in the very teeth of the gale and with the threat of death at any moment, the admiral went to his cabin and wrote an account of the voyage—in the most promising style—wrapped it in an oiled cloth, enclosed it in a cake of wax, put it into a cask, and threw it into the sea. He hoped the account would survive, redeeming his name even though the ship and all aboard were lost in the raging sea. The stubborn, unshakeable pride and sense of self that had kept him on his long quest for ships extended to his need that people know what he had done. He would not be robbed of his discoveries.

It is thus so ironic that his New World was named for someone else. Efforts to right that particular injustice have been many and unavailing. Whether Columbus was the first European who saw the mainland is now almost beside the point. The two continents of America should have been named Columbia. Short of that, the name the United States of Columbia should have been adopted at the time of the American Revolution.

That the land was named for Amerigo Vespucci, a provision merchant from Cádiz who joined the expedition of Alonzo de Hojeda, mounted on the basis of charts prepared by Columbus, is an accident of history. This sea voyage was Vespucci's first; he never claimed he was the first to see the land. His lively account of the voyage led German geographer Martin Waldseemüller, in his *Cosmographiae Introductio* published in 1507, to urge that some part of the new land be named America. A small part of South America was what he had in mind, and even then he was later convinced that the name was a mistake. But in 1538 Mercator, the great reformer of cartography who knew the New World to be a double continent, introduced the names North America and South America. Herbert Baxter Adams, the nineteenth-century historian, approved the name America, which he identified as a beautiful and worthy Germanic name meaning rich in industry. Adams' justification for approving the name was scientific and monkish: Europe was named after a woman; some lands should be named after men.[12]

In the early nineteenth century, the New-York Historical Society mounted an effort to adopt a new national name. The society recommended the republic of Washington. The Maryland Historical Society nominated Allegania as a name that would restore to the land a title suggesting its earlier inhabitants. The New Jersey Historical Society stuck by America, while other societies preferred Columbia. One of these, the Massachusetts Historical Society, wrote that "we cannot imagine any other name more appropriate or better suited to mark its distinctive character. The name of America irretrievably stamped by uncompromising usage upon both continents of the New Hemisphere as a perpetual memorial of human injustice by conferring upon one man a crown of glory justly due to another." But despite efforts now

In Sight of the New World, the grave and noble Columbus surveys the land, ignoring the repentent seamen who prostrate themselves at his feet, kissing his gown. John C. M. Rae engraved this image. Courtesy Library of Congress.

spanning almost five hundred years, Columbia did not last, and Allegania never began. While other citizens of the Americas are referred to as Canadians, Mexicans, or Brazilians, citizens in the United States call themselves Americans. Their country is America and will always be so.[13]

The Future

Weep for me, whoever has charity, truth and justice! I did not come on this voyage to navigate for gain, honor or wealth, that is certain; for then the hope of all such things was dead. I came to Your Highnesses with honest purpose and sincere zeal and I do not lie.

Christopher Columbus to his Sovereigns, 7 July 1503

By the beginning of the twenty-first century, a new chapter in the Columbian myth will be added to those of the past. How the five hundredth anniversary of the arrival of Columbus in the New World is commemorated will tell generations to come about America of the 1990s. On this anniversary, as before, commemoration will mirror contemporary interests. Columbus, the most protean of historic figures, will continue to serve the nationalistic, progressive, ethnic, and now environmental purposes that are of primary concern to the citizenry. Evaluations of Columbus will reflect what Americans think of themselves.

Americans are currently concerned with racial injustice and an endangered environment. The rights and feelings of groups previously ignored are being considered as never before. The wider significance and result of the voyage overshadow the personal qualities of the Admiral himself. Many events commemorating 1492 pointedly ignore the navigator. Columbus has not been invited to his own party.

To the extent that Columbus is recognized positively, it is as the first of many immigrants, not as a viceroy or an admiral. He instituted the multiculturalism that has been the nation's pride and that characterizes it to this day. The Columbian Quincentenary provides a medium for recognizing all immigrants and for celebrating cultural diversity.

Each person who steps on the shores of the United States reenacts the ritual of discovery, an entrance into a new life. All those who have come in the past, and those who continue to come, leave behind them an old world and embrace a new one.[14] They hope for a fresh, new life. Images of past immigrants may include ancestors or ethnic groups, but they begin with Columbus.

CHAPTER TWO

The Historical Record

In his character hardly is any one of the components of a truly great man wanting. For to the ideas of the most penetrating philosopher, and a scheme built upon them worthy of a great king, he joined a constancy and patience, which alone could carry it into execution, with the fortune of a private man.

Edmund Burke, *An Account of the European Settlements in America*, 1757

By the end of the eighteenth century, Christopher Columbus had become an important symbol for the New World. The achievement of that exalted status was the work of many hands, but much of the credit must be given to the English and European historians who crafted an historical figure worthy of a nation's admiration long before the United States recognized its own need for symbolic personification. The grooming of Columbus was not an altogether easy task, for he had to be distinguished from the other Spanish explorers who were tainted with "the black legend" of cruelty and greed, and then, beyond that, he had to be endowed with heroic qualities. Before all the parts were in place, his reputation went through a long evolution in Europe and was finally brought to America in the eighteenth century for adoption by the emerging young republic.

Little was written about Columbus in the colonies until the late eighteenth century; the great proliferation of Columbiana did not occur until the nineteenth century. Before 1750, most middling people were scarcely aware of the long-dead Italian explorer, and the learned few would have had some difficulty obtaining information if they had sought it.

The Early Records

The best early accounts of the adventures of Columbus were not available in America. His own account of his first voyage, in a letter to Luis de Santangel, the keeper of King Ferdinand's funds, was the first reliable report of the New World. This abstract of Columbus' journal from the first voyage, which puts the best face possible on the voyage, was the document Columbus copied and threw into the sea

A grave and visionary Columbus, "Who First Discovered the West Indies," was featured in *The General Biographical Dictionary: Containing an Historical and Critical Account of the Lives and Writings of the Most Eminent Persons in Every Nation* (RB 110474, vol. 10), edited by Alexander Chalmers and published in London in 1813. This item is reproduced by permission of The Huntington Library, San Marino, California.

on his first homeward voyage, lest the news of his exploits be lost. The letter in the cask was never recovered. The hand-carried original was lost, too, but not before it had been copied by Bartolomé de Las Casas. A copy of this document was published in Spain in 1493, and nine editions of a Latin translation were printed in major European cities; other versions in Spanish or Italian verse proliferated. The letter was not available in English, however, until December 1816 when the first English translation appeared in the *Edinburgh Review*.[1] So this first story of triumph was not accessible in America, and none of the other writings of Columbus had any general circulation.

From this first self-serving account of the journey, meant to be good news for the sovereigns, came the belief that the New World had been experiencing a golden age of civilization with its beautiful ("well made"), innocent, and generous natives. Columbus said of the Indians, "They are so ingenuous and free with all they have, that no one would believe it who has not seen it."[2] To match their pristine beauty, Columbus stressed his own kindness to them; thus his reputation for good treatment, distinguishing him from the "black legend" explorers, comes from his own writings.

The most important early account of his life was the positive biography written by his second son, Ferdinand. A young page at the court of Queen Isabella, Ferdinand accompanied his father on the fourth voyage and later sailed to Santo Domingo with his brother, before he retired to Spain as a prosperous man of letters. He collected a large library that aided in writing his *Historie*, the source of much of the personal detail of the legend. Ferdinand took pains to refute the inaccuracies of other writers, citing his father's papers and his own experience. The first English version of this biography, translated from a poor Italian translation of the Spanish original, was included in John Churchill's *Voyages* (1744–1746); a book not readily accessible in the colonies. A careful English edition of Ferdinand's work was not published until 1959. The original Spanish manuscript was lost.[3]

Another significant book, by a man who knew Columbus and was a resident of Hispaniola, was the account of Bartolomé de Las Casas. Las Casas wrote his *Historia de las Indias* from his experience as a colonist and a priest in the New World, as well as from many of Columbus' papers now lost. While in America, he ministered to the native population, occupying positions of importance while serving as the natives' protector and friend. He admired Columbus but deplored his policy toward the natives and was harshly critical of it. Las Casas' excellent first-hand account of the settlements was written in the mid-1500s and influenced some writers, but it was not published until 1875. Ferdinand, who wrote very sensitively about his father, was oblivious of the natives. These three early sources, Columbus' letter, Ferdinand's *Historie*, and Las Casas' *Historia* (generally positive and detailed), were not available to many people, certainly not to North Americans.

The best early use of these sources was in the *Historie general de los hechos de los Castellanos* of Antonio de Herrera, published between 1601 and 1615. Herrera relied heavily on Las Casas manuscript to produce a prolix, chronological account. But an English version, in which many liberties were taken, was not published in London until 1725–1726. Juan Bautista Muñoz published a volume of his *Historia del nuevo mundo* in 1793. He had the use of a large cache of documents that he copied, which have since been disbursed. An English translation of his book appeared in 1797. These books gradually made their way to the colonies in small numbers.[4]

Meanwhile, other Columbian accounts received some circulation in English. Peter Martyr d'Anghiera's *Decades* were manuscript newsletters sent to important churchmen, the pope included, between 1494 and 1526. Martyr was himself a humanist appointed by Queen Isabella to train young aristocrats, and he entertained the important leaders of Spain. He was among those welcoming Columbus, whom he interviewed for information upon his first return. Martyr's history of the exploration was published in 1511 and translated into English in 1555. He translated the reports of Vespucci, Columbus, and other explorers, often commenting on their adventures in terms of learned classical lore, but he spoke only briefly of the background and character of the explorer. This account, in good Elizabethan English, was a significant source of information, but only a few people were able to read his letters.[5]

Martyr evaluated the voyages of *"Colonus* the Genoese," in his letters to friends, filtering the admiral's claims through his own wide knowledge. Of Columbus' claim to have discovered the Indian coast, Martyr noted, "I do not wholly deny this, although the size of the globe seems to suggest otherwise." Martyr soon deduced that Columbus had not reached the Indies, for in a letter to Cardinal Sforza dated 1 November 1493, he spoke of *Colonus ille Novi Orbis repertor,* "that famous Columbus the discoverer of a New World." It was thus Martyr who coined that ringing phrase.[6]

The chroniclers who drew upon these sources about Columbus were no more neutral in their retelling of his adventures than are historians today. They used the story to promote their own special interests; but, as it happened, Columbus benefited from the early treatments. Prominent among the first historians writing in English were Christian apologists who wished to explain the explorations as part of a divine plan to extend Christianity. For that role, Columbus' character had to prove equal to his mission. His success was depicted as a triumph of the meek. The messenger for Christ was presented as the perfect Christian. Richard Hakluyt, the English cleric who wrote several volumes about voyages to the New World, regarded Columbus' achievements as providential. He was "the first instrument to manifest the great glory and mercie of Almightie God in planting the Christian faith, in those so long unknown regions." Hakluyt saw Columbus as a modest, good man who prevailed.

Some scorned the pildnes of his garments, some tooke occasion to jest at his simple and silly lookes, others asked if this were he, that lowts so lowe, which did take upon him to bring men into a Countrey that aboundeth with Golde, Pearle, and Precious stones. . . . This devise was then accounted a fantasticall imagination, and a drowsie dreame.

But the sequel thereof, hath since awaked out of dreames thousand of soules to knowe their Creator.

The spread of Christianity, as well as the great wealth brought home from the New World, testified to the righteousness of Columbus. Hakluyt encouraged the continuation of explorations following Columbus' example.[7]

Samuel Purchas, in his *Purchas His Pilgrimes*, also venerated the explorer of the Columbian World, more "fitlier named, than American," for his pious virtues. Columbus was "very devout, frequent in Prayer, observant of Fasts, temperate in Diet, modest in Attyre, gravely courteous in Behaviour, abstinent of Oathes, and abhominating Blasphemies." Columbus had to have been such a one for God to choose him for this great role. God would only work with the meek and humble. The lack of such qualities, according to Purchas, would naturally bring failure. The wrong kind of explorers were described as going forth

with high-swolne Sayles, filled with puffes of Pride, and blasts of Arrogance, addicting themselves to Swearing, Cursing, and other resolute Dissolutenesse (as if they sought Discoveries in the infernall Regions, and acquaintance with those Legions of Hell, rather then to discover Lands, and recover Infidels to internall peace by the eternall Gospell) eyther perish at Sea, or returne with the gaine of losse, and shame, in stead of glory.

Columbus, by contrast, had a "Dove-like lovely carriage in conversation," a metaphor adapted from the Latin name for the gentle dove— columba. This praise of Columbus' piety served Purchas' moral purposes more so than accurately delineating the character of the admiral himself.[8]

The Colonial American Story

This Christian justification of Columbus spilled over into the New World where Cotton Mather, in his great opus *Magnalia Christi Americana*, made mention of the admiral, although the scope of his book (1620 to 1698) covered a far later time. Mather not only emphasized the spread of Christianity, he interpreted Columbus' voyages as of providential advantage to the English, a common theme. Mather made note of the discovery by "this famous Man, acted by a most vehement and wonderful *Impulse*," and saw the hand of the Lord in the act of extending Christianity to prove the superiority of New England. He suggested that God had shown special regard for the English. "If this *New*

World were not found out first by the *English;* yet in those regards that are of all the *greatest,* it seems to be found out more *for* them than any other."[9] Mather included the Italian papist as part of God's plan for the English, thus legitimizing for the English colonial scene a person very foreign to its own style.

Mather's reference is useful as an early comment on what Americans knew about Columbus and how they regarded him. He apparently became a positive figure because of his religious connection, spreading Christianity to the New World and representing freedom of religion. This religious connection was sufficient to overcome the other major cultural differences that divided him from the protestant Americans, even though England was home and the Spanish explorers did not work over the northeastern seaboard. Other writers of historical books in the American colonies also recognized the admiral. For them, Columbus served as the person who started a new epoch. A survey of some of this material shows how Columbus fit into the historical organization of the colonists.

Thomas Prince, in his *Chronological History of New-England* of 1736, attempted to give a coherent shape to history. He ended one of his major sections with an account of Columbus' climactic achievement, naming him as the discoverer and paying him this dense tribute:

Being a skilful Geographer and Navigator, and of a very curious Mind, He becomes possess'd, with a strong perswasion, that in order to Ballance the Terraqueous Globe & Proportion the Seas and Lands to each other, there must needs be form'd a mighty *Continent* on the other Side, which Boldness, Art and Resolution will soon Discover. [Columbus proposed his scheme to various crowned heads], for this great Enterprize, [and despite] the growing Opposition of his fearful Mariners, he at length accomplishes [the voyage] to his own immortal fame, and the infinite Advantage of innumerable others.[10]

Columbus earned his own fame and provided a blessing for mankind.

William Stith, in his history of the first discovery and settlement of Virginia, published in 1747, gave Columbus a whole paragraph, calling him a "Person of great Knowledge and Experience in naval Affairs, of good Learning, and a comprehensive Mind," although he was "rejected as a whimsical and chimerical Man" by people in authority. His discovery bore bounteous fruit, described here a little too hungrily by Stith. Columbus, "being animated with a publick Spirit and a generous Principle of Glory, and the *Spaniards,* being as eagerly pushed on by an insatiable Thirst of Gold, so ardently pursued, and so successfully improved this first Discovery, that they soon became Masters of vast Tracts of rich and fertile Country, abounding in Gold, Silver, Pearls, Emeralds, and many other [of] the most precious and delicious Products of this Globe."[11] In Stith's account, the Spaniards suffered from excessive greed, not the virtuous Columbus.

The Stith and Prince accounts suggest that North American historians, although granting Columbus a role in the history of their land, did not envision a role that required extensive exposition. Their references tended to be short and positive. They did not play up his providential mission to expand the dominions of Christianity nor his heroic nature. Most of the early North American books dealing with Columbus were written from a very strong British, rather than Christian, point of view. They recognized Columbus as a necessary figure in opening up the New World but did not praise him as a superior person.

The first locally written, extended account of Columbus was published as part of the first American account of North America in *The New American Magazine* of 1758. Judge Samuel Nevill of Perth Amboy, New Jersey, served as a member of the New Jersey Assembly and later the speaker. He had lived in the colonies for nearly twenty-two years when he became a judge of the New Jersey Supreme Court and a magazine editor the same year. He edited *The New American Magazine* under the name "Sylvanus Americanus." His magazine digested material printed elsewhere, providing an invaluable, though short-lived, chronicle of the times. Abraham Baldwin suggested to Joel Barlow, that the *New American Magazine* would be a good place to publish Barlow's *Columbiad*. The magazine, Baldwin noted, contained "the best account he [had] ever seen of this continent."[12]

In 1758, the first part of Nevill's magazine, three half sheets, was devoted to a serial presentation of "A Complete History of the *Northern Continent of America*, from the Time of its first Discovery to the present: Compiled with that Impartiality and Regard to Truth which becomes a faithful Historian, and carefully extracted from the Authors of the best Credit both ancient and modern." The section was separately paged so that it could be bound after all the installments had been printed. The second half of the magazine contained essays, poetry, and other items. Nevill compiled his history of the continent from works supplying "the greatest Probability of Truth." His principal sources were Hakluyt and Purchas.[13]

Nevill wrote in 1758 from a prerevolutionary point of view. His aim was to justify the English presence in America by establishing the superiority of the English to the Spanish and the native Americans. He declared that the poor natives of North America were unable or unwilling to make good use of their land. The English, he said, had settled and subdued the wild deserts with great difficulty, rendering them fit for the use of man. "Thus the Right of Sovereign Princes to

The cover illustration from *The New American Magazine*, edited by Sylvanus Americanus [Samuel Nevill], includes the serialization of "History of North-America," the first extensive account written and published in the New World. The design, repeated monthly, indicates the American spirit, growing under the influence of rays from heaven and touched by the classical spirit of Mercury to the accompaniement of Triton's horn. Native and English Americans observe the development from their perch on the western shores. Courtesy, American Antiquarian Society.

new-discovered Lands, which lay waste and useless, and which were cultivated and improved by their Subjects, is made apparent, and in my Opinion, fully established. . . . Moreover, the Temporal Benefits which [the natives] receive from us will far out-balance any Damages they may pretend we have done to them."[14]

According to Nevill, things were different in South America where the natives were ingenious, inoffensive, and hospitable, except, of course, for human sacrifice and idolatrous worship.

What Right, divine or human, the *Spaniards* may claim to invade this Country, upon the Pretence of *Discovery*, and to massacre and murder Millions of the Inhabitants in cool Blood, in order to obtain Possession, at the same Time counterfeiting an earnest Zeal to propagate Christianity amongst the Heathens, I shall leave to the candid Reader to determine.[15]

In short, the English appropriation of land was a favor to natives; the Spanish intrusion, vicious and cruel.

With this interpretation, the English were not in need of Columbus to justify their presence. Although the first installment of Nevill's history recounted Columbus' story, he was treated as a representative of Spain and therefore an unsympathetic character. Nevill first defended England's rejection of Columbus' plan when it was put forth by his brother Bartholomew to the English monarch. "I know some Writers have made pretty smart Reflections upon King *Henry*, for his Dilateriousness." But Nevill revealed that the English course was the best, for the Spanish wore themselves out and squandered their naval power by purchasing Mexico and Peru too dearly.[16] Besides, although Columbus paved the way, John Cabot, who sailed for the English, made the first discovery of the main continent of America. Nevill, a good Englishman, justified his own history.

Columbus was no hero in this short and interesting account. Nevill repeated the charges of Columbus' enemies at court who represented him to the monarchs as ambitious, covetous, and tyrannical. According to Neville, Columbus had no true notion of how to govern, and he reduced both Spaniards and Indians to slavery, the results of which successfully worked Columbus out of the king's favor.

Nevill's early account, though refreshingly critical of Columbus, still sounds the note of personal tragedy. "Such a Train of Calamities, in which the Ingratitude of the *Spaniards* was not the least, sat heavy upon the Mind of *Columbus*. . . . [He died] with great Resignation, experimentally sensible, that the most important Services, attended by the most surprising Success, were thrown away upon an ungrateful nation."[17] With that note of sympathy, a basically critical story ended.

Nevill's account suggests that, on the eve of the American Revolution, Columbus' heroic qualities were muted in Americans' minds. Columbus was given a part, but not a leading role wherein his virtues could shine. How, then, could postrevolutionary writers, not two decades after Nevill published his account, place the explorer on a pedestal, making him the symbol of national confidence and independence?

The Influential Raynal

Actually, Americans were indebted more to European historians than to scholars on their own shores for the glorious Columbus of their postrevolutionary rhetoric. These books from across the sea, and particularly the works of the Abbé Raynal and William Robertson, greatly influenced their American audience.

The Abbé Raynal [Guillaume Thomas Francois] (1713–1796), a Jesuit and a literary figure, was also a prominent social and political leader.

He amassed a large fortune, perhaps through speculation in the slave trade, and used his funds for philanthropical purposes in France and Switzerland. His book, *A Philosophical and Political History of the Settlements and Trade of the Europeans in the East and West Indies,* much of it apparently written by other authors, was first published in 1770, then translated into other languages and reprinted many times. The anticlerical sentiment of the work provoked disapproval, and the author was sent into exile. The book was placed on the Index, banned by the Parlement of Paris, and burned by the public executioner. The famous and infamous "philosophic history" came out in an English translation in 1776 and went through fourteen editions before the end of the century.[18]

Raynal wrote with dignity and with a broad vision of the background of exploration. His references to Columbus were highly complimentary, filling twenty pages of his volumes. But it was not the admiral's part in spreading Christianity that garnered Raynal's respect. Raynal admired Columbus as a far-seeing visionary, a brave, mistreated hero. The proud ministers of Queen Isabella treated him with "contemptuous insolence" and regarded his theory as the "offspring of a distempered brain," while the superhero rose above them.

But Columbus was not to be discouraged by any difficulties; he possessed, as all men do who engage in extraordinary enterprises, a degree of enthusiasm, which renders them superior to the cavils of the ignorant, the contempt of the proud, the mean arts of the covetous, and the delays of the indolent. At length, by perseverance, spirit, and courage, joined to the arts of prudence and management, he surmounted every obstacle.[19]

Raynal thus established Columbus as a superior person, a man of vision and persistence, of genius and courage.

His relationship with the natives was more problematic. Raynal knew about the extensive abuses yet was determined to rid Columbus of the blame. He pointed out that a European visiting a place inhabited by non-Christians would naturally feel justified in taking possession in the name of his queen, as Columbus did when he met the natives of San Salvador, even though the New World seemed superior to the civilized one. Besides the understandable act of laying claim to the natives' land, Columbus himself was beyond reproach. All the evil was attributed to others.

On the first voyage, Raynal stressed Columbus' friendly attentions to the islanders and imputed the desire for gold to the Spanish crew. Cruel exploitation occurred after Columbus left for Spain. When he returned on the second voyage, paradise had disappeared. The blame for the disaster lay with his men, not with Columbus himself.

When Columbus did do battle with the natives, Raynal drew attention to his courage rather than to his rapacity. On one occasion, Columbus was forced to postpone his explorations to put down a native attempt to exterminate the Spaniards. Although his forces were reduced to two hundred infantry and twenty horses, "yet this extraordinary man was not afraid of attacking, in 1495, in the plains of Vega-Real, an army, which historians in general have computed at one hundred thousand men."[20]

Columbus attacked at night and won the day, using his horses and dogs to good advantage. To punish the natives for their rebellion, the Spaniards demanded that every Indian above fourteen pay a tribute in gold. Raynal acknowledged that this punishment was an imposition, because the people "were not used to be employed." Unsuccessful at passive resistance as well as force, the natives pulled up their crops and escaped to the hills, hoping to starve out their tormentors. The Spaniards then turned out their dogs to hunt down the hapless Indians. Raynal admitted that the colony was mismanaged, but he exempted Columbus, who was back in Spain for much of this period, from blame.

THIS extraordinary man purchased upon very hard terms the fame which his genius and industry had procured him. His life exhibited a perpetual contrast of elevation and depression. He was not only continually exposed to the cabals, calumnies, and ingratitude of individuals; but was also obliged to submit to the caprices of a haughty and turbulent court. . . .[21]

Bobadilla, the man who relieved Columbus, was described as "the most ambitious, self-interested, unjust, and violent man that had yet gone over to America," while Columbus was always depicted in a positive way. Always Raynal marveled at Columbus' great gifts and his fortitude in the face of adversity. Raynal did acknowledge the admiral's occasional failings though, saying that he brought some of his troubles on himself by enslaving the Indians. "His misfortunes had commenced with the discovery. Columbus, notwithstanding his humanity and his talents, increased them himself by fixing Americans upon the lands which he distributed to his soldiers."[22] This enslavement was more harshly extended by his successors Bobadilla and Ovando, until the native population was virtually decimated. But Raynal does not see this decimation as Columbus' fault. We hear instead of his vision and bravery. No one accords the same sympathy to Cortez or Pizarro. Raynal thus materially advanced the Columbus legend.

Robertson's History

Raynal's book was followed closely by the most significant of the early English historical works, the three volume *History of America* by

William Robertson. Robertson (1721–1793), a Scottish historian, Presbyterian minister, and politician, was trained at the University of Edinburgh. He became a minister in Gladsmuir in 1743 and, as a politician, served as a member of the General Assembly and later as elected moderator. He published the *History of Scotland during the Reigns of Queen Mary and King James VI* in 1759, becoming famous immediately. He was appointed Principal of the Edinburgh University in 1762 and Historiographer Royal in 1763.

His *History of the Reign of the Emperor Charles V* was published in 1769. In this work, Robertson omitted mention of the Spanish colonies in America, preferring to deal with them at length in another study. His *History of America* (1777) fulfilled that aim. That book, which has an inclusive title, actually dealt only with the Spanish discovery and presence in the New World. Robertson had intended to write the whole history of America, but he postponed writing the English sections because he felt the Revolutionary War would make major changes. "In whatever manner this unhappy contest may terminate," Robertson noted, "a new order of things must arise in North America." In the meantime, he published the first three Spanish-flavored volumes.

Robertson was an energetic and prolific scholar, and he was acquainted with England's ambassador to Spain. He enlisted the help of the ambassador's chaplain, Mr. Waddilove, and for five years the two worked closely together, collecting books and manuscripts and posing queries to Spaniards abroad. Robertson knew that the official archives near Valladolid were filled with papers about early America, "eight hundred and seventy-three large bundles." But Spain, by then embarrassed by the conquest of the New World, "with an excess of caution," had "uniformly thrown a veil over her transactions in America" and closed the archives. If Robertson had had access to the Spanish archives, the book would have been stronger, but his connections to crowned heads and diplomats, his assiduous inquiries, and his meticulous scholarship helped produce the best book on the subject written to that date. What is more pertinent to our inquiry, the book was available to Americans. The book's success in America was enormous and immediate, quickly becoming the standard work. In fact, it was the authority on Columbus until Washington Irving's biography was published in 1828.[23]

Discovery and conquest, not colonization, were Robertson's main themes. He acknowledged the blood-stained record of the Spaniards in the New World, perceiving their strangely mixed motives: "religious enthusiasm" mixed with both the spirit of adventure and with avarice. But throughout his account, he admired their "fortitude and perseverance."[24]

Robertson's dignified, decorous prose impressed the readers of his age. His account of Balboa's first sight of the mighty Pacific, "stretching in endless prospect before him," remained in the mind of Keats to inspire his famous lines about "stout Cortez"—whose name better fit the verse—and all his men, "silent, upon a peak in Darien."[25]

Because of the book's popularity, Robertson's treatment of Columbus was particularly important. Robertson relied heavily on early accounts published in Spanish. Among them were Ferdinand Columbus' biography, Anton. de Herrera's *Historia,* and Peter Martyr's *Decades.* Robertson's use of these sources provided their first widespread distribution in the English-speaking colonies.

Robertson recounted Columbus' life: his birth and education, his studies of navigation, his negotiations at court, his voyages, his colonizing efforts, his disgrace, and his death. Much of the action took place in the mind of Columbus, imagining him reviewing the evidence and concluding that sailing westward would take him to rich lands. Still more space was devoted to his unsuccessful efforts to sell his ideas to crowned heads. By contrast with the biographical treatment of Columbus, Cortez and Pizarro were considered only in connection with their conquests. This treatment of Columbus, which has become traditional, honored him for personal reasons as well as for his accomplishments, making him a much more flexible and durable symbol.

In Robertson's descriptions, Columbus became the driven explorer. "The study of these [Portuguese maps] soothed and inflamed [his] favourite passion; and while he contemplated the maps, and read the descriptions of the new countries which Perestrello had seen, his impatience to visit them became irresistible."[26] His peculiar combination of original thought and action was praised.

To a mind less capable of forming and of executing great designs than that of Columbus, all those reasonings and observations and authorities would have served only as the foundation of some plausible and fruitless theory, which might have furnished matter for ingenious discourse or fanciful conjecture. But with his sanguine and enterprising temper speculation led directly to action. Fully satisfied himself with respect to the truth of his system, he was impatient to bring it to the test of experiment, and to set out upon a voyage of discovery.[27]

Robertson made an admirable gentleman out of Columbus, here described in his visit to the Spanish court.

His character, however, was admirably adapted to that of the people whose confidence and protection he solicited. He was grave, though courteous in his deportment; circumspect in his words and actions, irreproachable in his morals, and exemplary in his attention to all the duties and functions of religion. By qualities so respectable, he not only gained many private friends, but acquired such general esteem, that, notwithstanding the plainness of his appearance, suitable to the mediocrity of his fortune, he was not considered as a mere adventurer, to whom indigence had suggested a visionary project, but was received as a person to whose propositions serious attention was due.[28]

Echoing the earlier Christian apologists, Robertson emphasized the religious nature of Columbus, who marched his whole band of sailors and adventurers into the monastery of La Rábida in solemn procession before setting out on his first voyage. "He would not set out upon an

Christopher Columbus, a woodcut engraved by Albert Alden, 1812–1883. The versatile Mr. Alden, bookseller, jeweler, and engraver, edited the *Barre Gazette*, illustrating it himself. He made and sold prints, the most important of which was *Alden's Pictorial Map of the United States.* Courtesy, American Antiquarian Society.

expedition so arduous, and of which one great object was to extend the knowledge of the Christian faith, without imploring publicly the guidance and protection of Heaven."[29]

Columbus immediately had difficulty with his men, who feared losing sight of land, notwithstanding the fact that they had signed on to a voyage to sail due west. Perhaps he was so weary of suing and placating the great people whose sponsorship he sought that he had no patience and understanding for the little men he had to command. In any case, Robertson made the best of it. Columbus' problems taught him

that he must prepare to struggle not only with the unavoidable difficulties which might be expected from the nature of his undertaking, but with such as were likely to arise from the ignorance and timidity of the people under his command; and he perceived that the art of governing the minds of men would be no less requisite for accomplishing the discoveries which he had in view, than naval skill and undaunted courage. Happily for himself, and for the country by which he was employed, he joined to the ardent temper and inventive genius of a projector, virtues of another species, which are rarely united with them. He possessed a thorough knowledge of mankind, an insinuating address, a patient perseverance in executing any plan, the perfect government of his own passions, and the talent of acquiring an ascendant over those of other men. All these qualities, which formed him for command, were accompanied with that superior knowledge of his profession, which begets confidence in times of difficulty and danger.[30]

These claims seem inflated considering the repeated mutinies he suffered, the fact that he needed to falsify the record of the distance traveled, and his poor success at colonization. It seems strange that the sailors should demand to turn back after traveling over seven hundred leagues or that they planned to throw Columbus into the sea. By disposing of him, they would only have made their own situations worse. Their mutiny in the face of these circumstances throws some doubt on his leadership abilities.

Robertson's plain account of the landfall of Columbus on 12 October 1492 was sufficiently majestic that the English Lord Wellesley confessed that he shed tears as he read it, that "it broke his rest at night." Despite some small inaccuracies, some still consider it the most moving account of the event in the English language.[31]

As soon as the sun arose, all their boats were manned and armed. They rowed towards the island with their colours displayed, with warlike music, and other martial pomp. As they approached the coast, they saw it covered with a multitude of people, whom the novelty of the spectacle had drawn together, whose attitudes and gestures expressed wonder and astonishment at the strange objects which presented themselves to their view. Columbus was the first European who set foot in the New World which he had discovered. He landed in a rich dress, and with a naked sword in his hand. His men followed, and kneeling down, they all kissed the ground which they had so long desired to see. They next erected a crucifix, and prostrating themselves before it, returned thanks to God for conducting their voyage to such a happy issue. They then took solemn possession of the country for the crown of Castile and Leon, with all the formalities which the Portuguese were accustomed to observe in acts of this kind, in their new discoveries.

Here Columbus enacted the role of the conquering hero, employing the European symbols of military rank and of Christian belief. Fate provided him with a large audience of curious and admiring natives, whom he completely ignored. The mythic rituals, kissing the ground, erecting a crucifix, and taking possession, all related to the Old World rather than to the New. He was oblivious to the culture of the New World and its peoples. Columbus was depicted as possessing a magnificent ceremonial sense of himself, which excluded concern for all others. The appeal of this passage to the Victorian Lord Wellesley, himself devoted to the building of empires in foreign climes, is understandable.

Columbus was always placed in a good light in Robertson's account. He justified the admiral's behavior, no matter what the evidence was. While out exploring for a gold mine on Christmas Eve of 1492, Columbus took to his bed at midnight. The careless pilot entrusted the ship to a cabin boy, and the ship was dashed against a rock and lost. Most captains would have been responsible for this calamity, sleeping or awake, but Columbus was portrayed as a victim of his disobedient men. "He alone retained presence of mind."

Soon after, he discovered that his "treacherous associate" Martin Pinzón had made off for Spain to be the first to tell of their discoveries. Most captains would have had to bear responsibility for such insubordination, but all fault was directed elsewhere. We are told, "The condition of Columbus was such that he stood in need of consolation." Not having space in his one remaining ship to take all his men home to Spain, Columbus decided to leave a colony, and he enlisted the native population to build a fort. Despite his respect for Columbus, Robertson saw clearly the future result of the colony. "In ten days the work was finished; that simple race of men labouring with inconsiderate assiduity in erecting this first monument of their own servitude."[32] But none of this "servitude" reflected badly on Columbus himself.

At the colony, in Columbus' absence the Spaniards reverted to evil ways in spite of his best efforts. Robertson noted that they behaved

The First Interview of Christopher Columbus with the Natives of America. Columbus distributes hawks' bells, gifts valued by the natives, which would later measure the gold tributes required of them. The beautiful, languid natives are here represented in romantic innocence. Charles Theodore Middleton, *A New and Complete System of Geography,* 1777–1778. Courtesy Library of Congress.

badly, "regardless of the prudent instructions which [Columbus] had given them." They mistreated the natives "as soon as the powerful restraint which the presence and authority of Columbus imposed was withdrawn."[33]

Robertson carried on this distinction between Columbus and his men. Columbus was always the gentleman, always using the pomp of military magnificence when he could to inspire the natives. "He did not neglect the arts of gaining their love and confidence. He adhered scrupulously to the principles of integrity and justice in all his transactions with them, and treated them, on every occasion, not only with humanity, but with indulgence."[34] When the native Americans were taxed each month for gold enough to fill a hawk's bell, Robertson tried to account for the change in Columbus' treatment of them.

Such an imposition was extremely contrary to those maxims which Columbus had hitherto inculcated with respect to the mode of treating [them]. But intrigues were carrying on in the court of Spain at this juncture, in order to undermine his power, and discredit his operations, which constrained him to depart from his own system of administration.[35]

Only gold would convince those at home of his success, and the need to obtain it forced him to impose this heavy tax and to exact payment rigorously. Robertson argued that this need excused Columbus for deviating "from the mildness and humanity with which he uniformly treated that unhappy people."[36]

When the complaints of Columbus' enemies at home persuaded Ferdinand and Isabella to send out Bobadilla to take charge of the colony, and when Bobadilla took possession of Columbus' house and sent him back to Spain in chains, Robertson turned him into a heroic and suffering victim.

Even under this humiliating reverse of fortune, the firmness of mind which distinguishes the character of Columbus did not forsake him. Conscious of his own integrity, and solacing himself with reflecting upon the great things which he had achieved, he endured this insult offered to his character, not only with composure but with dignity. Nor had he the consolation of sympathy to mitigate his sufferings.[37]

Robertson's Columbus was a towering figure, visionary and heroic, of finer quality than all those around him. He was forced to suffer for the inadequacies of his superiors and his men. No one suffered more than he. He wore himself out in the service of the ungrateful. Robertson told this story better and to a wider audience than had anyone before him.

In Robertson's hands, Columbus was a worthy national symbol for America. Made of finer stuff than the men around him, he was misunderstood and mistreated by his monarchs, even as the colonists were mistreated by the British Crown. He had found this New World, which had since been providentially populated by British subjects who were now led to seek their own independence. He had been separated from other wicked Spanish explorers, appropriated alone as a father figure for the American colonies. Such lapses as he was guilty of were either ignored or explained away.

Robertson's history was available to more American colonists than was any earlier source. His book was in the libraries of Harvard, Yale, and Princeton, where the learned young patriots who wrote about the explorer tended to study. Ordinary farmers would have had little access to such books, but a few citizens were accumulating large private libraries. Private proprietary libraries were beginning to be organized in the eighteenth century; Benjamin Franklin is generally credited with establishing the first in 1731. Connecticut had four subscription libraries by 1740. Many of these early institutions had small shelflists, few members, financial problems, and short lives, but Robertson's *History* was one volume likely to be included in them.

The Library Company of Wilmington, Delaware, established for a short period in 1763 and then reestablished in 1788, was typical of these intermittent institutions. An early shelflist, undated but probably from about 1800, lists about 336 titles. Not all volumes can be categorized, but fifty-two volumes were history, and the catalog listed both Robertson's *History of America* and Raynal's *History of the establishment of the Europeans in the Indies.*[38] William Byrd's fine library included *Purchas His Pilgrimes* and Hakluyt's edition of Peter Martyr's *Decades*, as well as several "Cosmographies" and histories of Spain and the New World.[39] The catalogue of books of the Columbian Peithologian Society of New York included Raynal and Robertson and two other histories of America without authors.[40] People who had access to books, then, would certainly have had books about Columbus available.

In these books, Americans would have found the discovery of their land attributed to a grave Italian sailing from Spain, whose courage and accomplishment were steadily accorded ever greater respect. When the stress of Revolution separated the colonies from Mother England, Columbus stood forth as an American hero of unblemished virtue. Historians who had written without thought for Columbus' subsequent appropriation had prepared a figure whom Americans could warmly embrace as a symbol of the courage and independence of their new nation.

CHAPTER THREE

Naming the Nation

Long has Columbia rung with dire alarms,
While Freedom call'd her injur'd sons to arms

Joel Barlow, "The Prospect of Peace," 1778

Hail, Columbia! happy land!
Hail, ye Heroes! heaven-born band!
Who fought and bled in freedom's cause.

Joseph Hopkinson (1720–1842), "Hail, Columbia," 1798

The Evolution of Columbia

The name Columbia was adopted as an alternative to America on the eve of the American Revolution. The name had not been heard for the first 150 years of settlement. The colonies had used names connecting them to Britain, just as they looked to the monarch, his colonial representatives, or to the poetic embodiment of Britannia as symbols of their nationhood. The invocation of Columbus by designating the colonies Columbia became relevant when the upstart settlements wished to distance themselves from Britain. Columbia provided a past that bypassed England.

The person who introduced the title that so helpfully provided an alternate identity to the scattered colonies should have been accorded fame and honor as a patriot. But, like many other developments important in retrospect, the origins of this usage are obscure and contradictory. The learned George H. Moore in a paper read before the Massachusetts Historical Society in the early 1880s specifically asked the question, "When and where did the name *Columbia* first appear in the land to which it justly belongs?" His answer was that it first appeared in a poetic tribute to George Washington written by Phillis Wheatley.[1]

Phillis Wheatley (ca. 1753–1784) was a black slave girl owned by Susanna and John Wheatley, a liberal Boston Methodist merchant. They encouraged Phillis during her early attempts to write religious poetry, and she published her first poem when she was thirteen. Her writing received considerable attention, largely because of her slave status and her ability to arrest the attention of the powerful. After the death of her mistress in 1774, she was freed and married John Peters, an ambitious free black man from Boston. Phillis Wheatley died when she was about thirty, after the death of her two children and the imprisonment of her husband for debt.[2]

The poem by Phillis Wheatley to which George H. Moore referred was written to "his Excellency Gen. Washington" at Providence on 26 October 1775, on the occasion of his elevation to what Wheatley called "Generalissimo of the armies of North America." Part of the poem reads as follows:

> One century scarce perform'd its destin'd round,
> When Gallic powers Columbia's fury found;
> And so may you, whoever dares disgrace
> The land of freedom's heaven-defended race!
> Fix'd are the eyes of nations on the scales,
> For in their hopes Columbia's arm prevails.
> Anon Britannia droops the pensive head,
> While round increase the rising hills of dead.
> Ah! cruel blindness to Columbia's state!
> Lament thy thirst of boundless power too late.

Washington was not unappreciative of the tribute and kindly invited the poetess to visit him at Cambridge in 1776. He also sent the poem to the press, and it was published that year in Pennsylvania.[3]

In this two-page poem, the name Columbia was used four times, three in the short passage above. Wheatley's poem would be a fitting beginning for this patriotic usage of the name. All the right associations are there, stated in the elevated poetic language of the time. The poem was a tribute to the glorious commander, yet warned him that he was subject to the "land of freedom's heaven-defended race." The revolutionary struggle was central to the "eyes of nations," who hoped that "Columbia's arm prevails." Columbia was equal to the "Gallic powers" subdued in the French and Indian Wars and to Britannia, drooping her "pensive head," suffering incredible losses with her "rising hills of dead," lamenting her "thirst of boundless power." Besides the perfection of the revolutionary message, the poem was written by a black woman, scarcely freed from slavery!

It would be very satisfying to announce that this sophisticated personification of Columbia, righteous in revolutionary fervor, was the first usage of the name in the New World. Alas, it was not to be.

Albert H. Hoyt located several earlier classical references to Columbia in the elegiac prerevolutionary verses of (gasp!) loyalists. One striking occurrence was in a poem celebrating the marriage and accession of George III, published in an elegant volume in 1761. The thirty-one compositions in the book were mostly the work of unidentified graduates of Harvard College in that year. Hoyt suggested that Thomas Oliver, lieutenant governor of Massachusetts in 1774 and subsequently a loyalist refugee, probably wrote this poem, which included the following lines:

> Hence, jarring discord, tumults, carnage, wars;
> Embattl'd nations! cease a while to deal
> Destruction; Peace! on balmy wings, descend;
> Let Hymen and the Paphian Goddess hold
> Imperial sway, soft'ning each heart to love.
> Behold, Britannia! in thy favour'd Isle;
> At distance, thou, Columbia! view thy Prince,
> For ancestors renown'd, for virtues more;
> At whose sole nod, grim tyranny aghast,
> With grudging strides, hies swift from British climes;
> While liberty undaunted rears her head.[4]

What irony, from the colonial point of view, that this early use of Columbia should honor George III, here presented as the monarch whose "sole nod" put "grim tyranny" to flight with "grudging strides" and who introduced "liberty, undaunted." "Carnage, wars; / Embattl'd nations" were to give way to peace for the wedding festivities. Britannia and Columbia were equally to behold their prince. Yet within fifteen years, these two would be locked in deadly combat.

Another Columbian poem, published on 26 April 1764 in the *Massachusetts Gazette*, lamented the destruction by fire of Harvard Hall and the college library. Unattributed and apolitical, the poem reads in part:

> Ye Flames, more merciless than the fell Hand
> Of all-devouring Time; more savage far
> Than Earthquake's horrid Shocks; why did ye not
> Recoil with Shame, when near the sacred Volumes,
> Arrang'd with Care, your pointed Spires approach'd?
> Why could ye not, the fam'd *Museum* spare,
> Unrivall'd in *Columbia*. . . .

This offhand reference indicates that the equation of Columbia with the colonies was easily understood among the learned in the 1760s. Additional references of this classical nature will very likely turn up in the future.

Within the next few years, this casual usage took on a more serious purpose. The name Columbia became useful to the patriots when the rhetoric of the Revolutionary War demanded justification for rebellion. Patriotic poetic evocations in the name of liberty and freedom roused the public, but such invocations left intact the relationship with a

This pillar honoring American heroes features three presidents, Benjamin Franklin, the Marquis de Lafayette, and, at the top in the primary position, Christopher Columbus. Engraved by O. Pelton, the image was published in *The Life of George Washington* by Washington Irving, volume 15, 1857 (RB 131135). This item is reproduced by permission of The Huntington Library, San Marino, California.

greater power from which the colonists were breaking away. The colonists needed a legitimate heritage that did not include Britain and a name that stood beside Britannia in equality, without the mother/child relationship. These they found in Columbus and Columbia.

Perhaps the first nationalistic use of the name Columbus was in "Liberty. A Poem" by "Rusticus," published in Philadelphia in 1768 during the Townshend Acts crisis. In that poem, Columbus appears and cautions the colonists that Grenville is preparing to "invade" their freedoms and that "On *Care* and *Union* your *Success* depends." This poem was attributed to a "New Jersey hermit," whose lack of ambition supposedly made him trustworthy, as opposed to the grasping and conspiratorial ministers. "America. A Poem" by Alexander Martin, published soon after the work of "Rusticus," allows Columbus and other New World explorers to regard the difficulties of the Townshend Acts and ask, "Was it for this?"[5] These appearances by Columbus were concerned with revolutionary activities rather than with the original exploration.

At this time, the form of the name was not yet settled. Columba was sometimes used instead of Columbia. The *Boston Gazette* of 7 September 1772 published a poem that adapted the name of the land from the "discoverer," referring to Grenville and Townshend as trying to "seize *Columba's* Money" and to Spain and France as attempting to divide "*Britain* and *Columba* fair."[6] Miles Parkin, an English writer, also used the less euphonious name in his "Columba, A Poetical Epistle, Heroic and Satirical," a poem of 1783. He chose "Columba," he said, because he found the nation's name "too trite and feeble to be admitted into a chaste English couplet." This preference for the lumbering Columba over the graceful America is difficult to understand, but perhaps he had the United States of America in mind. In his patriotic poem written from the British point of view, Parkin was angered by America's shameless alliance with France: "Columba's Hero [Washington] forges Britain's chain!" Still, he mourned the broken tie with Britain, which urged Columba to "Return . . . to thy parent's Arms," hoping she would join Britain " 'gainst Perfidious Gaul," so the two could dominate the world.[7]

James Allen, a Boston poet, also used the term Columba to refer to the American colonies in his long work "Retrospect." His friends brought out extracts of the work, along with his poem on the Boston Massacre, in 1772. Allen had been asked by his friend General Joseph Warren to write the poem on the massacre to accompany the general's commemorative oration. The work was suppressed, however, when the committee, chaired by Samuel Adams, suspected that Allen was not in true sympathy with the popular party.[8]

Cotton Mather recorded still another variant of the admiral's name. He noted that the learned English cleric Nicholas Fuller observed that America "might more justly be called Columbina."[9]

Columbia, however, was the more common usage by far. Mercy Otis Warren, the general's wife, wrote a poem with political overtones that used the name Columbia and was published on 13 February 1775 in the *Boston Gazette*. The poem was later revised and called "Poetical Reverie." Referring to the course of empire, Warren says,

> She, o'er the vast Atlantic surges rides,
> Visits *Columbia's* distant fertile Plains,
> Where LIBERTY, a happy Goddess, reigns;
> Where no proud Despot rules with lawless sway,
> Nor Orphan's spoils become the Minion's prey.

The headnote indicated that the piece had been written twelve months before and was being published as a "Prophecy hastening fast to a Completion."[10] After her husband, General Warren, was killed at the Battle of Bunker Hill and became a major American hero, his eulogy was written "by a Columbian."[11]

In July 1775, Philip Freneau, the most gifted of the early poets, published "American Liberty, A Poem," in the *New York Journal*. His use of Columbia here predated Phillis Wheatley by three months. In a footnote, he explains the meaning of Columbia: "America sometimes so called from Columbus the first discoverer."

> Where darling peace with smiling aspect stood,
> Lo! the grim soldier stalks in quest of blood:
> What madness, heaven, has made Britannia frown?
> Who plans our schemes to pull Columbia down?[12]

Freneau, who wrote a great deal of patriotic verse, can be profitably mined for additional references. In his "A Voyage to Boston" of 1775, is this couplet.

> 'Till then may heaven assert our injur'd claims,
> And second every stroke Columbia aims.[13]

John Anderson "humbly addressed" a poem in 1775 "to all true lovers of this once flourishing country":

> O Congress fam'd, accept this humble lay,
> The little tribute that the muse can pay,
> On you depends Columbia's future fate—
> A free asylum or a wretched state.[14]

A poetic parody of the popular work "Watery God" was called "The Jerseys of 1776." This poem celebrated the success of the Americans at Trenton and Princeton with these lines.

> Appall'd they view'd Columbia's sons,
> Deal death and slaughter from their guns. . . .
>
> The god with wonder heard the story,
> Astonish'd view'd Columbia's glory.[15]

The usage rapidly became commonplace and conventional. Colonel David Humphreys, a distinguished wit and Connecticut poet who became Washington's aide de camp, showed himself to be an eighteenth-century gentleman by penning a "Sonnet to my Friends at Yale College on my leaving them to join the Army." He chronicled his devotion to the "cause of liberty."

> While dear Columbia calls no danger awes,
> Though certain death to threaten'd chains be join'd.[16]

Military service did not dampen his poetic inclinations, and he recorded his departure from the military in 1783 with another sonnet, "On Disbanding the Army."

> Ye brave Columbian bands! a long farewell!
> Well have ye fought for freedom.[17]

The use of the name Columbia continued in some of the most engaging verses of the day—occasional lyrics set to popular songs. "The Dance" of 1781, to the tune of "Yankee Doodle," commemorated the campaign of Cornwallis in America and appeared soon after his surrender:

> And Washington, Columbia's son,
>   Whom easy nature taught, sir,
> That grace which can't by pains be won,
>   Or Plutus' gold be bought, sir.[18]

Jonathan M. Sewall, Esq., a poet from New Hampshire, wrote a song that was published on 19 December 1776 in *The Independent Chronicle*. The lyrics include this reference to Columbia.

> Michael! go forth! (the Godhead cry'd,)
> Wave thy dread Ensign o'er the Tide,
> And edge *Columbia's* Sword![19];

The name Columbia was well suited for replacing Britannia in many lines, having the same poetic resonance as well as the same rhythm and number of syllables. The resemblance made a somewhat mechanical substitution possible. "Britain's Glory, or Gallic Pride Humbled," written after the French and Indian War, was restyled by Benjamin Prime as "Columbia's Glory, or British Pride Humbled." Loyalties and pledges of devotion could easily be realigned.

> COLUMBIA only is my country now:
> To her alone my services belong:
> My head, my heart, my hands,
> My pen, my lyre, my tongue,
> COLUMBIA's interest now demands,
> Engrosses all my cares and claims my ev'ry song.[20]

Replacing Britannia with Columbia in songs that praised the king and the empire was deliberate and ironical. Tom Paine's setting of "The Great Republic: or, the Land of Love and Liberty" to the song "Rule, Britannia" was certainly calculated.

> Hail! Great Republic of the world,
> The rising empire of the West;
> Where fam'd Columbus, with a mighty mind inspir'd,
> Gave tortur'd Europe scenes of rest.
> *Be thou for ever, for ever great and free,*
> *The Land of Love and Liberty.*[21]

Here he characterized Columbus as a founder and indicated that America was not only equal but superior to Great Britain.

The Rising Glory

Long before independence, the term Columbia denoted more than just the gathered colonies and their revolutionary identity; Columbia was the utopian land, newborn and full of promise. A whole generation of poets, known as the "rising glory school," saw Columbia as the future hope of the world. In 1771, Freneau, along with his Princeton friend Hugh Brackenridge, wrote a stirring patriotic poem called "The Rising Glory of America." This prophetic poem included a reference to Columbus, perhaps Freneau's first. Freneau sang the story of America, beginning with

> The period famed when first Columbus touched
> These shores so long unknown—through various toils,
> Famine, and death, the hero forced his way,
> Through oceans pregnant with perpetual storms,
> And climates hostile to adventurous man.

Freneau dissociated Columbus from Cortez's bloody conquest, noting his intention only to discuss "these northern realms . . . designed by nature for the rural reign, / For agriculture's toil."

Cursed be that ore, which brutal makes our race
And prompts mankind to shed their kindred blood.[22]

This poem of Brackenridge and Freneau was one of the first written in America describing the actual historical Columbus, but the poets had an even more ambitious vision. They saw America as the last and best achievement of the civilized world, a mighty nation reaching from coast to coast, "warm in freedom's cause," and under the flag of Great

This fanciful engraving of Columbus, based on a painting by Mariano Maella and first published in *Historia del Nuevo Mundo* by Juan Muñoz, was sold in the United States in the early nineteenth century. Delaplaine used the image as the frontispiece of his *Gallery of Distinguished Americans*, 1814. A copy of the painting, presented to the Philadelphia Academy of Arts in 1818, has since disappeared. Courtesy, American Antiquarian Society.

Britain. These young collegians were loyal British subjects in 1771, yet their poetry prefigured the changes in the wind. Nationalistic and patriotic art and literature proliferated under this "rising glory" theme as the patriotic allegiances of the citizens shifted from King George to the new nation.[23] In a later practical example of the nation's "rising glory," the honored ship *Columbia* carried the stars and stripes around the globe in 1792. *Columbia*, the ship, extended the realm of the nation Columbia by exploring the land in the northwest of the continent. She gave her name to the great Columbia River and claimed the contiguous land, now Oregon, Washington, and Idaho.[24]

At the same time that Columbia, the new nation, was taking on a literary identity, the visual symbols by which she was represented were also taking form. Columbus himself did not represent the nation. In English prints and engravings, Columbia was often shown as an unclothed Indian princess. This female figure evoked the strangeness and wildness of a primitive land, but it lacked civilized culture and was not to the colonists' liking. During the Revolution, the female American symbol went through a number of changes, evolving into a decorous and attractive young goddess. This woman was known as Columbia, Liberty, or America. Modest in dress, sprightly in manner, holding a banner or flying on the back of an eagle, this fresh maiden symbolized a promising new nation, a rising glory herself.[25]

This sprightly miss was charmingly portrayed in a later patriotic pageant by John Brougham, which introduced Columbia as the female interest played against Columbus. Attired in cap and spangled bodice, she introduced herself as the niece of Uncle Sam: "In fact the genius of the mighty land / On which will rest your name and fame. / Myself and Liberty / Are one." She accompanied Columbus to the New World and back again, where she was introduced to the king and queen. She took the hands of the monarchs and energetically shook them. Told that she had outraged etiquette and should have knelt, she demurred, "I can't—my constitution wouldn't stand it."[26]

One of the best statements of the "rising glory" genre was the popular "Columbia," written by Timothy Dwight after the Revolution began. This poem combined the progress theme with that of independence from Britain. Dwight, the precocious grandson of eminent Puritan divine Jonathan Edwards, matriculated at Yale at age thirteen and distinguished himself as a student, becoming president there in 1795.[27] While an army chaplain at West Point in 1777, Dwight composed the song "Columbia" to remind the soldiers that they were heroes defending the rights of mankind. He had presented the same idea in his valedictory address to his Yale class of July 1776, just three weeks after Congress adopted the Declaration of Independence. He thought mankind would surely progress westward, toward perfection, and that America would be the most glorious land of all, where "the progress of temporal things toward perfection will undoubtedly be finished."[28] For Dwight, Columbia was an imaginary land rather than the one he lived in. He conjured up this new land from his dream by calling her name. Columbia no longer had an English past; in fact, she existed apart from history, with no ancestry whatsoever. The poem was predominantly secular, although it presented "Columbia" as a triumph in the unfolding of God's plan. The song struck many of the chords to which the patriots were most responsive and was singable and very popular, although it was not published until six years later.

The first stanza follows:

> COLUMBIA, Columbia, to glory arise,
> The queen of the world, and the child of the skies!
> Thy genius commands thee; with rapture behold,
> While ages on ages thy splendors unfold.
> Thy reign is the last, and the noblest of time,
> Most fruitful thy soil, most inviting thy clime;
> Let the crimes of the East ne'er encrimson thy name,
> Be freedom, and science, and virtue, thy fame.

Caleb Bingham, by the way, published this poem of Dwight's in 1794 in one of his schoolbooks, *The American Preceptor*, under the title "Columba." There the poem gracelessly read, "Columba, Columba, to glory arise, / The queen of the world, and the child of the skies."[29]

Another of Dwight's early works was "America, Or a Poem on the Settlement of British Colonies." He wrote most of this poem while he was a student at Yale but did not publish it until 1780. The colonial past was recounted, then Dwight went on to talk about the future, his vision of the millenium. His reference to Columbus was brief and glancing, only four lines set between "savage roarings" and "blest ELIZA." He indicated that the journey of Columbus was guided by heavenly forces, and he characterized the new lands as a promised place.

> At length (COLUMBUS taught by heaven to trace
> Far-distant lands, through unknown pathless seas)
> AMERICA's bright realms arose to view,
> And the *old* world rejoic'd to see the *new*.[30]

In 1787, Dwight published "Columbia," his lyrical hymn to patriotism, and his "Address of the Genius of Columbia, to the Members of the Continental Convention." Here, in the year of framing the Constitution, the founding fathers were given a choice of governmental styles: private interest, which was "rule unsystem'd," or a strong, central government.

Columbia's interests public sway demand,
Her commerce, impost, unlocated land,
Her war, her peace, her military power,
Treaties to deal with every distant shore—

Seize them oh! seize Columbia's golden hour,
Perfect her federal system, public power;
For this stupendous realm, this chosen race,
With all the improvements of all lands its base,
The glorious structure build.[31]

While some saw the limitless possibilities of the nation, others were motivated by the need to prove themselves equal to the British. Nathaniel Tucker, an American doctor practicing in England, wrote *Columbinus: A Mask* in 1783 as a patriotic gesture. His pride in independence was underscored by his realization that his countrymen were scorned by their British brothers.

for, believe me,
there's not a Cobler sitting in a stall
in England, but doth feel himself a sovereign
over this country; and the men that crawl on't
his subjects, that depend for life and property
on his good sufferance.[32]

Elhanan Winchester, another patriot in exile in England, predicted the nation's glorious future. He celebrated the three hundredth anniversary of the first landfall of Columbus with an oration praising the nation as *"the very birthplace of civil and religious liberty"* and suggested the adoption of the name THE UNITED STATES OF COLUMBIA. He had seen the colonies crushed and had lived to see them free and independent, "rising to glory and extensive empire." His prophetic vision of the future became fact.

Behold the whole continent highly cultivated and fertilized, full of cities, towns and villages, beautiful and lovely beyond expression. I hear the praises of my great Creator sung upon the banks of those rivers unknown to song. Behold the delightful prospect! see the silver and gold of America employed in the service of the Lord of the whole earth! See Slavery, with all it's train of attendant evils for ever abolished! See a communication opened through the whole continent from North to South, and from East to West, through a most fruitful country! Behold the glory of God extending, and the gospel spreading, through the whole land![33]

Columbus could be used as the leader with foresight, who took risks that improved mankind with inventions. He was the man with the active thirst for knowledge. His rashness was applauded in contrast to the prudence of those who hesitated to act.

> With cautious steps they tread secure from shame,
> But never, never feel a wish for FAME.

Risk was necessary, according to this unsigned author from the West Indies writing in the *Columbian Magazine* in 1791, for without it, progress would not take place. Would the prudent man ever have explored the wilds of science, "Or wander'd from his native shore?" The poet compares the prudent and the rash and names Columbus as an example of the latter and better group.

> Thy subjects are the spiritless and cold.
> The sons of genius are the rash and bold.
> Ye Indian realms, where fate has bid me steer.
> Did ever Prudence send Columbus here?

This poem illustrates the pride the young Americans felt in their daring and uses the mariner as an exemplar.[34]

The poetic fervor engendered by the Revolution led the country to think well of itself and to expect that high culture would follow. Some considered the writings of Trumbull, Dwight, Barlow, and Humphries to be equal to the works of the great English writers. This early enthusiasm for national culture, conjured up by ardor born from independence, lasted through the Revolution until about 1795, cooling considerably after the turn of the century. As the glories of the Revolution faded, the pressure for a new cultural nationalism was reduced.[35]

The Columbus—Washington Connection

Since the names Columbus and Columbia were invoked in connection with the American Revolution, they became linked with the name of George Washington. Washington was the father of the country; he was also of the present and of the place. Columbus was European and of the past. The combination of references to the new and old worlds gave stability to the nation's identity. The two intrepid leaders, Washington and Columbus, with their steely resolve, had much in common.[36]

Washington and Columbia were irretrievably linked in the spirit of the new nation. An example of this linkage can be seen in the Columbiads written to praise the mighty Washington. Richard Snowden, a New Jersey farmer, wrote such an epic in 1795.[37] Snowden's charming little epic looked forward to beyond the war period to a great day ahead, if only the faithful soldiers could carry on.

METHINKS I hear divine Columbia say:
Bear up, my sons, your valour still display;
The day draws near when peace shall bless the land,
And *Washington* shall rule with equal hand.[38]

This pairing of the names Washington and Columbus or Columbia
for patriotic and evocative purposes continued. When the ten mile
square for the national capital was ceded by Virginia and Maryland in
1791, the commissioners apparently had the power to name the new
entity. They named the capital city in a letter to Major L'Enfant, dated
from Georgetown on 9 September 1791: "We have agreed that the
federal district shall be called 'The Territory of Columbia,' and the
Federal City, 'The City of Washington': the title of the map, will, therefore, be 'A Map of the City of Washington, in the Territory of
Columbia.' "[39]

The two names linked with the national capital were frequently used
for institutions of higher learning. The British army had barely left
New York when Governor Clinton set out to reorganize King's College.
The legislators agreed to change the name to Columbia College to
symbolize "both the rejection of England and the glorification of
America."[40]

George Washington thought that the new national district should
have an institution of higher education and offered a gift toward its
establishment. Finally chartered as "Columbian College" in 1822, the
institution became Columbian University in 1873. In 1904, financial re-
organization plus confusion with New York's Columbia University led

The "Birthplace of Columbus" and the "Tomb of Columbus at Mt. Vernon" illustrate
the blending of the histories of notable men. Walt. McDougall, *The Un-Authorized History
of Columbus*, Newark, 1899.

to a name change. What else could Columbian University become but George Washington University?[41]

The names Washington and Columbia were frequently paired in poetry. Susanna Rowson, the educator and novelist, wrote an eulogy to "Columbia's guardian genius—WASHINGTON!"

> While Plenty decks Columbia's plains,
> Where'er the voice of Fame is heard,
> While love of Liberty remains,
> WASHINGTON's name shall be rever'd.[42]

When George Washington's farewell address, his "Valuable Advice to his fellow citizens," was published in 1796, the book was called *Columbia's Legacy*. The Columbian Anacreontic Society of New York, a choral group that flourished from 1795 to 1803, honored the memory of George Washington with a solemn service in St. Paul's Church in connection with the Philharmonic Society. The chorus of a song lamenting the hero's death, which identified the singers with their other father, was:

> Columbians weep! weep still in louder moan
> Your Hero, Patriot, Friend and Father's gone.[43]

A popular broadside, dated 1799, "LADY WASHINGTON'S LAMENTATION FOR THE DEATH OF HER HUSBAND," is supposedly from the lips of Martha Washington.

> When Columbia's brave sons sought my hero to lead them,
> To vanquish their foes and establish their freedom,
> I rejoic'd at his honors, my fears I dissembled,
> At the thought of his dangers my heart how it trembled,
> Oh, my Washington! Oh my Washington![44]

The Columbian Legacy

The idea of a glorious, culturally independent America may have wavered after the war, but once the word "Columbia" was entrenched, its use proliferated, and the word became associated with nationalistic aspirations. One of the best, though not the first, postwar periodicals was Mathew Carey's *Columbian Magazine*, which began publication in September 1786. The magazine gathered evidence of progress in all fields, spouting about what was best in the New World. Included was a section called "The Columbian Parnassiad," which presented poetry written in America.[45] Carey brought before the public a wide array of contemporary American writers and poets.

Artistic and cultural aspirations were frequently given a Columbian designation. The *Columbian Museum, or Universal Asylum*, a magazine with essays on agriculture, commerce, manufactures, politics, morals, and manners, published a single issue in 1793. The *Columbian Lady's and Gentleman's Magazine embracing literature in every department* reproduced engravings, music, and fashion and was published from 1844 to 1849.

Newspapers incorporating the name, including Massachusetts' *Columbian Centinel*, the *Columbian Phenix or Boston Review* (Boston, 1800), and the long-lived *Columbian Weekly Register* (New Haven, 1812–1911) sprang up. *The Columbian Muse* was a book of poetry published in 1794, and *The Columbian Lyre*, which included specimens of transatlantic poetry, was published in 1828. Noah Brashears' *Columbia's Wreath* dates from 1830.

Practical books exemplifying the hopeful, improvement ethos of the New World were similarly designated. *The Columbian Arithmetician*, written "by an American" in 1811, is an example of such patriotic improvement. *The Columbian Grammar, enlarged and approved* by Benjamin Dearborn also sounded the note of progress. Mathew Carey's *Columbian Spelling and Reading Book* of 1807; Benjamin Heaton's *Columbian Spelling Book* (1799); and Caleb Bingham's *The Columbian Orator containing a variety of original and selected pieces . . . calculated to improve youth and others in the ornamental and useful art of eloquence*, published in its sixth edition in 1804, are further examples. *The Columbian Orthographer* (1819) and many editions of *The Columbian Pocket Almanack* were also in this mode.

Musical books such as *The Columbian Songster, or Jovial Companion*, Pelissier's *Columbian Melodies* (1812), and *The Columbian and European Harmony* (1802) often used the name. *The Columbian Harmonist* of 1806 and 1816 set out to inculcate a "True Taste in Church Music."

Abner Kneeland's *The Columbian Miscellany*, published in 1804, gathered together some of the best material published in the magazines of 1788 and 1789. John Wilson Campbell's *The Columbian Reader*, published in 1814, was a selection of "Amusing and Instructive Lessons for Schools and Academies." Thomas Woodward's *The Columbian Plutarch or An Exemplification of Several Distinguished American Characters* (1819) was a collection of important biographies. *The Columbian Monitor*, Donald Fraser's book of 1797 that claimed to be "a Pleasant and Early Guide to Useful Knowledge," included information on religion, grammar, sample letters to copy, and rules for genteel behavior—everything a citizen of the new nation needed to know. The name added a patriotic and national touch to publications of all kinds.

A bloody battle with the Indians on 4 November 1791 was referred to as *The Columbian Tragedy.* Columbian societies were organized in Washington, D.C., in 1794 and in Marblehead, Massachusetts, by 1839. The Columbian Society of Artists in Philadelphia was holding exhibitions by 1807.[46]

For an exercise in name recognition, the adoption could hardly have been more successful. The rare classical reference of the 1760s became the most heartily adopted and commonly used allusion of the land. Cities, counties, ships, societies, clubs, museums, gas stations, stove companies, hotels, insurance companies, and schools chose this name for its overtones of combined solidity and daring, classical purity and ethnic warmth, historical origins and progress. Columbia transcended her origin to become an all-purpose name.

To Simon Willard, the name Columbia invoked a vision of the entire North American continent under a single government. He felt Canada should be annexed to make room for the poor. In an extended, rambling diatribe published in 1814, he evoked a mystical patriotism, which he saw as God's will. To him, Columbia meant equal rights for all. "Columbus was an ark of safety like the ancient Noah. He was a pilot, not a king; a friend to liberty, not a tyrant, but a Washington." Columbus came to America, opening the door to liberty for all Europe. The last verse of his final poem restated his thesis.

> By our God of rights Columbia
> Is promis'd free as sacred land,
> With glorious milk and honey,
>   As bravest fathers did command.
>   Free Columbia's constitution
>   One grand Columbian Union.[47]

A commercial note was also introduced. Susanna Rowson's rousing sailor song, "America, Commerce and Freedom," was not particularly patriotic, but it bound the nation, liberty, and good business together within the warm ambience and social life of the tavern. She used Columbia for poetic purposes, but for practical matters, she resorted to America, ending each verse with a variant of

> But toss off a glass, to a favourite lass,
> To America, Commerce, and Freedom.[48]

The nationalistic fervor, as well as the patriotic use of Columbia, arose again as America and Great Britain engaged in combat during the War of 1812. *Columbia's Naval Triumphs,* officially anonymous but probably written by Jonathan Seymour and published in 1813, was an epic recounting the naval battles of the War of 1812. Patrioticly praising

Columbia and her heroes, the poem was still faithful to England in style and tradition. The foe with her "haughty strength" was never directly named.

> Ye sons of Liberty! who fought and died,
>   When smiling vict'ry crown'd the righteous side;
> When a bright laurel fair Columbia bore,
>   Surpassing every wreath she ever wore.[49]

Battles were depicted, but only to praise Columbia's participants. The sketchily depicted enemy could forgive such an account after peace was made.

This ambivalence about American nationalism and subservience to British culture was reflected in a contest for new American naval songs sponsored by the *Port Folio*, an American magazine published during the era of the War of 1812. The editor went so far as to suggest borrowing English tunes for the purpose! He noted that the music "may be modelled on the airs most familiar to us, and even on those of the enemy to whose tunes of national triumph, we seem to have in some degree, succeeded by right of conquest, as well as of inheritance." A subscriber questioned whether a borrowed tune would accommodate the sought-after independence. More seriously, he questioned whether using such a song would not perpetuate "national enmities" arising "from circumstances merely of casual and transitory hostility."[50] Clearly the mood was to propitiate rather than anger Great Britain, a far cry from revolutionary sentiment.

Nevertheless, a national song did arise out of the conflict, and, notably, it was set to the English air "Anacreon in Heaven." Although originally published as "Hail Columbia," the song achieved fame as "The Star Spangled Banner." The original words of "Anacreon in Heaven," known as an English drinking song, were written by Ralph Tomlinson, president of the Anacreontic Society, a popular drinking club in London; the club's patron saint was Anacreon, the "convivial bard of Greece." The composer of the music may have been John Stafford Smith, although that honor is still contested.

Francis Scott Key was inspired by the tattered stars and stripes still flying over Fort McHenry in Baltimore in 1814 when he composed his immortal words, but the familiar melody had been used for many another occasional song and parody. In fact, patriotic Americans had been setting words to the melody, mostly using the name Columbia as a national designation, at least since the 1790s. Susanna Rowson had composed birthday lyrics to the tune for George Washington, sung in Boston on 11 February 1798. The chorus varied this repeated couplet.

The sons of Columbia forever shall be
From oppression secure, and from anarchy free.[51]

It is interesting and worthy of comment that Key's song, which began with a slang phrase, concentrated on the flag and avoided using the names Columbia, the United States, America, or anything else more specific than the vague "Land of the free, and the home of the brave" and the poetic "Heav'n rescued land."[52] The other primary patriotic song of the United States, "My Country! 'Tis of Thee," is in the same tradition, a blatant borrowing from the English national anthem, "God Save the King." Samuel Francis Smith, author of the words, claimed ignorance of the origin of the tune, which he found in a German songbook and believed to be a German patriotic air. In this song, first sung on 4 July 1831 in Boston,[53] once again no mention is made of the nation celebrated. "My country" is the "Sweet land of Liberty," the land "where my fathers died" and of "the pilgrim's pride," "my native country," the "Land of the noble free," and so on; but no specific nation is named. The same is true of Julia Ward Howe's elliptical "Battle Hymn of the Republic." Not until Katherine Lee Bates wrote "America, the Beautiful" did a widely accepted patriotic song specifically name the country. America worked very well in her lyrical song, although the name is confined to the chorus where it is set off by itself. Only the nation's greatest song writer, Irving Berlin, fully incorporated the country's name into a popular patriotic song. His simple and moving "God Bless America" is perhaps the unofficial national anthem. As poets have warned for some years, the appellation "The United States of America" discourages the muses.

The situation could have been different. We could just as easily have had a song that praised Columbia. Joseph Hopkinson's spirited, "Hail Columbia! happy land! / Hail, you Heroes! heaven-born band!" Won instant acclaim when published in 1798. Set to the music of Washington's inaugural march, the song combines references to Columbia and Washington and a significant historical event.[54]

"Columbia the Land of the Brave," now generally known as "Columbia the Gem of the Ocean," first published in 1843, would have been another excellent national anthem. Praising patriots, liberty, and the flag as well as actually naming the country, the song has the added advantages of being rhythmic, singable, and American in feeling. Though the authorship for this song has been contested, it is American in origin. To add to its virtues is its history: The music was later pirated back across the Atlantic and, in ironic reversal of American poets' earlier practices, published in England as "Britannia, the Pride of the Ocean."[55]

CHAPTER FOUR

Columbus in Poetry

Thus happy they dwelt in a rural domain
Uninstructed in commerce, unpractic'd in gain,
Till, taught by the lodestone to traverse the seas,
Columbus came over, that bold Genoese.

Yet the schemes of Columbus, however well plann'd
Were scarcely sufficient to find the main land;
On the *islands* alone with the natives he spoke,
Except when he enter'd the great *Oronoque:*

These islands and worlds in the wat'ry expanse,
Like most mighty things, were the offspring of chance,
Since steering for Asia, Columbus, they say,
Was astonish'd to find such a world in his way!

Where the sun in December appears to decline
Far off to the southward, and south of the line,
A merchant of Florence, more fortunate still,
Explor'd a new track, and discover'd Brazil:

Good fortune, *Vespucius,* pronounc'd thee her own,
Or else to mankind thou hadst scarcely been known—
By giving thy name, thou art ever reknown'd—
Thy *name* to a world that another had found!

Columbia the name was that merit decreed,
But Fortune and Merit have never agreed—
Yet the poets, alone, with commendable care
Are vainly attempting the wrong to repair.

Philip Freneau, selected passages from, "Sketches of American History"

Poets began to write about Columbus soon after his death. His story, with its excitement, triumph, and pathos as well as its patriotic overtones and historical aspects, is the stuff of literature. The rich and changeable aspects of the Columbian legend provided useful metaphors.

From the beginning, Columbus was an Italian hero. In the sixteenth century alone, three epic poems honoring the explorer were written in Italy, where the biography by Ferdinand Columbus was first published. Italians saw in Columbus a fellow countryman who had, in recent history, performed a deed of universal significance as well as of courage and merit. Though rich in the arts and sciences, Italy had for centuries been deprived of a political unity, without a national life or national heroes. Columbus was drafted for the role.[1] Italian immigrants brought him to America for that purpose, only to discover that he had been previously imported for patriotic purposes.

Epic tributes to the explorer were also written in Spain and France, where Columbus was portrayed as a tragic figure because his rewards fell short of his accomplishments. The admiration of poets was inspired by his bravery despite his apparent failure. This theme, of personal courage, extracted from the larger story of Columbus, was more attractive to the public than the narrative of seeking patronage or an account of his navigational skill. This emphasis on heroism in the face of difficulty made Columbus a model for courageous behavior.

An example of a typical European tribute to Columbus is the *Colombiade* of a French woman, Anne-Marie du Boccage (1710–1802), published in 1756.[2] The literary Madame du Boccage adopted Christopher Columbus as her personal hero, and she spent ten years describing his nobility in the ten songs of her long poem. She belonged to a circle that considered the unknown New World and its explorers a subject of rich imaginative and philosophical possibilities,[3] and in her poem she juxtaposed historically accurate and fictional scenes, reciting in long speeches the customs of the New and Old Worlds.

Madame du Boccage became famous, and her *Columbiade* went through three editions in France and was translated into several other languages.[4] Voltaire praised this fair poetess, put a laurel crown on her head when she visited him, and said she united the empire of beauty with that of mind and talent. Some of her other admirers enthusiastically declared that she was in person Venus and in art Minerva.[5] Although this poem does not seem to have been widely read in the New World, this epic is of the sort that learned young Americans might have seen. If they did not copy such models directly, they would have been familiar with the genre.

One of the poem's devices, which was not likely original with Madame du Boccage, was to show Columbus despondent at the end of his life, then to comfort him by disclosing a panorama of future events, indicating that all his suffering was not in vain. Though this device allowed writers to compensate for the injustice done to Columbus, it also gave poets free rein to tell any story they wanted, using Columbus as a visiting authority. After he would watch the ages unroll before him, he would break into generous tears of happiness, putting a stamp of approval on the author's interpretation of history.

American poets may not have discovered Columbus—who was the subject of many European works—but they certainly used him to achieve their aims. A basic historical account could be retrieved from Robertson, and the whole could be manipulated to serve the ends of the individual man of letters.

The attributes of the explorer attracted the two most prolific American poets of the revolutionary age, Philip Freneau and Joel Barlow, both of whom used Columbus in major works. Freneau attempted a psychological portrait; Barlow, using the popular format of Madame du Boccage, comforted the despondent Columbus with visions of the successful future of the land he explored.

Philip Morin Freneau (1752–1832) was a great and prolific poet who devoted some of his best efforts to Columbus. He was certainly the best American poet of the eighteenth century and perhaps the best American writer as well. Some of his graceful lyrics are still anthologized, but unfortunately Freneau is no longer widely read. He deserves rediscovery, for his sprightly poems bring pleasure to the reader and the ideas speak clearly to the present day. His language is apt, his syntax unlabored, and his lines reveal a meticulous metrical structure. He started young, writing a great deal of verse, both acknowledged and anonymous.

Freneau was a patriot. At Princeton, he was a close friend of James Madison. He bestowed the name and style on a whole genre of nationalistic and patriotic poetry with his commencement poem: "The Rising Glory of America." He should have been recognized as a great man.

But Freneau was emotional and impractical, a dreamer, a frustrated idealist. Freneau dissipated his estate. He made a precarious living teaching school, perhaps studying for the ministry, editing newspapers, captaining a schooner, and writing poetry for publication. He never prospered. He was a better protester than a fighter, and he did not take his place among the patriotic giants of his time. He was a college graduate and a fine scholar, but he was not accorded the rank of gentleman. He seemed to lack manner and substance.[6] He was a gifted but disappointed man who came to a sad end. As an old man of eighty years, he was walking across the lots toward his New Jersey home one evening and was mired in a bog meadow. He could not extricate himself, and his body was found there the next day.[7]

Perhaps his lack of heroic attributes and his grim view of the world allowed his writings to speak better to our twentieth century than to his own eighteenth. In his several poems that deal with Columbus and the exploration era, he revealed his vision of the dark side of the New World conquest. His poems could have been written today.

Freneau's poem "Discovery," written in 1772 but not published until fourteen years later, does not mention Columbus by name. Freneau's vision in this poem is a damning one. He castigates the exploring spirit that vanquished new lands for gain. He sees the discovery of America as nothing but looting by greedy Europeans, accompanied by the killing and enslaving of the natives. He views European civilization as being of no benefit to the New World.

Freneau declares that the explorers forgot "the social virtues of the heart."

> What are the arts that rise on Europe's plan
> But arts destructive to the bliss of man?
> What are all wars, where'er the tracks you trace,
> But the sad records of our world's disgrace.

In Freneau's view, exploration brought out the worst in the adventurers and despoiled the land; the conquest was damaging to the conquerers and to the conquered.

> Alas! how few of all that daring train
> That seek new worlds embosomed in the main,
> How few have sailed on virtue's nobler plan,
> How few with motives worthy of a man!

Man seemed incapable of contentment. Not happy at home, he set out to make people unhappy elsewhere.

> Slaves to their passions, man's imperious race,
> Born for contention, find no resting place,
> And the vain mind, bewildered and perplext,
> Makes this world wretched to enjoy the next.
> Tired of the scenes that Nature made their own,
> They rove to conquer what remains unknown:
> Avarice, undaunted, claims whate'er she sees,
> Surmounts earth's circle, and foregoes all ease;

These European marauders, in imposing their own laws and religion on other lands, destroyed what they found there. Freneau suggests that explorers should leave their own culture at home, that they should travel only to discover new ways of doing things rather than to impose their own unsuited customs upon others.

> Blest in their distance from that bloody scene,
> Why spread the sail to pass the gulphs between?—
> If winds can waft to ocean's utmost verge,

And there new islands and new worlds emerge—
If wealth, or war, or science bid thee roam,
Ah, leave religion and thy laws at home,
Leave the free native to enjoy his store,
Nor teach destructive arts, unknown before.

But Freneau did not exalt the native culture—which had its own problems—in comparison to the European. Unfortunately, even cultures protected from European powers were oppressed by their own leaders. With his unsentimental eye, Freneau damned human nature rather than Europeans. Oppressive leaders took command in every society. Throughout the world, the race of men was doomed to be "dupes to a few."

First Landing of Christopher Columbus; Frederick Kemmelmeyer; National Gallery of Art, Washington; Gift of Edgar William and Bernice Chrysler Garbisch.

> Howe'er [nature] smiles beneath those milder skies,
> Though men decay the monarch never dies!
> Howe'er the groves, howe'er the gardens bloom,
> A *monarch* and a *priest* is still their doom![8]

This grim vision, free from the exaggerated idealism that was to grow in the next century, was delineated when the poet was only twenty years old.

Columbus was among the Spanish adventurers whose influence Freneau deplored, and he went on to explore Columbus specifically in two more poems written in the 1770s, both published in his *Poems* of 1786. These remarkable poems are "Columbus to Ferdinand" (1770) and "The Pictures of Columbus" (1774). A complex, passionate Columbus emerged from Freneau's strongest early period. Freneau was less concerned about portraying a hero or a villain than in portraying a psychologically motivated explorer.

"Columbus to Ferdinand," written in 1770 and first published in June 1779 in the *United States Magazine* by Freneau's friend Hugh Brackenridge, was a mature work. Freneau imagined the entreaty of Columbus to the king and composed a monologue in which Columbus sued for support. "Illustrious monarch of Iberia's soil," he intoned, "While yet Columbus breathes the vital air, / Grant his request to pass the western main." This romantic and poetic imagining recalled the eager, visionary Columbus in a powerful psychological portrait. Columbus was believable, his arguments convincing, as he played on Ferdinand's vanity. Columbus himself was passionate and cunning as he tempted Ferdinand to action. The king took shape from the arguments that Columbus used to address him. This Columbus was not the devout gentleman of the religiously flavored accounts, but a cunning magician. Freneau used rich and persuasive language in painting the mysterious land. Ferdinand was urged to "Reserve this glory for thy native soil, / And what must please thee more, for thy own reign." Driven to seek this new route to the Indies, and drawing on a prophetic tradition, Columbus quoted lines from the *Medea* of Seneca. Freneau, a fine classical scholar, rendered the lines thus:

> Hear, in his tragic lay, Cordova's sage:
> *"The time shall come, when numerous years are past,*
> *"The ocean shall dissolve the bands of things,*
> *"And an extended region rise at last;*
>
> *"And Typhis shall disclose the mighty land,*
> *"Far, far away, where none have rov'd before;*
> *"Nor shall the world's remotest region be*
> *"Gibraltar's rock, or Thule's savage shore."*

Edward Moran painted *Debarkation of Columbus, Morning of October 12, 1492,* a marine ship painting of 1892. Courtesy United States Naval Academy Museum.

A 1510 copy of the tragedies of Seneca, here called Cordova's sage for his birthplace, is in the Columbian library at Valladolid. On the margin of the verse translated above, Ferdinand, the son of Columbus, has noted in Latin, "This prophecy was fulfilled by my father, Christopher Columbus, the admiral, in 1492."[9]

In his final anguished plea, the driven man promised success.

> —O grant my wish,
> Supply the barque, and bid Columbus sail;
> He dreads no tempests on the untravell'd deep,
> Reason shall steer, and shall disarm the gale.[10]

Freneau left the entreaty unresolved, but Ferdinand would have been hard pressed to resist this suit.

Freneau's *Pictures of Columbus*

Perhaps because Freneau found such good material in the relationship with Ferdinand, he undertook a more ambitious challenge in his *Pictures of Columbus*, a longer dramatic poem written in 1774 when the poet was twenty-two. This version exploited the whole Columbus legend by depicting the admiral from his first suspicion that a new continent existed to his last days. Freneau's interests here were not patriotic. He did not ally Columbus with the rising glory of America, a theme he did not pursue after his commencement effort, nor was he creating a heroic setting for America. His main interest again was a psychological portrait of the explorer.

Each of the eighteen pictures was a separate scene with a different setting, characters, poetic style, and believable insights. Freneau developed his characterization of Columbus by dramatizing his relations to the monarchs, to the witchlike Inchantress who tried to disuade him by showing him the future, to the priests who attacked him as a heretic, to the courtiers who laughed at him, to the sailors who refused to sail westward with a madman. Freneau drew Columbus, perhaps in his own image, as both an idealist and a practical man of action—an expert mapmaker, a businessman supervising the building of a ship and the hiring of a crew, a navigator, and a ship's captain who held his course and quelled a mutiny. Freneau liked the dramatic impact of the tragic ending; the ingratitude and cruelty of kings was one of his favorite themes. This streak of pessimism running through his character led him away from his early visionary optimism. His poem ends with stoic acceptance of the future.[11] Freneau was certainly not much like the admiral, but by examining his own motivations, he was able to project a recognizable and believable Columbus.

In the first scene of *Pictures of Columbus*, the navigator muses over maps, noting their disproportions. Thinking that the maps must have errors, he puts them aside, showing in this first picture his vaunting ambition.

> What can these idle charts avail—
> O'er real seas I mean to sail;
> If fortune aids the grand design,
> Worlds yet unthought of shall be mine.

In a scene reminiscent of *MacBeth*, Columbus next visits the dark and frightening "Cell of an Inchantress." This scene, not exactly historical, is set deep in a "gloomy grove." Columbus seeks to know

Whether phantoms I pursue,
Or if, as reason would persuade,
New worlds are on the ocean laid.

The Inchantress tries to discourage him from pursuing his plan, warning that ingratitude, "cold neglect," and "galling chains" will be his

Peter Frederick Rothermel's painting of 1842, *Columbus Before the Queen*, hints at a romantic relationship between the mariner and the monarch. Courtesy National Museum of American Art, Smithsonian Institution.

lot and that bitter, destructive results will come of his exploration. Once again, Freneau sounds the negative note of misery to come.

> The nations at the ocean's end,
> No longer destin'd to be free,
> Shall owe distress and death to thee!
> The seats of innocence and love
> Shall soon the scenes of horror prove.

But as he will not be swayed, she sends him beyond a "fatal curtain" to learn his future in picture three, "The Mirror." There he sees his voyage and the discovery of the New World but not the events that will result. Satisfied, he tells the Inchantress to veil her glass.

Picture four, the address of Columbus to Ferdinand, unfurls the navigator's plan. He appeals to the broader vision of the monarch—the likelihood of additional land masses and the chance to "plant your standards there." In beguiling language, Columbus urges his scheme onto Ferdinand.

> The time is come for some sublime event
> Of mighty fame:—mankind are children yet,
> And hardly dream what treasures they possess
> In the dark bosom of the fertile main,
> Unfathom'd, unattempted, unexplor'd.
> These, mighty prince, I offer to reveal,
> And by the magnet's aid, if you supply
> Ships and some gallant hearts, will hope to bring
> From distant climes, news worthy of a king.

In picture five, Ferdinand discusses the proposition with his first minister, who advises the king to send the fool Columbus off "to perish in his search." But Ferdinand, when he hears that Columbus has been pursuing this dream for many years, is intrigued by his dedication and ready to back the voyage.

In picture six, Columbus addresses Queen Isabella, spinning out his sweet dream, opening up to her visions of new kingdoms.

> Exalted thus, beyond all fame,
> Assist, fair lady, that proud aim
> Which would your native reign extend
> To the wide world's remotest end.

And later:

> Then, queen, supply the swelling sail,
> For eastward breathes the steady gale
> That shall the meanest barque convey
> To regions richer than Cathay.

In picture seven, Isabella's page of honour is writing a reply to Columbus. After outlining the many objections to the enterprise, the page writes:

> But you shall sail; I heard the queen declare
> That mere geography is not her care;—
> And thus she bids me say,
> "Columbus, haste away,"

She sends Columbus to Palos to look for some ships, and he urges some seamen to sail with him.

> "Embark, I say; and he that sails with me
> Shall reap a harvest of immortal honour:
> Wealthier he shall return than they that now
> Lounge in the lap of principalities,
> Hoarding the gorgeous treasures of the east."

But the sailors are not convinced:

> Alas, alas! they turn their backs upon me,
> And rather choose to wallow in the mire
> Of want, and torpid inactivity,
> Than by one bold and masterly exertion
> Themselves ennoble, and enrich their country!

Picture nine takes place in a sailor's hut near the shore. Thomas and Susan, a poor couple, consider whether Thomas, supposedly one of the men Columbus had addressed, should sail with him. This merry and rollicking poem was later reworked and published by itself in the newspapers. Freneau's successful vernacular verse is considered one of his major poetic contributions. These light-hearted stanzas of Thomas the sailor contrast nicely with the passionate outpourings of Columbus.

> I wish I was over the water again!
>   'Tis a pity we cannot agree;
> When I try to be merry 'tis labour in vain,
>   You always are scolding at me;
> Then what shall I do
> With this termagant Sue;
>   Tho' I hug her and squeeze her
>   I never can please her—
> Was there ever a devil like you!

In the final verse, Thomas notes:

> The man that you saw not a sailor can get,
> 'Tis a captain Columbus, they say;

> To fit out a ship he is running in debt,
> And our wages he never will pay:
> Yes, yes, it is he,
> And, Sue, do ye see,
> On a wild undertaking
> His heart he is breaking—
> The devil may take him for me!

Thomas remains at home.

In picture eleven, Orosio, a mathematician, is shown with his scales and compasses. In an anachronistic touch, while reading his gazette he notes in the news that the monarchs have decided to support Columbus. Orosio, the learned man, gives his assessment.

> THIS simple man would sail he knows not where;
> Building on fables, schemes of certainty;—
> Visions of *Plato*, mix'd with idle tales
> Of later date, intoxicate his brain.

Clearly the learned had no respect for the deluded explorer.

Columbus next meets with the pilot, who hopes to enlist a number of good seamen who are between voyages, and in the following picture, Columbus is at sea. The sailors outline their discontents, prepared to mutiny. Columbus puts them off for another few days, privately bemoaning his own problems. He has little sympathy for the fears of the men he had entreated to make the voyage, thinking only of himself.

> Why, nature, hast thou treated those so ill,
> Whose souls, capacious of immense designs,
> Leave ease and quiet for a nation's glory,
> Thus to subject them to these little things,
> Insects, by heaven's decree in shapes of men!

Intent on larger issues, he is disgusted at having to put up with his frightened sailors.

Since Freneau was exploring the interaction of characters in his small-scale scenes, he did not include the actual discovery and landfall in this poem. Those climactic moments took place outside the framework of the pictures. His next scene, picture fourteen, occurs after the landing at Cat Island, where Columbus wanders as in the Garden of Eden, enchanted by the beauties of nature and the freedom from civilization there.

> Sweet sylvan scenes of innocence and ease,
> How calm and joyous pass the seasons here!
> No splendid towns or spiry turrets rise,
> No lordly palaces—no tyrant kings

> Enact hard laws to crush fair freedom here;
> No gloomy jails to shut up wretched men;
> All, all are free!—here God and nature reign.

Then the snake enters the Garden of Eden. A Spaniard Hernando kills a native American for the gold trinkets in his ears. When Columbus comes upon the murdered man, he immediately foresees disaster. The total vision of the tragic future unfolds before him.

> Is this the fruit of my discovery!
> If the first scene is murder, what shall follow
> But havoc, slaughter, chains and devastation
> In every dress and form of cruelty!

Picture fifteen discloses Columbus as he is returning to Spain in a raging tempest. All hands are in danger of imminent death, and Columbus fears that his discovery will be lost. He seals his account of the voyage in a casket and throws it overboard.

> Then, must we die with our discovery!
> Must all my labours, all my pains, be lost,
> And my new world in old oblivion sleep?—
> My name forgot, or if it be remember'd,
> Only to have it said, "He was a madman
> Who perish'd as he ought—deservedly."

But the storm passes, and Columbus returns to the court at Barcelona. Ferdinand, Isabella, and Columbus sing a trio of great satisfaction, each in order.

> Let him be honour'd like a God, who brings
> Tidings of islands at the ocean's end! [Ferdinand]
>
> A woman, as his patroness, shall shine;
> And through the world the story shall be told,
> A woman gave new continents to Spain. [Isabella]
>
> A world, great prince, bright queen and royal lady,
> Discover'd now, has well repaid our toils;
> We to your bounty owe all that we are. [Columbus]

Ferdinand orders up fifteen more ships and bids Columbus to set out again.

But the next picture, having skipped over the colonization phase, reveals Columbus in chains, superseded by a cruel successor and bitterly resenting his humiliation. In Freneau's characterization, Columbus repents of his ambitions, though not accepting any responsibility for the difficulties that have come his way.

> Whoe'er thou art that shalt aspire to honour,
> And on the strength and vigour of the mind
> Vainly depending, court a monarch's favour,
> Pointing the way to vast extended empire;
> First count your pay to be ingratitude,
> Then chains and prisons, and disgrace like mine!

In the final picture, Columbus, at Valladolid, weary and broken-hearted, remembers the past and prepares for death.

> The winds blow high: one other world remains;
> Once more without a guide I find the way;
> In the dark tomb to slumber with my chains—
> Prais'd by no poet on my funeral day,
> Nor even allow'd one dearly purchas'd claim—
> My new found world not honour'd with my name.

The final verse accentuates the world's ill treatment of the explorer, who feels himself to be a just man.

> To shadowy forms, and ghosts and sleepy things,
> Columbus, now with dauntless heart repair;
> You liv'd to find new worlds for thankless kings,
> Write this upon my tomb—yes—tell it there—
> Tell of those chains that sullied all my glory—
> Not mine, but their's—ah, tell the shameful story.

Columbus was relatively blameless in Freneau's poem, and the poet clearly admired him. The navigator loved nature and deplored the bloodshed his travels brought, yet he had blundered into a world that brought sorrow to him. He seemed as much a victim as those whose lands he despoiled, and Freneau foretold the problems that the voyages of Columbus would bring to others.

This ambitious poem, in all its variety of styles, was impressive and moving, vigorous, supple, fanciful, and gracefully phrased as the material demanded. Believable characters were created and motivated, and the poem is dramatically powerful even though we are fully aware of the outcome. The young poet had created an original and sustained poem of which he and the new nation could be proud.[12]

The *Pictures of Columbus* is far more successful than most Columbus literature. It is the best of the Columbus poems and written by the best poet of the period; yet it was not published for more than ten years after it was written, and even then it received little attention. Little has been made of it in connection with Columbus ever since. The reason for this neglect is that the image portrayed is at variance with the heroic Columbus who burst onto the scene in the early nineteenth century.

Freneau's was a potent and complex figure that had brought sorrow to the New World. His story was not triumphant, and he ended his life bitter and forgotten without a compensatory view of a resplendent future. His voyages were not described as the heroic beginning of the new nation; they did not herald the success and happiness or the fertile fields and productive factories of America. The best eighteenth-century depiction of Columbus was virtually forgotten because it did not fit the patriotic stereotype.

Freneau had more to say of Columbus in an unsigned article in the Trenton (New Jersey) *True American* on 17 August 1822, almost fifty years after the earlier poems. As a sea captain, he had visited Santo Domingo twenty years before and had interviewed a former Jesuit who told him about the entombment of Columbus on Hispaniola. After Columbus died at Valladolid, his body was carried to Seville, then to the New World, and buried there. In February 1783, while repairing a church wall in Santo Domingo, workmen discovered a coffin, supposedly that of Columbus. The remains were later reinterred in Havana in 1795, although they were not likely those of Columbus at all. But in telling the story, Freneau included a short motto that was engraved on the coffin:

> A Castilla y Arragon
> Otro mondo dio Colon.

Translated, the motto reads, "Columbus gave a new world to the kingdoms of Castille and Arragon."

Freneau also included his own English translation of the Latin epitaph supposedly inscribed on the tomb of Columbus in Seville. The epitaph came from *Diccionario Geográfico-Histórico de las Indias* by Antonio de Alcedo and, according to Freneau, translates to the following:

> The dust of *Him*, whose fame the world resounds,
>   Whose name to heaven's celestial mansions soars,
> Here rests, concealed in these too narrow bounds;—
>   The bones of him, who first beheld these shores.—
> Old worlds, long known, too little for his mind,
>   He left, and unknown worlds disclosed to view:
> *He* wealth immense to thankless Spain assigned,
>   Spain! that her thousands *here*, her millions slew:
> Lands he explored, where Gods might legislate,
> To Spain gave Empires, and to thrones their state![13]

Philip Freneau's songs about another unappreciated voyager are better suited to the five hundredth anniversary of the voyages than to his own time. Perhaps the poetry of Freneau's youth will lead to his own rediscovery, and his star will rise. New honors are deserved by this best singer of the new American republic.

Barlow's *Columbiad*

The other major American poet of the period who used Columbus as a subject was Joel Barlow (1754–1812), and his Columbiad was the best known of the period. Barlow attempted more and accomplished less than Freneau. As a poet, he was more successful financially and less accomplished artistically.

Barlow was a Connecticut farm boy who studied at Yale and, along with Timothy Dwight, became one of the close-knit group of Connecticut Wits. Ambitious to write an epic poem, Barlow cast about for a topic that would consider "America at large," "the last greatest theatre for the improvement of mankind," and he found in the adventures of Columbus a perfect metaphor. "The discovery of America made an important revolution in the history of mankind," he said. "It served the purpose of displaying knowledge, liberty, and religion . . . perhaps as much as any human transaction."

Barlow thus produced the poetic statement that established Columbus in a major work. Freneau had portrayed Columbus as a tragic individual. Barlow, however, saw the "discovery of America" as setting the stage for all that was good in the nation. Columbus, as the godlike instigator, watched over the past and future of the world he discovered and therefore created. Barlow worked these ideas into two long poems, *The Vision of Columbus* (1787) and *The Columbiad* (1807).[14]

Barlow designed his poems in flashback style. The Columbus of these poems did not sue for support, scan the horizon, or subdue the natives. He was a pious, good man, who at the beginning and throughout was in jail and was forgotten.[15] He served as a framework for the narrative—the observer of history—and he had only two modes: benevolence and despondency. The narratives are without conflict. Columbus does not take part in the action, he reacts to it.

Barlow presented a virtuous America, vindicated from the excesses of decadent Europe. In *The Vision of Columbus*, an angel unrolls before the eyes of Columbus a panorama of the American continents, their geography, their recent past, and their prehistoric past. He sees the Golden Age in Mexico and Peru and follows the legendary Mano Capac, the first Inca, and his son Rocha. Six of the nine books of *The Vision of Columbus* are concerned with the past, primarily with the Incas and the Revolutionary War. Columbus, who was not active in either of these scenes, is exempted from responsibility and blame. Bar-

low separates him from the other exploring marauders, and allows him
to regard with sorrow the destruction of the Mexican civilization by
Cortez. Freneau, with the same materials to work from, implicated
Columbus in the black legend. Barlow, in order to provide a heroic
heritage for America, whitewashes Columbus.

Barlow's two poems are very similar; the second is a reworking of
the first. The major differences stem from the dates of creation. Barlow
began to organize *The Vision* in 1779 and continued to revise the plan,
influenced by current affairs, even as he wrote.[16] The first poem bears
the patriotic fervor of the American Revolution. The second reflects
the events of the French Revolution, after which Barlow became a
Republican, hostile to kings. The second version glorifies peace over
war; the improvement of civilization is linked to the advancement of
science rather than to faith. Man replaces providence as the instigator
of progress.[17]

Barlow's Columbus was a despondent observer. He could not act,
but eternally regretted his lack of appreciation. He thought he had
labored in vain, and the purpose of Barlow's poem was to show otherwise. Barlow outlined two purposes for writing his later work *The
Columbiad*. "The first of these is to sooth and satisfy the desponding
mind of Columbus; to show him . . . that he had opened the way to
the most extensive career of civilization and public happiness; and that
he would one day be recognized as the author of the great benefits to
the human race." The real object of the poem embraced a larger scope:
"To inculcate the love of rational liberty, and to discountenance the
deleterious passion for violence and war."[18] Once again, Barlow's vision was the reverse of Freneau's. While Freneau wrote of the driven
individual and his encounters, Barlow disregarded the character of
Columbus, presenting him as an inert symbol of national success.

In *The Columbiad*, Barlow replaced the angel narrator with a my-
thological figure and guide, Hesper, the spirit of the western world,
who resembled the Miltonic angel Michael in the last books of *Paradise
Lost*. Barlow expanded the narrative of the American Revolution into
three books to make the heroes of the war more heroic, the action
more epic, and the subject matter more detailed. Book eight was expanded to include an address to surviving patriots. The final, closing
vision of *The Columbiad* was more specific, as a great day of truth and
harmony dawns.[19]

The first quatrain of *The Columbiad* is illustrative of the poetry. The
first line captures the epic tone, the third and fourth lines are taken
directly from *The Vision of Columbus*, and the last is somewhat awkward
and obscure.

Hesper Appearing to Columbus in Prison. This engraving of the Miltonic figure of Hesper and the despairing, chained Columbus appeared in early editions of *The Columbiad* by Joel Barlow, either as the frontispiece or in the text. In a conventional format, the panorama of world history was paraded before the immobile Columbus. Courtesy Library of Congress.

> I SING the Mariner who first unfurl'd
> An eastern banner o'er the western world,
> And taught mankind where future empires lay
> In these fair confines of descending day.[20]

The enfeebled Columbus recounts his achievements.

> With full success I calm'd the clamorous race,
> Bade heaven's blue arch a second earth embrace;
> And gave the astonisht age that bounteous shore,
> Their wealth to nations, and to kings their power.[21]

Barlow's vision incorporated the future of America into the care of Columbus, so that he turns his gaze on the little settlements of colonists.

> Columbus hail'd them with a father's smile,
> Fruit of his cares and children of his toil.[22]

Barlow made an impassioned plea for equal rights in a hymn to peace, with Columbus looking on in approval. Barlow's views were those of his own time, and he created Columbus as equally convinced by the vision, appropriating him as the patron saint of the new nation.

> Ah, would you not be slaves, with lords and kings,
> Then be not masters; there the danger springs.
> The whole crude system that torments this earth,
> Of rank, privation, privilege of birth,
> False honor, fraud, corruption, civil jars,
> The rage of conquest and the curse of wars,
> Pandora's total shower, all ills combined
> That erst o'erwhelm'd and still distress mankind,
> Boxt up secure in your deliberate hand,
> Wait your behest to fix or fly this land.
>   Equality of Right is nature's plan;
> And following nature is the march of man.[23]

Barlow's assumption that Columbus, a devout monarchist, a goldseeker who demanded rank and instigated slavery in a small nation, would agree with him shows how far the myth had evolved from the historic man.

In conclusion, Hesper assures Columbus that his works are good, that all the world will benefit from his efforts.

> Here then, said Hesper, with a blissful smile,
> Behold the fruits of thy long years of toil.
> To yon bright borders of Atlantic day
> Thy swelling pinions led the trackless way. . . .
> Then let thy steadfast soul no more complain

Of dangers braved and griefs endured in vain, . . .
While these broad views thy better thoughts compose
To spurn the malice of insulting foes;
And all the joys descending ages gain,
Repay thy labors and remove thy pain.[24]

Barlow is sometimes given credit for the idea of the League of Nations or the United Nations because of his vision of unified government.
In imagining this unity, Barlow went beyond the conception of the
United States as the promised land, allowing for future evolution into
a single state. International cooperation, thus, is a very old American
idea. In book nine of *The Vision of Columbus*, Barlow's angel describes
a great building near the Garden of Eden where "delegated sires" meet
together. The version in *The Columbiad* is very similar.

High in the front, for manlier virtues known,
A sire elect, in peerless grandeur, shone;
And rising oped the universal cause,
To give each realm its limit and its laws;
Bid the last breath of dire contention cease,
And bind all regions in the leagues of peace,
Bid one great empire, with extensive sway,
Spread with the sun and bound the walks of day,
One centered system, one all-ruling soul,
Live through the parts, and regulate the whole.[25]

As mankind joins in brotherhood and the nations of the world meet
in congress, the emblems of superstition—stars, crowns, mitres, the
crescent, the pagoda, and the cross—are cast away. This godless vision
prompted considerable criticism of the rational rather than the religious
Barlow.[26]

Barlow borrowed ideas from many sources, weaving them together
successfully into a single vehicle. His first three books corresponded
closely in structure to sections of Robertson's *History of America*, and
he used material on the Incas from Garcilasso de la Vega and Mar-
montel that was available in the Yale library.[27] He also ranged widely
in seeking support for his work. He learned the patronage game well
enough to enlist a group of powerful subscribers, including Louis XVI,
Lafayette, and Washington.[28] An elaborate, later edition was dedicated
to Robert Fulton.

Barlow's two long Columbian poems did not succeed as poetry,
being somewhat turgid and plodding, but they did sustain an extended
vision that saw American independence as the climax of history, her-
alding a bright future. The evils of the past were presented as necessary

preparation for the triumph of free America and potential worldwide peace. The whole scenario was framed by Columbus who was satisfied at the story laid out before him.

Long before American poets discovered Columbus, his story was being sung by European poets. But when two major American poets did undertake belletristic treatments of the theme, their poetry diverged widely. Freneau traced the personal tragedy of a misunderstood man and the national tragedy of clashing cultures. Barlow elevated his static hero to a transcendant position. Freneau wrote the better poetry, but it was Barlow's vision that prevailed.

CHAPTER FIVE

The First Commemoration

Our society proposes celebrating the completion of the third century of the discovery of America, on the 12th of October, 1792, with some peculiar remark of respect to the memory of Columbus, who is our patron.

John Pintard to Jeremy Belknap, 1789

Here commerce shall her sails extend,
  Science diffuse her kindest ray;
Religion's purest flames ascend,
  And peace shall crown each happy day.
Then while we keep this jubilee,
While seated round this awful shrine,
  Columbus' deeds our theme shall be,
  And liberty that gift divine.

Columbian Ode, New York, 1792

The arrival of Columbus in the New World was first commemorated in the United States on the third centennial in 1792. The unusual event combined the talents of John Pintard, an extraordinarily public-spirited New York businessman, and the Tammany Society, in which he was an important leader. Pintard's missionary zeal carried the New York commemoration to Boston as well, where Jeremy Belknap took the lead. These two events, the first of their kind, defined Columbus celebrations for the future.

Columbus himself and various figures depicting Columbia had been represented in commemorative activity during the decade preceding the three hundredth anniversary. While celebrating the ratification of the Constitution of the United States, several states mounted processions in which pictures of national heroes, floats, and costumes were arranged to show how the Constitution stood as the last and climactic event in the long progress of history. In at least two of the parades, the figure of Columbus began the procession, continuing his role of providing a usable past for the new nation.[1]

In New York, the ratification procession took place on 23 July 1788, even though the debate at Poughkeepsie was still going on. Led by

"Four Foresters in Frocks, carrying Axes," Columbus made his appearance. "Columbus in his Ancient Dress—on Horseback" was followed by tradesmen with flags and mottos. The group of pewterers who were marching carried a silk banner that referred to Columbia.

> The Federal Plan Most Solid and Secure
> Americans Their Freedom Will Endure
> All Arts Shall Flourish in Columbia's Land
> And All her Son's Join as One Social Band

The students from Columbia College, renamed from King's College in 1784, also marched.[2]

Such ceremonial events, which include Columbus as a point of reference, a peripheral figure, have continued to this day. But it remained for John Pintard to make Columbus central, to pay him the sort of homage that later became mandatory. In 1892, one hundred years after that first event, Edward De Lancey paid John Pintard an extravagant compliment: It was to him that the world owed "the first movement in America to commemorate an anniversary of the greatest event in the history of mankind since the death of our Saviour."[3]

New York Commemorates Columbus

The Society of Tammany or Columbian Society had been established on 12 May 1789 at the City Tavern on lower Broadway soon after the United States adopted a national constitution. The organization aimed to "connect in the insoluble bonds of patriotic friendship American Brethren of known attachment to the political rights of human nature and the liberties of their country." With the motto "Freedom Our Rock," the society saw itself as the political successor to the Society of Cincinnati. The Society of Tammany had two patrons, Tammany, a fictive native American chieftain who represented the New World, and Columbus, an actual but already mythic figure who represented the Old World.[4] Both characters were invoked for ceremonial purposes, often at the same time, suitable symbols for this all male club.

From the start, Columbus played a role in the society's activities. The "Calendar of the Society, issued with the Public Constitution in 1790," specified 12 October, the anniversary of the discovery of America, as a day sacred to the memory of the society's second patron, Columbus. The event featured a "long talk" and a banquet. An ode or poem dedicated to the "great discoverer" and eulogizing the society was also included.[5]

On 12 May 1791, their second anniversary, the society recorded a tribute to Columbus. After dinner, the members drank toasts, and the eighth toast was to "the memory of the renowned Columbus—may our latest posterity inherit the goodly land which his intrepidity explored, and his sagacity discovered."[6]

John Pintard, the prosperous businessman and populist with antiquarian tastes who was involved in so many of New York's important organizations, was the first sagamore of the Society of Tammany or Columbian Order in the city of New York and the major power behind the organization and ritual. Pintard was an enthusiastic and energetic young man in his early thirties at this time. He had been orphaned at an early age and raised by his merchant uncle Lewis Pintard, who sent him to the College of New Jersey, later Princeton. Pintard inherited a fortune, which he then improved with his business successes, meanwhile promoting public projects of civic benefit.[7]

Pintard had a vision, and he began to collect interesting Americana in the name of the American Museum instituted by the Tammany Society.[8] On 6 April 1789, Pintard wrote to his friend Dr. Jeremy Belknap, a clergyman and doctor of divinity as well as an eminent scholar in Boston. "My avocations, especially as a citizen, are numerous. . . . My passion for American history increases, tho' I have but detached moments and scant means of gratifying it. . . . [Our Tammany Society] being a strong national society, I engrafted an antiquarian scheme of a museum upon it." He went on to say, "Our society purposes celebrating the completion of the third century of the discovery of America, on the 12th of October, 1792, with some peculiar remark of respect to the memory of Columbus, who is our patron." He proposed a procession and an oration, as well as a memorial monument.[9]

In Pintard's plans were thus the elements that have been used to commemorate Columbus to this day: orations, odes, monuments, parades, toasts. This commemorative plan was originated by the patrician and energetic organizer of a patriotic and political fraternal order. Nothing in it was related to the Renaissance court of Ferdinand and Isabella or to the ethnic groups who had adopted Columbus as their American hero. Yet these elements have been adopted by thousands of ethnic, patriotic, religious, and school groups, and the ceremonial aspects have been adapted to impressive commercial traditions as well. The Columbus Day / Thanksgiving parades that introduce holiday sales are later evolutions of the Tammany Society's processions.

The proposed celebration marking the three hundredth anniversary was heralded by the *New York Journal and Patriotic Register* for 10 October 1792 in the following announcement.

Notice: The members of the Tammany Society or Columbian Order, are hereby notified that an extra meeting will be held in the Wigwam the 12th inst. at seven o'clock, to celebrate the third century since the discovery of America by Columbus.
By Order of the Grand Sachem
Benjamin Strong, Secretary.[10]

The members gathered in their Wigwam, a communal house, to celebrate in "that style of sentiment which distinguishes this social and patriotic institution." The event consisted of a dinner and an oration; in addition, Columbian odes were recited, patriotic songs were sung, and the patron was toasted. "The event was marked by a stately ceremony in which the Society eclipsed all former efforts in the dignity and pomp displayed."[11] This was the first ambitious celebration devoted chiefly to Columbus in the New World.

The press praised the event. The *New York Journal and Patriotic Register* of 13 October 1792 noted that on the previous day, "Brother J[ohn] B[arent] Johnson addressed the Society with an animated eulogy on this nautical hero and astonishing adventurer [Columbus] with great applause."[12] Unfortunately, no copy of this "animated eulogy" can be found. The same paper referred to the event four days later, elaborating on the address.

An elegant oration was delivered by Mr. J. B. Johnson, in which several of the principle events in the life of this remarkable man [Columbus] were pathetically described and the interesting consequences to which his great achievements had already, and must still conduct the affairs of mankind, were pointed out in a manner extremely satisfactory.[13]

This pathetic description portrayed in an "extremely satisfactory" manner must have brought great pleasure to the Tammany crowd. Columbus was shown both as a hero and a victim. The speech was probably of the same level as the ode and toasts, some of which are quoted here for antiquarian interest. The toasts, probably written by Pintard, were of higher literary quality than the verses. Though many can be repeated without pain, twentieth-century critics of the admiral will find fault with calling Columbus the discoverer of the world and with the intimation that the New World under a European-based civilization was an improvement over the original. The reference to the United Columbian States is interesting, as is the encouragement of immigration and abolition. Tammany toasted

The memory of Christopher Columbus, the discoverer of this new world.
May the new world never experience the vices and miseries of the old; and be a happy asylum for the oppressed of all nations and of all religions.

May peace and liberty ever pervade the United Columbian States.

May this be the last centenary festival of the Columbian Order that finds a slave on this globe.

May the fourth century be as remarkable for the improvement and knowledge of the rights of man, as the first was for discovery, and the improvement of nautic science.

May the deliverers of America never experience that ingratitude from their country, which Columbus experienced from his King.

May the genius of liberty, as she has conducted the sons of Columbia with glory to the commencement of the fourth century, guard their fame to the end of time.[14]

The ode, sung on this occasion in New York in 1792, was a loose doggerel account relating Columbus to the nation's success in the Revolutionary War. After patriotic rhetoric, the ode invoked the current catchwords: commerce, science, freedom of religion, and peace. All these American notions were remarkably related to the freelance explorer who never came anywhere near New York. But once linked to American causes, the name of Columbus came to invoke all matters which concerned the nation, and his interest in the profits of his enterprise was, after all, similar to their own economic ambitions.

> Ye sons of freedom, hail the day,
>   That brought a second world to view;
> To great Columbus' mem'ry pay
>   The praise and honor justly due.
> *Chorus*
>   Let the important theme inspire
>   Each breast with patriotic fire.
>
>   . . .
>
> Hark! from above, the great decree
>   Floats in celestial notes along,
> "Columbia ever shall be free,"
>   Exulting thousands swell the song.
>   Patriots revere the great decree,
>   Columbia ever shall be free.
>
> Here shall enthusiastic love,
>   Which freemen to their country owe;
> Enkindled, glorious from above,
>   In every patriot bosom glow.
>   Inspire the heart, the arm extend,
>   The rights of freedom to defend.
>
>   . . .
>
> Here commerce shall her sails extend,
>   Science diffuse her kindest ray;
> Religion's purest flames ascend,
>   And peace shall crown each happy day.
> Then while we keep this jubilee,

While seated round this awful shrine,
Columbus' deeds our theme shall be,
And liberty that gift divine.[15]

As part of his commemoration, Pintard arranged for a monument to be created, a modest and didactic, fifteen-foot column that has disappeared completely. When Pintard wrote to Jeremy Belknap in Boston on 6 April 1789 disclosing his plans for commemorating Columbus, he proposed to erect "a column to his memory. I wish to know, if possible, the dimensions and cast of your monument on Beacon Hill, to guide our calculations."[16]

Pintard must have had ambitious plans, for a fifty-seven-foot Boston Monument had recently replaced the century-old beacon light, which had blown down in a gale in 1789. Charles Bulfinch designed the Doric column topped by a gilt wooden eagle, which was built of brick and stone, "encrusted by cement." The monument only lasted until 1811, when the hillside was dug away and sold to fill in low land elsewhere in Boston.

The Boston Monument was a didactic memorial with long inscriptions engraved on plaques, poetically retelling the story of the Revolution. Jeremy Belknap noted that he had been consulted about the inscriptions.[17]

Pintard adopted Boston's idea of a public sculpture that told a story and created a much less ambitious monument in New York. The monument was "upwards of fourteen feet in height," being well illuminated and resembling black marble. The monument was "exposed for the gratification of public curiosity some time previous to the meeting."[18] The shaft was only a quarter the size of the column in Boston, but it was probably "encrusted with cement" in the same way. The shaft was "ornamented with a number of transparent devices depicting the principle events in the career of Columbus." The monument blended a "grave and solemn with a brilliant appearance."[19]

Images and information appeared on each busy face. At the base a globe emerged from clouds and chaos presenting a "rude sketch of the once uncultivated coast of America." On the pyramidal part, History drew up the curtain of oblivion, revealing four representations.

On the right side of the obelisk was a commercial port and expanding ocean where Columbus mused on the insignia of geometry and navigation, his youthful studies. Science, meanwhile, instructed him to cross the great Atlantic. Science, in luminous clouds, handed him a compass and pointed to the setting sun. Under her feet was a globe of the world representing then-known lands with the western half blank. On the upper part of the obelisk, an eagle supported the arms of Genoa. An inscription gave the date of the monument and credited the Tammany Society.

The second side of the monument showed the first landing, with Columbus in a state of adoration, his followers prostrate around him, and a group of native Americans at a distance. Above, the arms of Europe and America were blended and supported by an eagle. The inscription read

> Sacred to the Memory
> Of
> Christopher Columbus,
> The Discoverer of a New World
> October 12, 1492

The third side exhibited the splendid reception of Columbus by the court of Spain on his first return from America. He sat at the right hand of Ferdinand and Isabella. A map of the western countries and "some of their peculiar productions" laid at his feet. The prone eagle supported the arms of Isabella as the inscription read

> Columbus
> Was Born at Genoa,
> 1447,
> Was Received by the Court of Spain
> In Triumph,
> 1493;
> Was Put in Chains by its Order,
> September, 1500;
> Died at Valladollid
> May 20, 1506.

The fourth side showed Columbus in his chamber, pensive and neglected, the chains with which "he had been cruelly loaded" hung against his bare walls on which was written, "The Ingratitude of Kings." His declining moments were cheered by the Genius of Liberty whose glory illuminated his solitary habitation. The emblems of despotism and superstition "were crushed beneath her feet," intimating the "gratitude and respect of posterity." On the pedestal, Nature caressed her various progeny; "her tawny offspring seem to mourn over the urn of Columbus." The eagle, no longer prone or loaded with decorations of heraldry, soared in an open sky, "grasping in her talons a ferrule inscribed, THE RIGHTS OF MAN."[20]

Pintard's sympathetic scenario was balanced in depicting both the triumph and disgrace of Columbus, his achievement and his ignominy. No criticism was directed at Columbus himself, depicted as the bringer of "the rights of man," mourned, after his passing, by nature's "tawny offspring." The monarchs were blamed for their "ingratitude." A bookful of text, symbols, and pictures was included on this shaft.

The monument was placed in the American Museum of the Tammany Society, which Pintard had begun. The museum then occupied a large room in the Exchange, a building on arches that stood at the south side of Pearl Street, facing up Broad Street. The monument, which was annually illuminated on the twelfth day of October, was given prominence in the advertisements for the museum. It was built, however, as a "portable monument" and was removed after 1792 to be exhibited in a museum and waxwork establishment.[21] The collection eventually went to P. T. Barnum, and the monument disappeared.

Pintard's connection with Belknap bore additional fruit however. Pintard hoped to found a national organization, and, when visiting Belknap in Boston in 1789, he disclosed his scheme for such a society. Belknap shared Pintard's enthusiasm for collecting historical documents; he had often traveled to repositories to do research and had watched with dismay as valuable collections were disbursed or accidentally destroyed. He had collected many important documents on his own. Pintard and Belknap got along well together, and following Pintard's visit, the Massachusetts Historical Society, the dean of such organizations, was founded in Boston on 24 January 1791 with Dr. Belknap as its first corresponding secretary.[22] Pintard was later instrumental in founding the New-York Historical Society.

Boston Commemorates Columbus

In Boston, the Massachusetts Historical Society, fired up by the New York Columbian commemoration, honored the admiral with a procession, an address, and a poem on 23 October 1792.[23] The Boston society had planned to celebrate on the actual three hundredth anniversary, but members made a mistake in adapting the old calendar to the new. There were nine days between the old and new calendars,[24] and their celebration should have been held on 21 October. This small error gave New York the uncontested honor of being the first group to organize a commemoration in honor of Columbus.

During the 1792 celebration, the Massachusetts Historical Society in Boston met at the house of the Reverend Dr. Peter Thacher, where they formed ranks and proceeded to the Brattle Street Church. There they heard an address and a poem. The governor of Massachusetts, the lieutenant governor, and the councillors who were in town accompanied the members of the society to a dinner at the home of James Sullivan, where the memory of Columbus was "toasted in convivial enjoyment." "The warmest wishes were expressed that the blessings now distinguishing the United States might be extended to every part of the world he has discovered."[25]

A Mr. Rea and a "select Choir" sang the ode that told the story of a promised land. This new land was protected from European corruption, which consisted of war, superstition, and the alliance of "crown and mitre" that stifled political and religious freedom. Some of its verses follow.

III.
Whilst *Ocean* kept his sacred charge,
    And fair COLUMBIA lay conceal'd;
Through Europe, *Discord* roam'd at large,
    Til *War* had crimson'd every field.
IV.
Black *Superstition's* dismal night
    Extinguish'd *Reason's* golden ray;
And *Science,* driven from the light,
    Beneath monastic rubbish lay.
V.
The *Crown* and *Mitre,* close ally'd,
    Trampeled whole nations to the dust;
Whilst FREEDOM, wandering far and wide,
    And pure RELIGION, quite were lost.
VI.
Then, guided by th' Almighty Hand,
    COLUMBUS spread his daring sail;
Ocean receiv'd a new command,
    And *Zephyrs* breath'd a gentle gale.
VII.
The Western World appear'd to view,
    Her friendly arms extended wide;
Then FREEDOM, o'er th' Atlantic flew,
    With pure RELIGION by her side.
VIII.
Tyrants with mortal hate pursu'd;
    In vain their forces they employ;
In vain the Serpent pours his flood,*
    Those heaven-born Exiles to destroy.

. . .

*Rev. 12:15.

X.
"Sweet peace and heav'nly truth shall shine
    "On fair COLUMBIA's happy ground;
"There FREEDOM and RELIGION join,
    "And spread their influence all around."

CHORUS
Hail "GREAT COLUMBIA!" favour'd foil;
  Thy fields with plenty crown thy toil;
  Thy shore, the seat of growing wealth;
  Thy clime the source of balmy health.

From thee proceeds the virtuous plan,
  To vindicate the *Rights of Man.*
  Thy fame shall spread from pole to pole,
  Whilst everlasting ages role.[26]

The speaker for the evening was none other than Jeremy Belknap, who gave an extensive sermon using a text from Daniel—"Many shall run to and fro, and knowledge shall be increased." After speaking on Columbus, Belknap used the occasion to affirm that the new Massachusetts Historical Society would promote useful knowledge and serve as a vehicle for disseminating historical information to the masses, helping to educate and improve mankind.[27] While writing his address, he told his friend Ebenezer Hazard in a letter of 27 August 1792,

My labour for October 23rd is nearly accomplished. I find myself obliged to dip deeper into antiquity than I was first aware, but I think I can vindicate Columbus against those who would rob him of his fame, not excepting Mr. Otto. [Lewis William Otto had recently published a paper in the *Transactions of the American Philosophical Society* arguing that Martin Behaim of Nuremburg had discovered South America before Columbus embarked on his first voyage.][28]

Belknap's speech on the first European to set foot on the new land was reasoned and fair, and he couched it in elegant English prose. He correctly noted that the sum of twenty-five hundred crowns to finance the voyage, which was to have been raised by the pawning of Queen Isabella's jewels, had actually been advanced by Luis de Santangel, the keeper of King Ferdinand's privy purse. "Thus," he gallantly concluded, "to the generous decision of a female mind, we owe the discovery of America."

His ponderous paragraphs were filled with weighty and sonorous pronouncements, a series in almost every sentence. Columbus spent twenty years in preparation for his first voyage, Belknap noted, "a voyage which opened to the Europeans a new world; which gave a new turn to their thoughts, to their spirit of enterprise and commerce; which enlarged the empire of Spain and stamped with immortality the name of Columbus."[29] Belknap had once again struck the commercial note so sympathetic to the business interests of the new nation.

Belknap dwelt primarily on the achievements of Columbus, saying little of his failures. He concentrated his efforts on the quest for support,

the voyage, and the landing. By contrasting his early notable achievements with the stern punishment from his sovereigns—which came, in
fact, as a result of his misgovernment—Columbus was portrayed as a
tragic figure. "Let it suffice to observe that his latter days were em-
bittered by the envy of his rivals, the death of his patroness and the
jealousy of his sovereign. Though he merited the honor of giving his
own name to the continent which he discovered, yet it was called after
an inferior, that very fortunate adventurer."[30]

When Belknap included Columbus in his volume *American Biography*, a collection of sketches first published in 1794, he portrayed the
admiral as a misunderstood hero. In fact, the very inclusion of Columbus in this volume is further evidence of his adoption as the founder
of American culture. Belknap's account lacked originality, relying heavily on previously published works, but it was much admired in his
day.[31] Belknap respected Christopher Columbus so much for his
achievement that he made him practically perfect.

In the life of this remarkable man there is no deficiency of any quality which
can constitute a truly great character. . . . His constancy and patience were equal
to the most hazardous undertakings. . . . His prudence enabled him to conceal
or subdue his own infirmities; whilst he took advantage of the passions of
others, adjusting his behaviour to his circumstances; temporizing, or acting
with vigour, as the occasion required.[32]

Belknap followed the tradition of Raynal and Robertson in steadfastly defending Columbus against charges of inhumanity against the
Indians. Belknap admitted that Columbus had carried dogs to the West
Indies and used them against the natives, but he justified the behavior
by noting that "gentlemen of the best families in Spain" had accompanied Columbus and that the dogs and horses belonged to them. The
animals had proved effective in dividing the Indians, but, if Columbus
had had any preconceived designs against the natives with the dogs,
he would have brought many more with him. A century before Belknap, by the way, the Reverend Solomon Stoddard had advocated the
use of dogs to protect the citizens of Deerfield, Massachusetts, against
the Indians. Stoddard argued persuasively for their fearsomeness and
tracking ability, citing previous successful use in Virginia.[33] Stoddard
would have warred with the natives. Columbus, on the other hand,
according to Belknap, "endeavored as far as possible to treat [the na-
tives] with justice and gentleness. The same cannot be said of those
who succeeded him."[34]

Two other cities managed Columbian commemorations worthy of
note in 1792. Philadelphia published a speech, and Baltimore erected

a monument. In Philadelphia on 23 October, the *Daily American Advertiser* published a special Columbian edition. An oration that Joseph Reed of Philadelphia had delivered at Princeton was published in the paper. Reed pictured a Columbus surveying the greatness of the New World from "his empyreal height"; but no honor was being paid to him, and Reed counted the ways in which the public had failed him. There were no statues erected, no inscriptions made, and no honors decreed to celebrate this great event. "Illustrious shade," Reed intoned, "my feeble voice shall announce thy praise; and this enlightened audience, kindling at thy name, will inscribe upon their hearts the honors due to thy exalted worth!"[35] He and others thought it unseemly that the admiral had been ignored in the past and proposed making up for past slights.

A Private Tribute in Baltimore

In Baltimore, the first American monument to Columbus was erected, the creation of a patriotic Frenchman, Charles Francis Adrian le Paulmier, Chevalier d'Anmour. M. d'Anmour was a shadowy figure whose name has been found spelled in a variety of ways. According to historian Herbert Baxter Adams, he was the first French consul in Baltimore. He was mentioned in the *Journals* of Congress in 1778, soon after the first treaty with France, and thereafter. He acquired a Maryland estate in 1789 and held it until 1796. His marriage to a young lady from the West Indies was announced in the Maryland newspapers in 1782.[36] One story held that he had belonged to a society in France that perpetuated the memory of Columbus and that he erected the monument because of "his admiration for Columbus' bravery in the face of apparent failure." This evident French regard for the admiral preceded American interest.[37]

A man of wealth and style, Chevalier d'Anmour entertained lavishly and often. Lafayette had been feted at his house. During one of his parties in 1792, someone mentioned that there was no monument to commemorate Columbus in all of the new United States. Shocked by this discovery, M. d'Anmour made a solemn vow that this neglect should be immediately remedied by the erection of an enduring shaft upon his own estate. He was said to have unveiled his monument to Columbus on the three hundredth anniversary of the discovery, although no newspapers mentioned the event.

The monument consisted of a tapering quadrangular shaft, twenty-eight-feet tall, rising from a sloping pedestal. The shaft was surmounted by an ornamental cornice, about three feet in height. The monument was built of molded bricks covered with mortar or cement, appearing to be grey sandstone. The daughter of a later owner of the property said that the monument was erected at a cost of eight hundred pounds or four thousand dollars.

A marble slab on this chaste and graceful column, modest but impressive, was incised with easily read letters.

Sacred
to the
Memory
of
CHRIS.
COLUMBUS,
Oct. XII,
MDCC VIIIC.

The date in Roman numerals was formed in a quaint form rather than the October 12, MDCCXCII we would expect. Possibly the column was erected after the date indicated, but this monument seems more likely to be what it claims to be.[38]

One hundred years later, when New Yorker Edward De Lancey described Columbian commemorations for 1792, he noted that Balti-

This Columbus obelisk was erected by Charles Francis Adrian le Paulmier, Chevalier d'Anmour on his estate in Baltimore in 1792, the first permanent monument to Christopher Columbus in the New World. In 1964, the monument was moved to stand in a grove of pine trees on the edge of Herring Park. Courtesy Maryland Historical Society, Baltimore.

more had commemorated the event by laying an obelisk in the garden of a villa called Belmont, the country seat of the Chevalier de Nemours, a significant variant of the name. De Lancey had never seen the monument and was uncertain that it existed.[39]

The property on which Baltimore's Columbus monument stood was located on the east side of the Hartford turnpike, fronting on North Avenue. The property passed through the hands of Zenos Barnum, and the monument became known to the public when North Avenue through the Barnum estate was opened. The property was later purchased by Samuel Ready, and the house became a hotel and later the Samuel Ready Orphan Asylum. The monument stood in the southeast corner of an attractive enclosure on an elevated, terraced plateau. In the hands of Samuel Ready's heirs, the monument was honored, the surroundings beautified, and the public invited to visit.

Mysterious stories about the significance of the monument circulated. It was rumoured that the monument was actually erected to honor a favorite horse of Zenos Barnum. Herbert Baxter Adams took pains to dispel this notion, attributing it to confusion with a later horse monument and thinking it unlikely that a horse of that name would die on that date. He also located the monument on a map of 1801 that predated Barnum's ownership of the land.[40]

Another old tale was that d'Anmour had died at the old mansion and was interred near the base of the shaft. Buried treasure also figured in the tales.[41] These colorful legends still persist.

The monument's location at some distance from a thoroughfare and hidden in the woods caused it to be forgotten for some years. Arthur Wellington Tyler, the librarian of Johns Hopkins University, chanced upon the obelisk one day in 1876 while out walking, rediscovering it for the Johns Hopkins historians who trooped out as a group to look it over. The daughter of a former owner returned to visit, remembering that during her childhood visitors from Italy and France often came to see the monument, which seemed to be known in Europe, probably the oldest in the New World.[42]

The monument stands as an eighteenth-century Frenchman's expression of regard for Columbus, antedating by over half a century the Columbian monument in Genoa, dedicated in 1862.[43] The monument was moved in 1964 to stand in a grove of pine trees on the edge of Herring Park.

In the summer of 1792, the impending celebrations in New York and Boston were written up in newspapers, and, intrigued by Pintard's imaginative plans, others organized events. Windsborough, South Carolina; Providence, Rhode Island; Richmond, Virginia; and other towns held military parades, dinners, and toasts in honor of the occasion.[44]

The Tammany Society continued to honor their patron on dates close to the landfall anniversary. On 11 October 1809, William L. Marcy delivered "An oration on the Three Hundred and Eighteenth anniversary of the Discovery of America" before the Tammany Society, or Columbian Order. He included an account of the life of Tammany, the Indian chief.[45] Rather than looking back to the boyhood of Columbus, the speaker honored the explorer by referring to an imaginary native past, which had been appropriated by this patriotic society. These orators envisioned a mixed group of highlighted heroes who could be woven together into a rich pastiche of a fictive past for the new nation and society.

Two years later, in 1811, the Tammany Society mounted a special Columbus commemoration when laying the cornerstone of Tammany Hall at Naussau and Frankford streets in New York City. The building was later purchased by Charles A. Dana for the New York *Sun*. The procession on that occasion was picturesque and attractive, and in the center of the ninth division, between the files of the first six tribes, Tammany and Columbus appeared together in their colorful characterizations. Columbus was carrying the ancient flag of Christendom with its cross; Tammany carried the stars and stripes. The two represented the promise of improved civilization and its realization. Columbus and Tammany sat on a raised seat at the rear of an extensive stage, alternately smoking a peace pipe. In the center appeared the Genius of America, attended by her "attributes" who fed the flames of liberty burning on an altar dedicated to freedom. The stage was designed as an open field covered with grass and shrubbery, with an oak tree in the rear under which Tammany and Columbus sat. This whole float was drawn by six white horses guided by postillions; a grand band of music preceded the car, playing native airs.[46]

Columbus here occupied a position representing the Old World in harmony with the New. Neither Columbus nor Tammany participated in the action. Instead, they looked on approvingly, supervising the symbolic "Genius of America" posed before the sacrificial fires of freedom and liberty.

The interest of the Tammany Society in their secondary patron began to wane as politics waxed ever more important.[47] The Tammany Society part of the name eclipsed the Columbian Order part. Artist John Vanderlyn, who was a member of the society, inscribed a decorative crest in a shield shape. This specimen of his artistic penmanship, dating

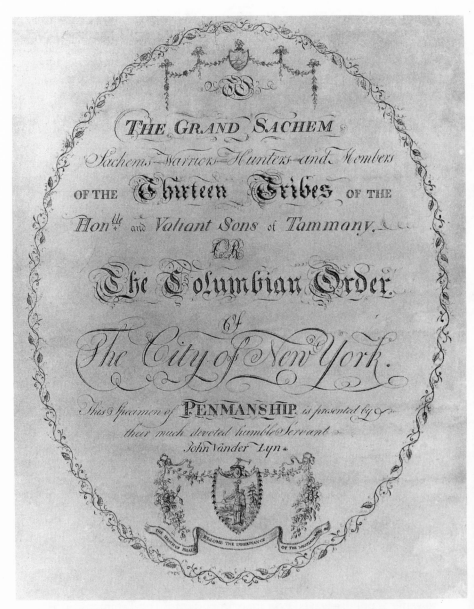

John Vanderlyn drew a possible emblem for the Tammany Society or Columbian Order in this penmanship sample. He represented the native chieftain Tammany but not the society's other patron Columbus. Depicting Tammany gave Vanderlyn early practice in drawing natives, which he was to use in his Columbus painting. Courtesy New York State Office of Parks, Recreation and Historic Preservation, Senate House State Historic Site.

from about 1795, included Tammany but, alas, not Columbus who was cast into the shade by the native patron.[48] Responsibility for organizing Columbian commemorations was transferred to other patriotic and ethnic groups. The neglect, however, cannot dim the Tammany Society's part in establishing the central role of Columbus in the nation's past, making him share figuratively with native Americans the foundation on which the new nation was established. Columbus brought Christianity; the Indians provided peace; and their joint presence allowed freedom and liberty to flourish. The celebrators, spurred by patriotic optimism and wishful thinking rather than documentary evidence, freely invented historical situations to meet their needs. By staging commemorations and by creating a human representation of Columbus, the Tammany Society played a major part in creating America's fictive past.

CHAPTER SIX

The Heroic Image

In the life of this remarkable man, there was no deficiency of any quality, which can constitute a great character. He was grave, though courteous in his deportment, circumspect in his words and actions, irreproachable in his morals, and exemplary in all the duties of religion.

Caleb Bingham, 1794

A Moral Model for the Young

Most people who think of Columbus as a hero learned that lesson in school. For shaping the collective memory of the nation, the stories told to the children were probably more important than those told to their parents. Children remembered the mythical Columbus as the model of bravery and perseverance, the all-wise navigator whose nobility was equal to the discovery, almost to the creation, of a New World.

How could this romantic, idealized image persist when the actual historical record was filled with cruelty and horror? The Columbus of history, including his human imperfections and serious weaknesses, had been disclosed repeatedly, and his shortcomings had not been hidden. But children's books offered Columbus as an example of good character for young readers, distorting history in the interest of inspiring children. The writers conflated the development of the New World with the development of their readers' moral resolves.

Columbus was not automatically envisioned as a model for children. At first, he was an abstraction rather than a person. The first books in English available to the children of the New World stressed the discovery rather than the discoverer. These straightforward accounts, devoid of sentimentality, narrated the patterns of exploration, portraying the explorers as instruments of the nations they represented. *The World Displayed*, a series of voyage descriptions in many volumes assembled by Christopher Smart, Oliver Goldsmith, and Samuel Johnson and published in 1759, was one of these popular publications.

The tiny volumes of *The World Displayed*, nicely bound in leather, were published in England by J. Newbery, who was the first to make books for children his business. One of these handsomely illustrated

Columbus is poised, ready to leap ashore in this picture engraved for the *New York Mirror*. Courtesy The Library of Congress.

volumes, although not obviously nor exclusively a child's book, could fit easily into a boy's pocket, to be carried along on his outings. Washington Irving owned and loved these books. He took them to school and read them instead of doing his schoolwork. Here he came to know the Columbus he later fleshed out and romanticized.

The World Displayed first mentioned Columbus in a long introduction outlining the state of Portuguese navigation in 1492. The explorer was introduced in an even-handed statement that balanced the good and the ill of his venture. "Columbus made the daring and prosperous voyage, which gave a new world to *European* curiosity and *European* cruelty." The authors dealt with action, not characterization, and did not judge Columbus for his decisions. The malcontents sent home to Spain during the rebellion represented him as "an insolent alien, ignorant of the laws and customs of the Spanish nation." But for all its cool tone, the book finally granted Columbus high marks: "Thus died this truly great man" who, by his abilities, "not only raised himself

and his family to nobility, but rendered himself by his discoveries the
greatest man of the age in which he lived."[1] Irving could be expected
to speak well of a man to whom he was so introduced.

After the Revolutionary War, even though Columbia had been
adopted as the poetic name of the nation, the explorer was a faceless
symbol, and children's literature did not refer to him. *The American
Primer Improved* of 1776 and *The Columbian Primer, enlarged and improved* of 1799, with their nationalistic titles, would seem particularly
promising places for including information about Columbus. But both
were primarily religious volumes with long catechisms and dialogues
between Christ, youth, and the devil. The volumes were prefaced with
small amounts of ABC material, but included nothing at all about
Columbus.[2]

Even more promising was the book titled *The Columbian Reading
Book or Historical Preceptor: A Collection of Authentic Histories, Anecdotes, Characters*. This anonymous book of 1802, published by Matthew
Carey, related virtuous incidents in the lives of important historical
heroes, aiming to improve young people. One hundred and sixty four
vignettes from Roman, English, Chinese, Spanish, Greek, and Persian
history illustrated virtues such as friendship and modesty. American
stories about natives and black slavery were even included. But this
Columbian volume, probably copied from English sources, contained
nothing about either Columbus or Washington, the two beings most
apt to be included in a book of this sort.[3]

Though absent from these early, religiously based primers, the admiral began to make a strong appearance in the secular schoolbooks
of such pioneering American educators as Noah Webster, Caleb
Bingham, and Jedidiah Morse and in the first history books. These
books borrowed from many other sources, eventually going back to
the biographical detail of the work of Columbus' son Ferdinand and
the history of Herrera, based on the Las Casas manuscript. Positive
aspects of these early sources were rendered in a still more positive
fashion in the American books.

Actual history books for children came late to the schools. Only
eight or nine American history texts were published in the United States
before 1820, and none were circulated widely. These books were highly
derivative and, because of their borrowings, were often published
anonymously. The publishers saw them as filling specific patriotic and
moral needs. Columbus was incorporated as marking the beginning of
national history and was honored as a form of national chauvinism.[4]
From his premiere position, he was used to demonstrate the virtues
young citizens should exhibit

"Columbus' first interview with the natives of America," the frontispiece of one of the first American history texts published for children. Courtesy Rare Book Department, Free Library of Philadelphia.

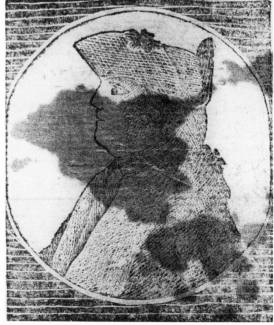

A portrait of Christopher Columbus, shown here as a gentleman of the new republic appeared in *The History of America*, Philadelphia, 1795. Courtesy, American Antiquarian Society.

The spirit of patriotism "excited" the author of *The History of America, abridged for the use of children of all denominations* to produce this work for his young readers in 1795. He noted that the mind "takes a turn in future life, suitable to the tincture it hath received in youth." His book was to furnish children with an account of past human actions so that they might be able to project the future. The book made no attempt at synthesis but instead began with geographical description, then presenting short biographical sections and pieces on the states. Columbus was given just a few pages, in lofty language. "However sanguine Columbus might be in his expectations, it appears that his proposals for carrying his bold schemes into execution was [sic] treated with cool indifference." The book was "adorned with cuts" of discoverers, heroes, and governors, and in a charming confusion of styles, a primitively drawn Columbus appeared in the frock coat and ruffles of an eighteenth-century gentleman.[5]

In some books, Columbus transcended the contents of the book as the only person worthy of note, almost more important than the nation itself. In another American history book for children, *A Concise History of the United States, From the Discovery of America till 1795,* the writer saw the discovery of America as a "curious and interesting object of enquiry." Understanding it, the author went on, required a knowledge of "that eminent man, who first brought the new world to the knowledge of the old." Why should it be necessary to know the personal history of Columbus? The assumed answer was that his character, his achievement, and his successful recognition by the powerful of his age echoed the experience of the new nation. His story was part of the national story. This ambitious narrative, described as "especially for schools," gave him the whole first chapter.

The discoverer was created to make him worthy of a great new country.

His genius was too vigorous and persevering to suffer an idea of this importance to rest merely in speculation. . . . Happily for mankind, in this instance, a genius capable of devising the greatest undertakings, associated in itself a degree of patience and enterprize, modesty and confidence, which rendered him superior, not only to these misfortunes, but to all the future calamities of his life.[6]

The book was assembled by publisher John M'Culloch, who borrowed freely from other printed sources including Barlow and Webster. The facts, and often the phrases and sentences themselves, were copied from earlier publications.[7] M'Culloch took care to choose and repeat the most flattering remarks.

More knowledge of American history was provided by geography and reading books. One such was the pathbreaking *Geography Made*

Easy, published in 1784 by Jedidiah Morse. Definitely for children, the book asserted that geography was not only a polite and agreeable pursuit but also a very necessary and important part of education. Morse described the solar system and defined clouds, tides, and bays in a scientific tone far distant from the old religious schoolbooks. Morse then launched into the discovery of America, beginning in the most personal way with the birth of Christopher Columbus. He mentioned Columbus' knowledge of geography but did not discuss his actual theories, concentrating on the familiar journey from court to court to sell his scheme. Besides an account of the voyages, the book provides an assessment of his character—grave, courteous, circumspect, and irreproachable in morals—before moving on to describe the physical characteristics of the natives of the Americas and the standard geographical aspects of the United States and the individual states. The biographical section on Columbus was a contrast in style and tone and was out of place among the rest of the subject matter. No other characters emerged from the book. Other continents and nations were discussed, but Columbus stood alone as a man worthy of note.[8]

The same unexpected attention was given the explorer in Noah Webster's collection of pieces for recitation published in 1787. The book, titled *An American Selection of Lessons in Reading and Speaking*, which proposed to instruct young people in geography, history, and politics as well, was made up of little Roman moral tales about honesty and kindness. Here, among the classics, was a surprisingly extensive biographical section on Columbus written by Joel Barlow. This account was much longer than the other pieces, running on for a dozen closely printed pages, and he took up half a page on the table of contents in subheads, included for him alone. The piece was apparently inserted into an already existing manuscript. Webster's biographer claimed that this schoolbook was the first in the United States to record the history of the events that led to the formation of the nation.[9]

In this piece, Barlow, already noted as the author of two long poems about Columbus, asserted that every circumstance relating to the discovery and settlement of America was interesting. Yet he presumed that few persons were acquainted with the character of that man "whose extraordinary genius led him to the discovery of the continent, and whose singular sufferings ought to excite the indignation of the world." Both Barlow's emphasis on the sufferings of the admiral and his assertion that Columbus was little known are worthy of notice. Webster's inclusion of this material represented the adoption of Columbus into the schoolboy's canon of literature, as well as a move toward nationalism.

Barlow praised the admiral, using Robertson as his source. "Every talent, requisite for governing, soothing and tempering the passions of men, is conspicuous in the conduct of Columbus." Here, in this book of moral tales, was a long, sympathetic, and emotional treatment of Columbus, more extravagant in every way than the other pieces in the book.[10]

Caleb Bingham, an educator whose schoolbooks were reprinted year after year, published *The American Preceptor, Being a New Selection of Lessons for Reading and Speaking, Designed for the Use of Schools* in 1794. He also collected moral stories in his effort to "Train Up a Child in the Way he Should Go," giving preference to productions of "American genius." His book was meant to be useful and inoffensive, eschewing romantic fiction and tales of love. An unattributed "Account of Columbus" fit right in.

This complimentary account of Columbus set him in place as the father of American progress. His "discovery" "opened to mankind a new region of science, commerce, and enterprize; and stamped with immortality the name of its projector." The account was broken up into paragraph-sized pieces and numbered for the use of students in large classes who might declaim it. We can imagine a child standing at the front of a class singsonging, "In the life of this remarkable man, there was no deficiency of any quality, which can constitute a great character. He was grave, though courteous in his deportment, circumspect in his words and actions, irreproachable in his morals, and exemplary in all the duties of religion." Students who memorized and recited this litany of virtues were not likely to forget them.[11]

The emphasis on character went even farther in another book of the same genre, *The Columbian Reader Containing a New and Choice Collection of Descriptive, Narrative, Argumentative, Pathetic, Humourous, and Entertaining Pieces, Together With Speeches, Orations, Addresses, & Harangues, to Which is Added, A New Collection of Dialogues Designed for the Use of Schools,* of 1811. The compiler saw the need for a new collection of pieces to instill virtue, morality, and ambition in students by studying the best examples of composition and oratory. "The Character of Columbus," included here without an author, repeated the regular cliches, but left out all accomplishment. This account recited nothing about geographical theories, nothing about suing for support around the courts of Europe, nothing about the voyages, the natives, or the colonies, nothing about the great future of the nation. Only the character and the nobility of the explorer and the injustices perpetrated against him were described.

Considerable space was devoted to the apocryphal egg anecdote. In this story about Columbus, some people at a public dinner insinuated that anyone could have found the New World. Columbus sent for an egg and asked whether anyone could stand it on its small end. When all failed to manage the feat, Columbus took the egg, cracked it a little so that the end was flat, and stood it upright. Again the company scoffed, saying that anyone could have done that. Columbus agreed, but noted that none of them had thought of it. "So I discovered the Indies, and now every pilot can steer the same course. Many things seem easy when once performed, though before they were thought impossible." Columbus was thus specifically quoted, and the moral blatantly drawn from a fictitious tale. This sort of story showed Columbus to be not only noble, but clever and tricky, presumably a good lesson for America's youth.[12]

This same emphasis on shrewdness came up again in a simple biography of the admiral written for school use by 1837. The preface of this anonymously written series of life stories stated that the United

The gentlemanly Columbus challenges grotesque scoffers to stand an egg on its end and illustrates the solution. This apocryphal moral tale was supposedly offered as a parallel to assertions that anyone could have found the New World. Michel Felice Corne created this image in 1805 after an engraving by William Hogarth. Courtesy Essex Institute, Salem, Massachusetts.

States boasted of excellent subjects for national biographies. Columbus, who never ventured to nor dreamt of the United States, was accorded the whole first volume of the series, which also included Washington and Franklin.[13]

This spirited biography was written in a matter-of-fact style, uncloyed by overzealous praise. Adapted for the hard-working sons of the new republic, the book criticized Columbus' son Ferdinand for denying that his father had followed a mechanical employment in his youth. "This discovers a very false pride."[14] Equally pertinent for young Americans, Columbus was presented as a canny trader. In negotiating terms with Queen Isabella, he would "listen only to princely conditions." "A meaner spirit," after all those years of poverty and disappointment, would have been glad to get any help from the Crown. But Columbus would consent only to the rewards and honors that he proposed, demanding them as if already successful, a useful model it would seem for young people in a booming nation built on dreams and speculation.[15]

Evidence that Columbus made appearances in other classrooms is found in Susanna Rowson's, *A Present for Young Ladies; Containing Poems, Dialogues, Addresses.* This successful novelist was also a schoolteacher, and she wrote and collected recitation pieces for her students. The explorer was mentioned several times in these learned readings and given considerable space in her extended treatise on the "Rise and Progress of Navigation." The discoverer was subordinated to the discovery, but the "eminently conspicuous" explorer's story was told, concluding with Columbus' loss of reputation and death, "as superior merit ever excites envy in little minds."[16]

Meanwhile, Columbus was taking his place in books of world history as well as in the nationalistic American schoolbooks. Serious history books such as Benjamin Tucker's, *Sacred and Profane History Epitomized, with a Continuation of Modern History to the Present Time*, published in 1806, figured him prominently. The book was written in the catechetical method borrowed from religious education, in which questions and answers are written out and learned by rote. The first question in the American section was about the identity of the discoverer. How, to whom he applied, and when he began his voyage were next asked. Tucker acknowledged his debt to Robertson. Again, the history of the nation was considered in a peculiarly personal style.[17]

All this adulation in the school prepared the way for a major work of scholarship for grownups, the most important in installing the historical Columbus as a mythic and celebrated figure on the American scene. The importance of Washington Irving's biography in establishing the mariner as an American hero cannot be overestimated.

Irving on Columbus

There is a certain meddlesome spirit, which, in the garb of learned research, goes prying about the traces of history, casting down its monuments, and marring and mutilating its fairest trophies. Care should be taken to vindicate great names from such pernicious erudition. It defeats one of the most salutary purposes of history, that of furnishing examples of what human genius and laudable enterprise may accomplish.

Washington Irving, *The Life and Voyages of Christopher Columbus*

If Columbus had wanted to become an American hero and had mounted a campaign for the position, he could not have chosen a better biographer than Washington Irving. Irving, one of the new nation's most accomplished men of letters, wrote the first full-scale, exclusively Columbian biography produced in English, establishing the benevolent, wise and heroic Columbus for a wide American reading audience. Although Columbus had been written about in many places, he owes his favored position in the United States to this long and enthusiastic biography, which enjoyed immediate and lasting success. Yet, positive as Irving is, even he could not conceal Columbus' failings and the havoc he wrought on the native population of America.

Irving's youth had directed him toward this biographical task. He had been a great reader as a child in New York and was particularly drawn to the romance of foreign travel. He had poured over collections of travel literature and taken his little volumes of *The World Displayed* to school with him, where he slyly read them instead of working at his lessons. He believed the voyages of Columbus and the conquests of Mexico and Peru more wonderful than fairy tales. He considered a book of travel like a coach at the door; "he must jump in and take a ride."[18]

This fanciful attitude carried over into his mature works. Named for that other American hero, George Washington, whose life's history he also wrote, Irving was the first to romanticize peculiarly American subjects. *The Sketch Book* made him and Rip Van Winkle famous. Though he was a successful writer of American material, he was also aware of European culture and aimed to emulate it. He saw himself as a wanderer, drawn by nations on both shores of the Atlantic Ocean. Columbus had acted out the same wandering impulse, driven to seek new lands. Amiable, articulate, and very much in awe of great men, Irving seemed to move naturally toward the composition of *The Life and Voyages of Christopher Columbus.* In fact, the idea of the biography evolved from coincidence borne through desperation.

Irving was attracted to the romanticism of Europe and particularly of Spain and had studied that nation's language and literature. In 1825 he heard from Alexander Everett, minister plenipotentiary of the United States at Madrid, that a collection of Spanish materials on Columbus was then in the press. Everett encouraged Irving to translate the documents into English, suggesting that the project might be profitable and the publication successful in the United States. Irving was tempted by the project and wrote to Everett asking whether he might be attached to the embassy in some way. Everett urged him to come and provided some nominal connection to the legation. He introduced Irving and his brother Pierre into the warm expatriate society and particularly to the wealthy American book collector Obadiah Rich, then American consul. Rich invited the Irvings to stay with him in his large house.

The materials that Everett had brought to Irving's attention had been gathered by the Spanish historian, Don Martín Fernández de Navarrete. Navarrete had spent years searching out these original materials after he had accidentally stumbled on the Las Casas copy of Columbus' journal of his first voyage. Three volumes of original documents that Navarrete had gathered were published in 1826. Irving was enthused about Everett's suggestion that he translate the documents into English, and he sent off letters to publishers, urging their support. But the publishers were not encouraging; the documents were dry. Irving's enthusiasm for the translation faded when told that general readers would not be interested. He later justified his own narrative by saying that "the sight of disconnected papers and official documents is apt to be repulsive to the general reader, who seeks for clear and continued narrative."[19]

Irving was in a quandary. His reputation was at a low ebb, and he badly needed a popular and financial success. Critics at home carped about his long silence, and he knew that he must find a topic soon—a book that was his own and that capitalized on American themes. Columbus could be that subject, if he could only enliven the dull documents. Irving had the support of the American minister, and Irving's own official connection and genteel status could open doors to Spanish officials. He was already settled in Madrid, where he had the rich trove of Navarrete's materials as well as the library of Obadiah Rich. Unlike any writer in English before, he had but to reach out his hand to grasp the Columbian materials. Under these circumstances, he resolved to write the life of Columbus.[20]

F. O. C. Darley's drawing of the first landfall would have illustrated an edition of Washington Irving's biography of Columbus, which was never published. This image is similar to many others of the first landing, with the kneeling Columbus planting his flag. But Darley, who also illustrated Irving's *Sketchbook*, shows Columbus as a slightly comic figure, as if Don Quixote were acting the part. Courtesy Washington Irving Papers, Rare Books and Manuscript Division, The New York Public Library, Astor, Lemox and Tilden Foundations.

Irving was not suited by training or temperament to write serious historical biography, and the work was hard-going for him. He wrote easily and gracefully, although his style was not appropriate for this project. Irving borrowed the manuscript of the Las Casas journal on Columbus from Obadiah Rich on 16 February 1826. From that date, his journal entries recorded working on the Columbian materials almost daily. Though he continued his pleasant social dinners and evening calls, his tourist visits and correspondence, and although he often noted his weariness and depression, his listlessness and low spirits, he logged in longer and longer days at his work.[21] He read, he checked and outlined, and he began to write. Henry Wadsworth Longfellow, touring Europe before assuming a professorship at Harvard, called on him and was received graciously. Longfellow later remembered Irving as a handsome man, cheerful in society, who began his work by six in the morning.[22]

On 29 July 1827, after twenty-one months of the most strenuous literary labor he had ever known, Irving completed his manuscript and sent it off to publishers in New York and London. His English publisher John Murray had some doubts about the book but decided to publish it anyway, sending Irving a handsome advance. The American and English editions both came out in 1828.[23]

Irving said his history would combine all that had been related by different historians as well as the minor facts found in various documents recently discovered. He compared and collated every source he could find, expecting to arrive at the truth. He was a master compiler, and he patched together all the facts and evidence into a seamless whole.[24] He felt that his historical researches were meticulous and exhaustive—but he did not differentiate between his sources. All accounts were of equal weight to him. If he found something in print, he felt justified in using it. The apocryphal stories that had crept into the legend of Columbus also crept into Irving's book. The legendary matter, which included Columbus' youthful piratical voyages, his university career, his appearance at the council of Salamanca University, and his triumphant return to Barcelona (and all the embroideries thereon) were retained despite the lack of evidence for them. They were too good to lose.[25]

He manipulated the facts he found for romantic purposes. One example is found in a letter to Alexander H. Everett of 31 July 1828. Irving had located a source that placed the birthdate of Columbus at about 1435 instead of ten years later in 1445, as Robertson indicated, or the later 1451 that Morison suggested. Irving jumped at the earlier date for dramatic effect. "I think all the actions of Columbus, his perseverance, his fortitude, his undaunted enterprises, receive wonderful additional force from his advanced age."[26] When he found a source he preferred, he was willing to dismiss others that did not suit him.

He put in everything he could find and added more besides. He imaginatively recreated the life of Columbus, conceiving new details to flesh out his scenes in dramatic and colorful ways and to weave together his historical episodes. Gone were all the comic elements of his earlier work. He borrowed from others, concentrating on the idealized figure of Columbus, enhancing the humorous and picturesque details. The story was familiar, but Irving shaped and colored the events. His nonfiction narrative read more like a gentle romantic fiction than a history. The style has been called "ornamented and gaudy and meretricious," but the *Life* was also a beautiful story, gracefully told, always smooth, always dignified.[27]

For fifty years, American authors had been transforming Columbus into an American symbol, using him abstractly to represent the New World. Irving was the first to concentrate so much space and effort on the man. His multivolume work followed Columbus step by step through his life, incorporating every scrap of known evidence. This extended work by a specifically American writer brought the whole of Columbus' life and adventure into the canon of American literature. Irving had captured the hero for American purposes, making this noble human being an American personage. Paintings, sculpture, tales, poems, pageants, and plays were inspired by this book, many authors paying specific tribute to Irving's work as the primary source. Irving had crystallized an abiding interest of the age in this graceful, pseudohistory of the discovery of America.

Irving planned

to relate the deeds and fortunes of the mariner who first had the judgment to divine, and the intrepidity to brave the mysteries of this perilous deep; and who, by his hardy genius, his inflexible constancy, and his heroic courage, brought the ends of the earth into communication with each other. The narrative of his troubled life is the link which connects the history of the old world with that of the new.[28]

While narrating the life of the explorer, Irving stressed both the mental powers and the actions of Columbus, his inner and outer selves. He was the symbol, with his "heroic courage" and his "troubled life," that brought Europe and America together.

Irving created a person worthy of this heavy freight, and he endowed his Columbus with high powers that combined vision with action. He said that Columbus "singularly combined the practical and the poetical." "His conduct was characterized by the grandeur of his views, and the magnanimity of his spirit." This colossal man had envisioned and then had gotten down to work. His dream was to colonize, cultivate, civilize, build cities, and introduce useful arts, bringing everything under law, order, and religion. Irving concluded one section: "In every undertaking, the scantiness and apparent insufficiency of his means enhance the grandeur of his achievements."[29]

Irving aimed to create a hero. To attain this end, he downplayed evidence that contradicted his characterization. For Irving, history's major purpose was to provide example, and great men deserved protection from criticism to encourage others to succeed. Historians since have rightly bridled at Irving's characterization of meticulous research as "pernicious erudition."

Irving created a Columbus who was much like himself. The polite gentleman of letters who felt adrift between the cultures of Europe and America identified with his hero, the daring explorer. His Columbus suffered American-style angst. Columbus' voyages to the New World paralleled Irving's quests in the Old. Critic Jeffrey Rubin-Dorsky asserted that Irving held his readers in thrall because his tales "reenacted their doubts about identity and their fantasies about escape." He held that Irving, like many of the disaffected idealistic Americans of the early nineteenth century, sorrowed over the failure of the nation to live up to her promise. Irving's most compelling theme as a writer, according to the critic, was the displaced person at sea in a changeable world. This homelessness and longing for stability reflected the situation of American intellectuals as well as that of the Italian mariner. Rubin-Dorsky interpreted the book as a romantic quest for the unattainable, full of religious allusion, rather than a Renaissance voyage of discovery. He read the voyages as "emblems of loss and unfulfilled possibilities," seeing Columbus as a mythic hero on a fated journey. On his third voyage, Columbus believed that he had reached the outskirts of a blessed kingdom. As Columbus brought the Old World to the New, he brought evil and a sense of loss to this promising and pure place.[30]

This failure to arrive at peace in the promised land was depicted throughout the book. Irving put himself inside the mind of Columbus, seeing through the eyes of the explorer as he portrayed his romantic images. Irving and Columbus both yearned to journey to magical places, to somewhere besides where they actually were. Columbus' mind perpetually leapt beyond his actual vision, and he saw each place in terms of somewhere else. When he was gliding along the "smooth and glassy canals" separating the verdant islands, he thought he was in the Orient. The magnificent vegetation, the odors wafting from soft flowers, the splendid plumage of the scarlet cranes all persuaded him he had reached his goal. If the place was not the Orient, Columbus saw its beauties in terms of Spain. The softness and sweetness of the country equaled the delights of spring in Valencia. His mind was always traveling beyond the ship. He was excited by the constant hope of soon arriving at the known parts of India and circumnavigating the globe on the way home. He imagined he had found the mines of the Aurea Chersonesus, whence "Solomon had derived such wealth for the building of the Temple." His ardent imagination was always out in front of his ship, thinking up new schemes. He thought he might return to Spain via Jerusalem or sail around the whole coast of Africa, and having circled the globe "furl his adventurous sails at the Pillars of Hercules." Irving was right beside him while painting the images of his dreams. Columbus maintained this eager, restless vision—an inspiration to Irving—even when broken down by infirmities, old, in pain, confined to his bed, and marooned on a remote island. Irving marveled, "What an instance of soaring enthusiasm and irrepressible enterprise is here exhibited!"[31] There was no rest for the minds of these wanderers.

Irving's incorporation of American character into this story was perhaps unconscious, but he nevertheless made the "troubled life" of Columbus the connecting link between the history of the Old World and the New.[32] On the first voyage, he created two counterbalancing celebratory rituals: the first landing and the triumphant return. The first landing was a conquest and a discovery. Columbus himself saw to it that his first appearance was dramatic and auspicious, a high ceremonial occasion. But it was also a glorious moment when the New World first appeared in its splendor before European eyes. The triumphant return, largely manufactured for the purpose by Irving, showed Europe in royal magnificence honoring the new land—through the person of Columbus. The latter acted out the linkage by claiming the New World in the name of the Old and then returning to Spain to take possession of the Old World in the name of the New one. What made him great was that he had found America, and in bowing to him, Isabella bowed to the glories of the New World.

Irving's account of the first landfall showed a victorious Columbus. He had accomplished his objective. "The great mystery of the ocean was revealed; his theory, which had been the scoff of sages, was triumphantly established; he had secured to himself a glory durable as the world itself." Columbus reached the shore in his own boat, "richly attired in scarlet," holding the royal standard. This New World was presented as belonging to him. His "heart was full to overflowing" as he enjoyed this fulfillment of all his hopes—his glorious and deserved reward. He beheld the land with an "enamored and exulting eye," his triumph mingling with admiration. He was exploring "the charms of a virgin world, won by his enterprise and valor."[33]

Following his New World accomplishment, Columbus returned home to conquer Spain, where he was hitherto a stranger and a suppliant. Irving pictured the kind of reception Columbus should have had. Columbus' fame had resounded throughout the land, and he

The First Landing by Leopold Flameng portrays a small but graceful and commanding Columbus at the center of a busy scene. The chaotic Spanish activity is played off against the romantic foliage of the New World. Flameng's beautiful etchings make the descriptions of Washington Irving visual. Marquis Auguste de Belloy, *The Life of Columbus*, 1885.

progressed through the country like a sovereign. Eager citizens along the roads and in the villages filled the streets, windows, and balconies and "rent the air with acclamations." The sovereigns, in order to receive him with "suitable pomp and distinction," ordered their thrones placed in "a vast and splendid saloon" under a "rich canopy of brocade of gold." They sat in state, awaiting his arrival, attended by Prince Juan and their court dignitaries as well as the principal nobility of Spain. All were "impatient to behold the man who had conferred so incalculable a benefit upon the nation." At length Columbus appeared, surrounded by a brilliant crowd of cavaliers, among whom he was "conspicuous for his stately and commanding person." His venerable aspect gave him the noble appearance of a Roman senator. "A modest smile" exhibited his pleasure at this glory. Irving commented that nothing could be more moving to or deserved by a "mind inflamed by noble ambition" than "these testimonials of the admiration and gratitude of a nation, or rather of a world." As the conquering discoverer approached, the sovereigns stood, as they would for a person of the highest rank. Columbus knelt and offered to kiss their hands, but they hesitated to permit such an act of homage from one who had become so grand. They raised him and seated him in their presence, an unusual honor in this "proud and punctilious court." How delicious for the admiral. Actually, the return received little attention. Peter Martyr noted that Columbus reported to the monarchs, who allowed him to sit in their presence, but the rest of this tale was history retold as it should have been rather than as it was.

According to Irving, Columbus displayed to the monarchs the glories of the newfound Orient, the natives he had brought, as well as the strange birds, animals, rare plants, and gold in many forms. These colorful curiosities he pronounced as mere harbingers of greater discoveries yet to be made, which would add whole new realms of wealth to the dominions of Spain. Irving then had the proud sovereigns behave in a manner similar to the natives of the New World. They sank to their knees and, "raising their clasped hands to heaven, their eyes filled with tears of joy and gratitude, poured forth thanks and praises to God for so great a providence."[34] Irving's imagination was equal to the occasion.

Irving's Columbus took ownership of the land in two great ceremonies: He took possession of the New World in the name of the Old; he then returned to Spain and laid claim to the Old World in the name of the New, linking the two by his travel between them. The natives looked on in wonderment at the first; the sovereigns, at the second. How could a stranger and outsider have experienced more complete triumph?

The Triumphal Return by Leopold Flameng, with its vast crowds and graceful storybook buildings, puts Irving's fanciful description into visual form. Columbus is the center of interest. Critic Néstor Ponce de León grumbled at Flameng's inaccuracies, but he was visualizing the myth rather than reality. Marquis Auguste de Belloy, *The Life of Columbus,* 1885.

These events climaxed the explorer's career. In retrospect, Irving wished he could end his story there. "Well would it be for the honor of human nature, could history, like romance, close with the consummation of the hero's wishes; we should then leave Columbus in the full fruition of great and well-merited prosperity." The triumph of his return, as written in this account, had been complete. But as Irving continued to glorify the return from the first voyage, he allowed sorrowful aspects to creep in. "Thus honored by the sovereigns, courted by the great, idolized by the people," the explorer "drank the honeyed draught of popularity, before enmity and detraction had time to drug it with bitterness." The discovery had burst with "sudden splendor upon the world," encouraging envy.[35]

Irving was most criticized for rewriting the record to excuse Columbus' weaknesses. Irving in turn criticized historians who were overly critical of historical figures like Columbus, "marring and mutilating" them in the public eye.[36] Through Irving's eyes, Columbus was seen as a great man whose failures were due to his compatriots and the

Columbus reports to his sovereigns in the engraving of Leopold Flameng. Here is Irvingesque idealization, as the gallant Columbus kneels to his beautiful sovereigns. The exotic natives have brought the tokens of their land with them. Flameng focuses the light on these visitors from the New World. The Old World is in shadow. Critic de León found the artistic merit of Flameng's etchings in inverse ratio to their historical worth. Marquis Auguste de Belloy, *The Life of Columbus*, 1885.

inconstancy of public favor. Irving reported that the "illustrious merit" of the great man energized the "rancorous passions of low and groveling minds."[37] Irving wanted to create a heroic Columbus. He did not, however, completely whitewash the explorer's record.

When Columbus first sent natives off to Spain as captives, Irving put the best possible face on the situation. Columbus ordered that the men, women, and children be instructed in Christian teachings and the Spanish language. His idea was that the fierce Caribs, who were already familiar with a number of the native tongues, would be used as interpreters and as Christian missionaries after religion and civilization had reformed their "savage manners and cannibal propensities." Irving was willing to recognize that this proposal had some benefits, but he was critical.

He pointed out a suggestion of a "most pernicious tendency" in Columbus' plan. Columbus had held a "mistaken view of natural rights prevalent at the day, but fruitful of much wrong and misery in the world." Having suggested that Christianity would save the natives, Columbus then proposed to exchange them as slaves for farm animals. "In this way the colony would be furnished with all kinds of live stock free of expense; the peaceful islanders would be freed from warlike and inhuman neighbors; the royal treasury would be greatly enriched; and a vast number of souls would be snatched from perdition, and carried, as it were, by main force to heaven." This modest proposal for profiting from the lives of slaves was too much even for the hero-worshipping Irving. "It is painful," he noted, "to find the brilliant renown of Columbus sullied by so foul a stain."[38]

Irving could only palliate rather than vindicate the behavior of Columbus by saying that he acted in conformity to the times, sanctioned by the example of the sovereign. Irving found his behavior at "variance with his usual benignity of feeling, and his paternal conduct towards these unfortunate people."[39] He did not ignore Columbus' attitude toward the enslavement and mistreatment of the natives, but he recorded it with sorrow. He even implicated Columbus in the Black Legend. When Caonabó, one of the native caciques, organized an attack to surprise and overwhelm the Spanish settlement, the native planned to slaughter the intruders, trusting that the island would then be delivered from unwelcome Europeans. Irving recognized the hopeless nature of the contest, noting that "where the civilized man once plants his foot, the power of the savage is gone for ever."[40]

The strength of Columbus was as a mariner and navigator, not as a governor or colonizer. He would sail away from his colonies for long periods during which everything would go to rack and ruin. During his third voyage, he left his brother Bartholomew, known as the Adelantado, in charge of Hispaniola while he explored the vicinity. During this time, Roldán, the chief judge of the island, a man raised from obscurity by Columbus, defied the leaders and raised a force of disaffected Spaniards to back him. They roamed the countryside making trouble. On his return, Columbus made peace with the impudent upstarts, forgiving their infractions of the rules, restoring the insolent Roldán to his judgeship, dismissing all charges, and deeding land to the mutineers. Irving praised this magnanimity of Columbus with consternation. He related, "The mind grows wearied and impatient with recording, and the heart of the generous reader must burn with indignation at perusing, this protracted and ineffectual struggle of a man of the exalted merits and matchless services of Columbus, in the toils of such miscreants."[41] Columbus forgave too many times, Irving thought. Then, his patience finally exhausted, he leaped on offenders with undue ferocity, executing rebels. He was weak and firm at the wrong times. The colony was in the midst of hanging Spaniards when Bobadilla arrived from Spain, looked over the chaotic situation, took control, and sent Columbus and his two brothers back home in chains. Perhaps no one could have governed this colony of lazy and greedy adventurers; certainly Columbus could not.

Irving stressed Columbus' devotion to Christianity. A major theme was the transportation of Christian culture and belief to the New World. Irving made much of Columbus' identification of himself with St. Christopher, the hearty saint who bore the Christ child over the waters. The piety of Columbus came out frequently as he trooped his men to church and had them sing *Te Deums*. Irving assured us that the propagation of the faith in distant climes was one of Columbus' major motivations. Columbus felt divine direction in his life. He believed that "he had been chosen by Heaven for the accomplishment of those two great designs, the discovery of the New World, and the rescue of the holy sepulchre."[42] Irving gave Columbus full credit for his Christian impulses. Irving also acknowledged the mystical propensities of Columbus, about which he was less enthused.[43]

Columbus' "troubled life" was such that he lost everything. He took possession of both worlds; he stood astride the Atlantic Ocean, laying claim to both sides. Then he lost it all. Irving made a final, more tragic judgment. Although Columbus was always thinking grandly beyond where he was, Irving thought that his imagination was not up to envisioning his actual achievement. He did not realize what he had done. "With all the visionary fervor of his imagination, its fondest dreams fell short of the reality. He died in ignorance of the real grandeur of his discovery."[44]

Irving continued the story of the Spanish colonies after Columbus

This sepia water-color version of a much copied early portrait of Columbus, with his spaniel curls and familiar black hat, adds romantic native Americans and a heroic wreath overhead as well as the egg scene below. The original painting of this image by Deveria was bound into an 1831 edition of *The Voyages and Discoveries of the Companions of Columbus* by Washington Irving (RB 22799). This item was reproduced by permission of The Huntington Library, San Marino, California.

was relieved from governing responsibility. With the records before him, he acknowledged the results of Columbus' policies. The gentle romancer could scarcely stomach some of the horrors of colonial rule under Columbus' successors. Las Casas left accounts that were abhorrent to him. Bartolomé de Las Casas had come to Hispaniola in 1500, at the age of twenty-six, to make his fortune. Instead, he was converted and became the first priest ordained in the New World. As a priest and missionary, he came to love the natives and to regard them as his brothers. He recorded and decried the ways of Spain in the New World. He admired Columbus but reproved his policies.

Irving had to deal with Las Casas' reports of the government in the New World. In 1499, when Columbus pacified Roldán's mutineers by giving them land, he bound native workers to cultivate the Spanish estates. This system of slavery was known as "repartimientos." The system was also exercised in the mines, extending the oppression of the natives. Isabella objected to this system as practiced by Columbus and his successor Bobadilla, and when Ovando succeeded to the local governorship, the natives were freed. But Ovando later reinstituted the program in a more strict and cruel form.[45]

Irving told how the native men were sent to mine for gold, laboring under the lash with little food. After their six- or eight-month enlistment in the mines, they returned home, many dying on the way, to find their families dead or gone. "Nature and humanity revolt at the details." The sufferings inflicted on the natives were intolerable, and, along with the illnesses brought by the Spaniards, the system was ruinous to the native population. In less than twelve years after the discovery of Hispaniola, Irving noted, several hundred thousand of its native inhabitants had perished, "miserable victims to the grasping avarice of the white men." He recorded the "tragical history of the delightful region of Xaragua," inhabited by "amiable and hospitable people." Here the Europeans, by their own account, found "a perfect paradise," which, "by their vile passions, they filled with horror and desolation."[46]

In vain did Irving regret his inclusion of these details as "disgraceful to human nature" and likely to stigmatize Spain, that "brave and generous nation." But he could not pass silently over "transactions so atrocious," witnessed "beyond all suspicion of falsehood." He described the massacre of women and children and the punishment of natives captured in the countryside by the amputation of both hands, acts inspiring terror throughout the land. He told how the Spaniards hung their victims on low gibbets so that their feet would reach the ground, prolonging their deaths, and hacked at the sufferers with their swords. He told how the Spaniards wrapped their victims in straw and set fire to them. In a judgment powerful for this mild narrative, Irving noted that "such occurrences show the extremity to which human cruelty may extend, when stimulated by avidity of gain; by a thirst of vengeance; or even by a perverted zeal in the holy cause of religion."

Having condemned the practice, he proceeded to excuse the instigator, distinguishing between the policy and its later extension. "The system of Columbus may have borne hard upon the Indians, born and brought up in untasked freedom, but it was never cruel nor sanguinary. He inflicted no wanton massacres nor vindictive punishments; his desire was to cherish and civilize the Indians, and to render them useful subjects; not to oppress and persecute, and destroy them." His Indian slaves were sent to Spain to be civilized and Christianized.[47] This policy, of course, does not explain how the natives, after having been traded for cows and horses (if they did not die in crowded vessels at sea), could ever be regathered and retransported back to Hispaniola where their knowledge of civilization could improve their savage brothers.

Besides the slavery issue, Irving also palliated his hero's greed. When Columbus first anticipated great wealth from the New World, he immediately planned to fund a crusade to deliver the Holy Sepulchre. Irving approved the "visionary, yet generous, enthusiasm of Columbus." But his search for gold doomed him to misery. The Spaniards refused to cultivate the earth, wasting their time hunting for mines and golden streams, "starving in the midst of fertility." On his fourth voyage, after sailing along the coast of South America looking for a passage through to India, Columbus decided to abandon the search and return to the promising mines reported at Xaragua so he could finance a triumphant return to Spain. "Here, then, ended the lofty anticipations which had elevated Columbus above all mercenary interests," which had "given an heroic character to the early part of this voyage." He abandoned his pursuit of a passage through Central America and went back to hunt for gold. Irving was disappointed.[48]

Irving considered Columbus a great man despite these weaknesses. His behavior was characterized by grand views and a magnanimous spirit. He was silent when injuries were heaped upon him. Irving noted that when a truly great person endures the "insults of the unworthy," a noble scorn will swell and support the heart, silencing the tongue. Irving thought that Columbus was defeated by his associates, that "dissolute rabble which it was his misfortune to command; with whom all law was tyranny, and all order restraint." Still, Irving admitted that Columbus erred in feeling that non-Christians had no natural rights.

In enslaving natives against their wishes, "he sinned against the natural goodness of his character, and against the feelings which he had originally entertained and expressed towards this gentle and hospitable people." But again, he was not entirely to blame. "He was goaded on

This image of an old Columbus harmonizes with early physical descriptions of the man with his broad, grave face and prematurely white hair. Painted and engraved by G. Silvani, the image comes from Pierre M. Irving's 1864 book on his uncle, *The Life and Letters of Washington Irving* (RB 386281, vol. 4). This item is reproduced by permission of The Huntington Library, San Marino, California.

by the mercenary impatience of the crown, and by the sneers of his enemies at the unprofitable result of his enterprises."[49]

Irving's book was an admirable literary achievement, but his style and diction were not suited to the story he had to tell. Many neat chapters include information high in drama and horror, but they tell the tale without suspense or climax. The ornamented style partially accounts for the book's lack of popularity. Few literary historians read it. Although it is a substantial contribution by a significant American writer, this long and old-fashioned book lulls the reader to sleep with the gentle undulations of the narrative. Historians dismiss it because of Irving's cavalier treatment of the evidence.

The voyages and discoveries, played out by tragic figures over half the world and resulting in towering hopes and immense despoilation and disaster, changed the course of world history. These events constituted a magnificent and tragic episode in human history; the events were glorious and ignominious for the admiral himself, for the nations he represented and explored, and for most of the individuals concerned. All were caught up in forces outside their own understanding; all suffered from the conflict of the Old World with the New. This epic cries out for a dramatic treatment, for heroic language more worthy of the triumphant achievement and the bitter despair than Irving's nice account.

Irving's book was nonetheless commercially successful and enthusiastically received. The *Kaleidoscope* hailed Irving in his new role as biographer and historian and stressed the importance of his research. The *London Weekly Review* praised the style and treatment. The author was ranked "among the ablest historians of the age." The *New York Mirror* noted that Irving had turned to great advantage his movement toward serious history, although no one could have expected that development. The Columbus work "guarantee[d] Irving's literary immortality." The *Southern Review* rejoiced at the "vivacity and racy humor" of Irving when he dealt with American themes.[50]

Alexander Everett, instrumental in the creation of the volume, found the book "nearly perfect," leaving him little to say. He thought the work would "supersede the necessity of any future labors in the same field." Irving, in his treatment of this happy and splendid subject, had "brought out the full force of his genius as far as a just regard for the principles of historical writing would admit."[51]

Some anonymous contemporary reviewers were less impressed and more critical. The *Monthly Review* objected to Irving's romanticizing of Columbus, who seemed more like the hero of an historical novel

Johann Michael Enzing-Müller engraved, painted, and published this *Family Monument from the History of our Country*, an allegorical scene encompassing all of American history, in 1858. Largest and most prominent is Columbus in the act of laying claim to the New World. The artist also included scenes from the War for Independence, the western movement, and technological advances. George Washington leads a row of the first thirteen presidents of the United States toward an altar bearing the Constitution. Courtesy of The New-York Historical Society, New York City.

than the object of a serious historical inquiry. Also, the book was too long. The *London Magazine* called this agreeable narrative "somewhat too prolix, and in many places feeble; but on the whole, four pleasant volumes, which would be much pleasanter if they were only three." The reviewer further probed Irving's sensitive core by pointing out the major fault of the book: the "absence of all manly opinion—that skinless sensitiveness, that shuddering dread of giving offence, by which all the former productions of this writer are marked." The *Athenaeum* further complained that Irving's recent works had been insipid and his reputation, inflated even at first, had declined. The Columbus book did benefit from a clear, unaffected style, but the reviewer found little new in it. He also castigated Irving for weakly excusing Spanish atrocities against the Indians.[52] Although most critics offered general acclaim for the book, its faults were clear to discriminating readers from the beginning.

The historians who followed Irving would cast a more critical eye on the sources. Instead of excusing weaknesses, historians would deplore them. Irving himself they largely dismissed. Still, it was he who fixed the explorer firmly in the public regard, he who influenced the artistic productions to come, and he against whom they had to speak.

CHAPTER SEVEN

Glory and Gloom: Columbus after Irving

She comes! She comes!
With her white sails spread,
With her banners proudly streaming,
With a haughty brow, and an eye of dream,
Through its dark enfringes beaming.
And who is she, 'mid these island shades,
Unshielded from wrong or danger,
Who hastes from the depth of her forest glades
To welcome the stately stranger?
Her glance heeds not the gathering storm;
In its simple joy it blesses,
And the grasp of her hand is as free and warm
As the wealth of her ebon tresses.
But the gold of her rivers shall turn to dust,
Ere from history's scroll hath faded
The deeds of that visitant's savage lust,
Who thus her realm invaded.
Yes, many a pitying eye must weep
O'er the Old World's shameful story:
At the scourge which you raise o'er her sisters' sleep,
And the blood that stained her glory.

Lydia Huntley Sigourney, "On the Meeting of the Old
and New Worlds, 1492," 1834

The Columbian art work that followed Washington Irving's biography was marked by extravagance and a heightened emotion. The popular biography inspired poets and artists to create a transcendant Columbus. An increasingly visual aspect to the literary work can be traced to the scenic richness of the Irving work. The majority of Columbian literature, painting, and sculpture, much of it used ceremonially or to further other interests, was enthusiastic and patriotic, but the dark tale was also told.

Too much Columbian material from this period exists to be considered in this brief study, which is primarily concerned with the beginning of the legend rather than its development, but some interesting examples are cited as illustration.

In this depiction of *Columbus Before the Council at Salamanca*, an aged mariner describes his plan for sailing west to a bored and disdainful group of learned men. Robert Walter Weir, a former professor of drawing at the Military Academy, painted this picture in 1884. Courtesy The West Point Museum, United States Military Academy, West Point, New York.

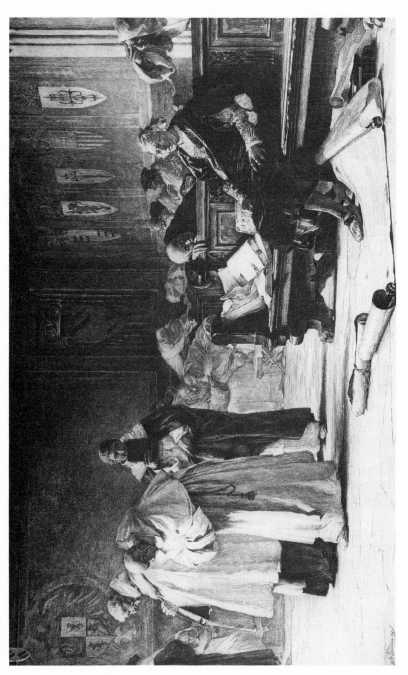

An aged and bitterly disappointed Columbus stares into space after hearing that his plan for the Enterprise of the Indies has been turned down by the council at Salamanca. Courtesy Library of Congress.

Lydia Huntley Sigourney, quoted above, with her heightened dramatic and visual sensitivities, created effective poetry perfectly suited to the Columbian style. Her poem "On the Meeting of the Old and New World, 1492," captured the excitement of the encounter, personified the two worlds as the "stately stranger" and the native maiden, and frankly related the bloody results of their clash.

The popular poetess portrayed an Irvingesque Columbus in her poem "Columbus Before the University of Salamanca," dramatizing the fictive encounter between the humble mariner and the proud, learned scholars who dismissed his theories. She created a visual scene as her "mariner with simple chart" confronted "a robed and stately crowd," and noted that "The Inquisition's mystic doom / Sits on their brows severe." Simple humility was pitted against the pride of the earth. An interesting head-note credited Washington Irving with this statement: "Columbus found that in advocating the spherical figure of the earth, [Columbus] was in danger of being convicted not merely of *error*, but even of *heterodoxy*." Here, several layers of Columbian myth-building were exposed. First, Irving incorrectly asserted that the wise of the world believed the world to be flat and that Columbus was in religious danger. Sigourney then accepted Irving's book and went on to create and dramatize the significant scene. She counseled her Columbus:

> Courage, World-finder! Thou hast need!
> In Fates' unfolding scroll,
> Dark woes, and ingrate wrongs I read,
> That rack the noble soul.[1]

Artistic representations were also influenced by the heroic Irving images. Since no actual likeness of the mariner was known to exist, artists relied on published descriptions or their own imaginations. Most of the bronze, marble, and painted effigies were recognizable as Columbus, despite their wild variations. When presented visually, certain similarities linked the representations of him: a grim purpose in the expression, a steely gaze for scanning the horizon, a set jaw that no circumstance would alter. This firm expression plus the stocky middle age at which he was usually shown and his Renaissance costume generally set him off from other notables. This artistic representation of Columbus was fabricated from historical fact and wishful thinking.

In America, the three hundredth anniversary of the landing in the New World was commemorated with faceless monuments: one in Baltimore and one in New York. After that, the monuments had faces and bodies, and the major patron for Columbus memorials was the gov-

A kindly gentleman in the ermine robes of royalty was painted by Emile Chaese, adapted from the Yanez and Puebla portraits of Columbus found in the National Museum of Madrid. Currier and Ives presented this idealized image to the American public as a standard. Courtesy Library of Congress.

ernment of the United States, through symbols installed in the United States Capitol building.

The National Capitol as Columbian Shrine

By the time the Capitol was being erected, Columbus was already enthroned as the noble and wise spiritual father of the New World, and nowhere is it clearer that Columbus is a creation of the American imagination. When the decorative scheme of the Capitol was finally completed, several accomplished and dramatic works of art honoring the admiral were installed in it;[2] all located in the very District of Columbia. The symbolic purpose of the Capitol was to provide visiting citizens with an altar for patriotic veneration. Columbus worked perfectly at invoking that mythic meaning, and he was prominently featured in several locations.

Even today visitors to the United States Capitol symbolically enter by way of the experience of Columbus: through the huge and heavy bronze double doors that depict the story of the admiral. Designed by the American artist, Randolph Rogers, at Rome in 1858, these doors are nineteen-feet high and nine-feet wide. Crafted of solid bronze and weighing twenty thousand pounds, the heavy doors swing wide for visitors at the main entrance to the huge Rotunda. The doors were cast by Von Miller at Munich in 1861 at a cost of thirty thousand dollars. They are said to compare favorably to the Ghiberti doors in Florence, a judgment invoking European standards for an artwork illustrating American superiority.[3]

The doors were originally installed in 1863 between Statuary Hall and the House extension in the Capitol, but because of "their massiveness and great beauty," they were moved in 1871 to the focal location at the entrance to the Rotunda.[4] These Rogers doors are the largest of four sets of bronze doors in the Capitol, and they tell the best integrated story. The House and Senate bronze doors, designed by Thomas Crawford, depict mixed revolutionary scenes and allegorical medallions. The doors designed by L. Amateis installed at the center of the West Front show the "Apotheosis of America" in mixed scenes representing agriculture, jurisprudence, fine arts, and so on.[5] These vignettes now seem dated and oddly chosen, while the Columbus doors still seem integrated, organized by the life of the explorer. While the myth of Columbus may not be perfect for American purposes, it has been better developed and wears better than any other we have.

In high relief and surrounding decorative borders, the Rogers doors tell all the best of the Columbus stories. These include the triumphal entry to Barcelona after the first voyage and the appearance before the council at Salamanca University.[6] Of the scenes, four took place before the first voyage; two, including the tympanum above the door, depict his landing and his first encounter with the Indians in the New World; and the final three include his return in chains and his death. The story presented portrays his whole life rather than just his exploration.

The bronze doors depicting events in the life of Columbus by Randolph Rogers date from 1863. Citizens symbolically enter the Capitol and the United States through these doors, which detail the real and mythical experience of Columbus. The doors are located at the east entrance to the Rotunda. Rogers incorporated scenes, symbols, and personalities into this rich design. Courtesy Architect of the Capitol.

In this detail from the Rogers doors, the *Audience at the Court of Ferdinand and Isabella* allows a youthful mariner to present his plan. The king and queen are shown separately in relief at the sides of the scene, and Rogers' signature plaque is on the left. Courtesy Architect of the Capitol.

In this detail from the Rogers doors, *Columbus' First Encounter with the Indians*, the static and clothed Europeans meet the active and unclothed natives. The cross in the background represents the Old World; the wild foliage, the New. The large figure on the right titled Africa is one of four representing the continents. Courtesy Architect of the Capitol.

His portrait is worked into the transom arch, above a figure of the American eagle. Portraits of the individuals who played parts in the memorable world drama are worked into the panel borders; these include ecclesiastical dignitaries as well as six sovereigns, several patrons, his companions on the voyage, his fellow explorers, and even portraits of his historians. Anchors, rudders, and armor are worked into the decorative scheme, and figures representing the peoples of the continents of Asia, Africa, Europe, and America frame the panels.[7] At the center of the figurative world is the bold Genoese, a genuine American hero. Rather than content himself with a single Columbian image, Rogers assembled and organized all the elements of the Columbian myth to fashion the symbolic entrance to the United States.

Once through the doors, the visitor stands in the great Rotunda. A guidebook of the late 1860s described the planned decoration as depicting the gradual progress of the continent "from the depths of barbarism to the height of civilization": from the wild state of the hunter tribes, through the "advance of the white and retreat of the red races" and on beyond the Revolution. This treatment promised to "afford a richness and variety of costume, character, and incident, which may worthily employ our best sculptors in its execution," and will form for future ages a monument of the present state of the arts in this country.[8]

The massive Rotunda features eight huge paintings, each twelve by eighteen feet. Visitors can almost enter into these paintings, symbolically experiencing the action of the picture. The Rotunda seems to be the world in which the action occurs. Four paintings by John Trumbull on revolutionary themes include the signing of the Declaration of Independence, two British surrenders, and the resignation of Washington. The other four sentimental favorites include Robert W. Weir's *The Embarcation of the Pilgrims in the "Speedwell," at Delft Haven*, William H. Powell's *De Soto Discovering the Mississippi River*, John Gadsby Chapman's *The Baptism of Pocahontas*, and John Vanderlyn's *The Landing of Columbus*.[9] All these paintings represent the triumph of America—over the British, over enemies of Christianity, over the New World itself. Columbus could have been interpreted as part of the old order over which the genius of America triumphed, but instead he is appropriated into the American system.

John Vanderlyn, who painted the massive Columbian scene, was a country boy from a Dutch farming family in Kingston, New York, where he displayed precocious artistic talent. Although accounts of his early years disagree, he became a protege of Aaron Burr and studied abroad with his support, remaining faithful to Burr after the latter's troubles. Vanderlyn was a very promising artist in his early years, and he was awarded a gold medal from the hand of Napoleon Bonaparte for his historical painting *Marius on the Ruins of Carthage.*[10]

Vanderlyn petitioned Congress for a commission, respectfully soliciting "the honor of being employed by Congress to execute a picture commemorative of some national event worthy of being transmitted to posterity, and occupying a place on the walls of the Capitol." He was ambitious to have "at least one production of [his] pencil in so distinguished an edifice." In 1836, nearly twenty years after his letter when the artist had turned sixty, Congress appropriated fifty thousand dollars to fill the four vacant panels in the Rotunda of the Capitol with historical paintings; twelve thousand went to Vanderlyn.[11] He moved to Paris to paint the picture, which he completed in 1844. Critics accused

This engraving was taken from John Vanderlyn's *Landing of Columbus at the Island of Guanahani, West Indies, October 12th, 1492.* The painting was installed in the United States Capitol in 1847. Measuring twelve-by-eighteen feet, the painting dominates the east wall of the Rotunda. Visitors to the Capitol, the nation's patriotic shrine, think of this image when they think of the explorer. Courtesy Library of Congress.

him of using French artists to help him, a charge he substantially denied.

Vanderlyn did not paint quickly, and he disliked painting portraits. Consequently he was less than successful as an artist. His plan for a national gallery behind City Hall in New York, for which he constructed a rotunda and painted a circular view of Versailles, was unsuccessful. He criticized the public for lack of taste, but in actuality, he was just a poor businessman. For the twenty years that preceded receiving the Columbus commission, he had accomplished little.[12]

In his painting of Columbus, Vanderlyn gave visual form to the landing as described by Washington Irving in his history. This picture, in turn, influenced the way Americans from then on understood Columbus. When Levi Morton, vice president of the United States, opened the Columbian Exposition grounds in Chicago in 1893, he praised the artists of the past. Vanderlyn's was his idea of Columbus. "I see him as in the great picture under the dome of the Capitol with kneeling figures about him, betokening no longer the contrition of his followers but the homage of mankind with erect form and lofty mien animating these children of a new world to higher facts and bolder theories."[13] Vanderlyn embellished his image in accordance with the Columbian myth by including a Franciscan monk at the landfall, although none was present on the voyage. Since bringing Christianity to the natives was accepted as a prime purpose for the voyage, the visual evidence of such a wish was frequently included.[14] The heroic qualities ascribed to Columbus, aided by Vanderlyn's grand conception and artistic execution and seen by millions of citizens in an imposing state building where they had gone to pledge their sentimental allegiance, significantly added to the reputation of Columbus.

An anonymous account of the painting, probably published about 1846 and given out at the Capitol, described the painting in terms so reverential as to be cloying. And where did the information come from? It was slightly paraphrased from the biography of Washington Irving.

No sooner did he land, than he threw himself upon his knees, kissed the earth, and returned thanks to God with tears of joy. His example was followed by the rest, whose hearts indeed overflowed with the same feelings of gratitude.

Then, rising and drawing his sword, Columbus solemnly took possession of the land and, having complied with the requisite forms and ceremonies, called upon all present to take the oath of obedience to him as admiral and viceroy, representing the persons of the sovereigns. The Amerindians were described in all the childish naivety so offensive to readers today.

During the ceremonies of taking possession, they remained gazing in timid admiration at the complexion, the beards, the shining armour, and splendid dresses of the Spaniards. The admiral particularly attracted their attention, from his commanding height, his air of authority, his dress of scarlet, and the deference which was paid him by his companions.

Columbus was then summed up as a successor to Moses.

The bold Genoese launched his frail barks upon the trackless waters, and pursued his mysterious voyage, with no cloud by day, no pillar of fire by night, to guide his path through the wilderness of waves. His daring adventure was crowned with the grandest of human discoveries; great in itself and in its consequences; the expansion of mind, the enlargement of knowledge, the perfection of art, the promotion of comfort, the advancement of liberty.[15]

Another contemporary account was less enthusiastic. The New York diarist Philip Hone noted that "it is a striking picture, the grouping well imagined and the story well told, and on the whole will be approved, though it has many faults." With its prominent leg and well-formed calf, the picture qualified as a "shin piece."[16] Vanderlyn played up the highlighted leg and daintily pointed toe, in an unlikely and awkward position, as Columbus too easily hefts his two heavy items. The romantic and sentimental pose may be amusing to us today, and sophisticates like Philip Hone had reservations back then. Néstor Ponce de León, who evaluated many of the artistic Columbian images in 1892, considered the Vanderlyn picture "worthless," but his major objections were the inclusion of the friar and the lack of resemblance to descriptions written by contemporaries. De León admitted that the ship in the background and the foliage were rendered well.[17]

Art critic Kenneth Lindsay, in his description of the painting, commented on the symbolic use of light. Light infuses the civilizing influences in the picture—the visitors from Spain and their ensigns. The source of light is the Old World, represented to the left behind the boats. The natives peer from the shadows of the benighted jungle. Columbus, in a "figural gestalt" with his flag and sword, commands with authority both the painting and the vast space of the Rotunda. Vanderlyn included a "greed motif" in the background of the picture, as two sailors, inattentive to the solemnity of the moment, shove each other.[18] Still, the picture works in presenting the heroic Columbus, bringer of civilization to the New World, and many visitors have found the image inspiring.

Above some of these large paintings in the Rotunda are reliefs of important explorers created by or attributed to Enrico Causici and Antonio Capellano. Columbus, with long curly hair and a beard, is shown

A stone relief-bust of Christopher Columbus, surrounded by a floriated wreath panel, is located on the east wall of the Rotunda of the United States Capitol and attributed to Enrico Causici and Antonio Capellano. Columbus wears armor as an honored soldier. The relief dates from 1825. Courtesy Architect of the Capitol.

in profile in a suit of armor. Wreathed in classical foliage, he appears to be an honored military man.[19]

The Rotunda contains another significant Columbian work, the immense frescoed frieze that tells the story of the nation in nineteen scenes. This frieze is more than eight-feet high and three hundred-feet long, circling the Rotunda fifty-eight feet above the floor. Constantino Brumidi created the designs and completed about a third of the frieze before his death. After the first scene—a general "America in History" depiction—comes the mariner. The imperial Columbus, gazing into heaven, descends a gangplank as all kneel in homage before him.[20]

Constantino Brumidi painted a massive frieze in fresco around the walls of the Rotunda in the United States Capitol telling the history of the nation in classic episodes. Columbus figures prominently in the second vignette located over the west door. He looks to the heavens as others kneel before him. This part of the frieze was completed in 1878. Courtesy Architect of the Capitol.

Given the Rogers doors, the Vanderlyn painting, the relief portrait, and the frieze, the Rotunda alone has four depictions of Columbus, all in heroic style.

Constantino Brumidi, who did much of the decorative painting in the Capitol building, painted two other Columbian images. The mariner is included in an unlikely group of four single portraits: William Brewster, the pilgrim divine, represents religion; Benjamin Franklin represents history; and, although Christopher Columbus represents discovery, Amerigo Vespucci was chosen for exploration.

The Columbus seen in this grouping is probably the most successful in the Capitol building in uniting legend and reality. His recognizable stocky body is clothed in modest dark costume, his linen shirt shows at the neck of his dark coat, his pointed dark hat sits atop a rugged, black-haired head. His attention is absorbed in a world globe; both hands explore it, encompassing it as if possessing it, while he refers to a chart in his lap. The whole scene is then enhanced by casual touches of grandeur. A silken cape, fallen from his shoulders, is draped over his lap. His globe sits on a marble column. His instruments of navigation lie at his feet. The common man, here intent on the world, is enriched by his accessories.[21]

Another of Brumidi's paintings, *Columbus and the Indian Maiden,* is found in the Senate wing on the first floor. In this mural, the recognizable explorer is lifting a veil covering the head of an Indian maiden who sits on a rock, recoiling slightly and turning away from him at this uninvited intimacy.[22] Probably meant figuratively as in drawing away the veil hiding the New World and opening it to view, this painting is nonetheless unfortunate. Columbus looks a little silly, and his actions toward the maiden are offensively familiar. Meanwhile, the maiden's drapery trails on the ground in a way that suggests an extra foot.

Capitol organizers, in providing a useful heritage for Americans, did not feel obliged to choose a single past. Within a few feet of each other on the East Gallery corridor can be found two pictures whose myths contradict each other. A. G. Heaton's oil mural, *The Recall of Columbus,* which refers to Isabella's agreement to support the voyage and her invitation to return to court, is not far from an idealized mural by Per Krohg, adapted from an image by Christian Krohg, portraying *Leif Erickson Discovering America.* The hopes of Americans from northern and southern Europe are soothed by the inclusion of their "discoverers."[23]

One Columbus monument created for the Capitol can no longer be found there. The sculpture *Discovery of America* was executed in Naples

This recognizable image of Columbus absorbed in the globe of the world is found in a fresco by Constantino Brumidi, located in the southeast corner of room S-216 of the Capitol. In a juxtaposition meant to emphasize the seriousness of the mariner, the modest man in severe black is surrounded by decorated surfaces and elegant accessories. Courtesy Architect of the Capitol.

by Luigi Persico in 1844 and was placed at the east central portico of the Capitol above the south end of the steps. This marble statue featured two figures: Columbus, stern and haughty, triumphantly holding a globe aloft, and beside him a female figure who symbolized the Amerindians.[24] The slightly clothed figure of the maiden knelt in a subordinate and worshipful pose.[25]

Columbus was dressed in a suit of armor modeled on one that supposedly belonged to him and is held by his descendants to this day. Unfortunately, the armor came from a period one hundred years after his time. Néstor Ponce de León regretted that the visage bore no resemblance to the description of the mariner and that, in his unnatural position, "he looks like a warrior of the XVIIth century, playing baseball with a preposterously large ball." In a tantalizing comment, de León noted that he could not "find words to express [his] surprise at the inartistic handling of the figure of the Indian maiden." Persico worked for five years on this grouping, which cost twenty-four thousand dollars. The critic thought it unworthy of reproduction.[26]

President James Buchanan, while a Senator from Pennsylvania in 1836, had recommended that *Discovery of America* be ordered from its sculptor, Luigi Persico. Persico, a native of Naples, had emigrated to

Constantino Brumidi's fresco *Columbus and the Maiden* is located on the west corridor of the first floor in the Senate wing of the United States Capitol. Columbus here officiously draws the veil from the New World, a maiden who retreats from this intrusion. Courtesy Architect of the Capitol.

America in 1818 and had already furnished several large sculptures for the east facade of the United States Capitol. Buchanan described the statue as representing

the great discoverer when he first bounded with ecstacy upon the shore, all his toils past, presenting a hemisphere to the astonished world, with the name America inscribed upon it. Whilst he is thus standing upon the shore, a female savage, with awe and wonder depicted in her countenance, is gazing upon him.[27]

Some concern that native artists rather than Europeans should be employed led President Martin van Buren to invite Horatio Greenough to do a companion piece depicting the rescue of a white female captive from a fierce Indian brave.

The Discovery Group, a marble sculpture by Luigi Persico, indicates Christopher Columbus holding aloft the globe while an Indian maiden cowers at his side. This sculpture used to be on the east side of the United States Capitol but has since been withdrawn, illustrating changing interpretations of the Columbian myth. Courtesy Library of Congress.

While the artistic merit of the Persico statue was debated, the political merit also became the subject of controversy. The theme of the domination of native American civilization by European civilization was an unfortunate one. Regardless of what inspired Persico to adopt this theme in the first place, the statue was used as justification of the westward roll of civilization afterwards. In 1845, a Democratic congressman from Alabama stated:

The artist, when he made Columbus the superior of the Indian princess in every respect, knew what he was doing. And when he likewise placed the ball in his hand, he intended further to represent the power of civilization, and what were to be the effects of the discovery of that wonderful man. . . . Freedom's pure and heavenly light . . . would continue to burn, with increasing brightness, till it had illumined this entire continent.[28]

This sculpture represented domination, not assimilation. The sculpture underscored and supported the government's Indian removal policy.[29] Both the Persico and the Greenough sculptures proved offensive to Americans, and in 1939 it was suggested that the Persico statue, an unfortunate reminder of a "barbaric past," be "ground into dust." In 1958 when the building was to be extended, the government removed all the sculptural works in the vicinity. Most of the art works were later returned to their places, but the two offending works, which had deteriorated and which represented politically incorrect views, disappeared forever.[30]

The monuments to Columbus in the New World showed him as a man of his time, enhanced by his particularly honorific position. These pictures inspired further descriptions and legends. Writers and artists, always hoping to create a Columbus worthy of discovering and founding a great nation, went beyond reality to further the reputation of the admiral. The Columbus they created only circumstantially resembled the Columbus of history, but he remained a real presence.

Columbus for Children

He was courageous and resolute, contemned idleness and effeminacy, disdained to pamper his appetite with dainties, which, while they please the palate, destroy the health; in short, he was the declared enemy of luxury and frivolity, and constantly employed in some study that might render him hereafter useful to his fellow creatures.

Joachim Campe, 1826

During the middle half of the nineteenth century, schoolbooks dealing with Christopher Columbus proliferated. Many of these books were turned out by the Goodrich brothers, Charles Augustus and Samuel Griswold. The indefatigable brothers, chroniclers of lively popular history, turned American educational history into an industry, publishing improved volumes in all sizes for many purposes. Charles Goodrich was the son-in-law of Noah Webster, marrying into the educational literature business. His brother, Samuel Griswold Goodrich, was the most prolific textbook writer in America. He wrote at least eighty-four text and reading books for children, many under the name of Peter Parley. He adopted the name when he was still in his twenties to give himself a grandfatherly aspect. Goodrich turned out his many books, which repeated and duplicated each other, with the help of hired assistants, including Nathaniel Hawthorne.[31]

The Goodrich brothers made their books attractive with engravings and a lively style, but their attempts to add interest met with some derision. Critics deemed the introduction of engravings "a fatal facility," because the appeal to the senses would leave the understanding to "indolence and emaciation."[32] Still, these history books were the first to achieve national popularity; they formed part of the educational movement in which the type became larger, the text more interesting, the illustrations more numerous, and the content more bland and inoffensive. The books were lively and dramatic. When hard facts were not available, they waxed fictional and flowery.

The Goodrich brothers stressed the saving qualities of history. Charles Augustus Goodrich, in his durable and popular *The Child's History of the United States*, first published in 1822 and popular throughout the century, claimed that history had benefits beyond knowing about the past; it could "chasten the imagination, improve taste and conversations, and discipline the mind." Goodrich opened his lengthy history with Christopher Columbus and closed with Andrew Jackson.[33]

In another of his books specifically including the explorer in his title, Charles A. Goodrich incorporated a number of enlightened learning aids. His *History of the United States of America; from The Discovery of the Continent by Christopher Columbus, to the Present Time*, first published about 1823, used two sizes of type on each page, the larger type for the basics and the smaller to fill in with details. In his first chapter, he honored Columbus for making the western continent known to the inhabitants of Europe. Goodrich also drew moral conclusions and invited readers to regard Columbus as a man of genius and enterprise, to "emulate his decision, energy, and perseverance," and to summon these qualities to accomplish useful objects.[34]

Goodrich, in a subsequent edition, reworked his title to keep up with historical developments, including the likelihood that Columbus had been preceded to western shores. His *Great Events in the History of North and South America; from the Alleged Discovery of the Continent by the Northmen, in the Tenth Century to the Present Time,* published in 1851, gave equal billing to the northmen, to Columbus, and to John Cabot; but Columbus still got most of the space and the credit for awakening the world to the new lands.[35]

Samuel Goodrich's *First Book of History for Children and Youth* had appeared in nearly three hundred editions by 1850. The book was full of pictures and maps and divided into brief, attractive sections. This *First Book* divided history into units by states. His last unit was on the West Indies, so Columbus, in a real first, ended this book rather than beginning it.[36]

The Goodrich attitude toward the admiral, mass-produced for nineteenth-century children, could be found in Peter Parley's *Tales About America and Australia,* written by Samuel Griswold Goodrich and published in London about 1842. The book, in large type and breezy style, credited Christopher Columbus with "the boldest enterprise that human genius ever conceived, or human talent and fortitude ever accomplished." This lively book was full of phrases like "that very night," and "Columbus was the first to leap on shore." His enemies at court were described as "a gang of disorderly ruffians."[37]

The movement to simplify schoolbooks continued, and by the end of the century, genuine first books about the explorer could be found. An anonymous series, *The Stories of Great Men,* published in 1895, featured in very big type and simple sentences the stories of Washington, Penn, Franklin, and Israel Putnam. These stories reduced facts to a basic few while also inventing material to bring the stories into children's experience. Although the school life of Columbus was completely unknown, the author imagined a possible scenario that would be familiar to teachers and students. "His teachers were glad to teach him all they knew. 'He will be a great man some day,' the teachers used to say."

Even for primary schoolchildren, the sorrow and the pity of the tale was exploited. The end of Columbus was interpreted this way.

When he died, no one cared. Hundreds of years after, people began to understand what a great man Columbus was. . . . If he had been treated fairly, perhaps he would have reached our great continent. Don't you think our country should have been named for him, instead of being called America?

I am always glad when I hear it called COLUMBIA.[38]

People had taken liberties before with the story of the explorer, whether on purpose or accidentally. That this abbreviated account should wander so far from the record is evidence of how fully the story was exploited for educational and patriotic purposes.

Another significant textbook was written by Emma Willard, the influential principal of the seminary for young women at Troy, New York. Her progressive *History of the United States, or, Republic of America*, first published in 1828, appeared in fifty-three printings before 1873 and was also translated into German and Spanish. Her text, which made her rich and famous, abounded in chronological aids to learning, and she was the first American history textbook writer to include historical maps. Unlike earlier compilers, she presented a sweep of history, beginning her account of America with the first inhabitants. She described the characteristics and locations of the various tribes and traced possible routes by which they first arrived on the continent. The personal Columbus was subordinated to her greater scheme, his story allowed only a couple of pages. She did not deal at length with his sorrows, but, eschewing sentimentality, she rendered into her own elegant prose the familiar descriptions. "He possessed a teeming imagination, an ardent courage, a glowing zeal, and all those energetic impulses of the soul which lead to high achievement."[39]

Clearly, the textbooks of the new nation were teaching about the voyages of exploration and, particularly, about the character of the admiral. Beyond the textbooks, he was also the subject of biographical treatments in children's gift books. Extended retellings of the old story stressed wholesome adventure and serious moral training. These extended moral tales did not always repress the dark side of Columbus' record but made an effort to deal with it. Columbus' part in enslaving the Indians was directly acknowledged and judged reprehensible. The contradiction between these good and evil qualities required considerable explanation, particularly during the Civil War.

One widely circulated book was Joachim Heinrich Campe's framed tale in which a father tells the history of Columbus to his children who urge him on, ask him questions, and beg him not to stop. The book, translated from the original German in the 1820s by Elizabeth Helme, allowed the adventurers from Spain full merit for courage, patience, perseverence, and genius while, according to the translator, "retracing with a merciful hand the deeds that disgraced them."

Campe drew a moral from each incident in a florid style, believing that adventure stories would arm young men against the romantic reveries of fashionable books. Adventure stories gave a boy "a salutary contempt for the affected jargon or frivolity, or sentiment," protecting him from "a false delicacy" and inspiring him with a taste for "chaste and profitable amusements."[40]

Campe's framework of a family discussion allowed him to air different opinions. When the mother noted that the kind natives were

The title page for *History of the United States*, painted by Alonzo Chappel, features a commanding Columbus, sword drawn, planting the colors of history instead of Spain. All defer to him here, including other explorers. The friar represents the church, and the maiden represents the New World. Courtesy Library of Congress.

"savages, men without education, without even the knowledge of God," the father retorted that we should be shamed and disgraced to be less humane than the Indians. "With how many more motives to act well has Providence furnished us than those poor Indians, deprived of all instruction! Oh my children!" We should steadfastly endeavor to render ourselves worthy of the many advantages that come to us. "What will become of us, if, one day weighed in the balance with these good savages, we are found wanting in rectitude and generosity!"[41] Campe condescended to the native culture.

In the most dramatic portion of the book, the father appears with gloomy aspect. The children look on in anxious silence. Campe must reveal the weaknesses of his hero. Finally, the father in a voice of sorrow says,

Oh my children! Why cannot I now draw the curtain and conceal from you for ever the atrocities that have been committed in the New World? But why should I conceal them? Soon or late you must know them; for the voice of innocence and humanity cries aloud, and will announce to the remotest posterity the injustice and barbarity of which the Christians have been guilty.

After terrible suspense, Campe admits that the Spaniards loosed some fierce mastiff dogs on the Indians during the military encounter on Vega Real. After the Indians lost the fight, they were forced to pay a gold tribute. Misery, slavery, and extinction eventually resulted. "Here we lose sight of the humanity which has hither to distinguished Columbus." The father wonders what necessity could force a just or virtuous man to deviate from his principles of rectitude and humanity and cannot excuse him. "Is it virtue to perform our duty as long only as we find it accord with our temporal interest? True virtue, as I have often told you, demands sacrifices." The father concludes that the conduct of the admiral was, in this instance, selfish and "wholly contrary to the principles of Christian charity."[42]

The necessity of reporting historical events while maintaining the admiral's hero status created tensions for other authors writing on Columbus. Eliza Robbins, in her book of 1829, *Tales from American History*, was another who wished to provide a model of improvement for young men. She considered "the discovery of America" the most extraordinary event in modern history," and the "first discoverer of the American continent" one of the greatest men that ever lived; she presented his noble character as a model for the boys and hoped that they would possess the same virtues when they become men.[43] He had the "noble and praiseworthy desire to benefit mankind."[44]

As the story progressed, her difficulties increased. She considered Columbus' achievement greatest at the completion of his first voyage.

"Tears and regrets made no part of the triumph of Columbus," she said. So far, the discovery had "done no evil, had destroyed no happiness." He had intended to "confer blessings on his fellow men," and so far had done so. Columbus "believed that he was appointed by Providence to render still higher services to mankind."[45]

After detailing some of the bloody events resulting from the clash between the adventurers and the natives, Robbins noted that the history of southern America was one of the saddest with which she was acquainted. She was forced to observe that the "character of Columbus, so grand and elevated among men," must compensate "for all the painful feelings excited by the cruel, selfish, ignorant Spaniards, with whom he was associated." She sternly reproved his practices, grieving that so great a benefactor of mankind as Columbus should "not have better understood the rights of man, than to suppose himself justified in tearing the poor Indians from their country, their families, and all the objects of their affections, and causing them to be sold to the service of strangers." Columbus could only have "encouraged this traffick in men" because it was an established practice. "The manner in which Columbus exercised the power of a conqueror, was neither wise nor kind."[46]

Sarah E. Bradford in her book *The Story of Columbus, Simplified for the Young Folks*, published in 1863, hoped to encourage young people to patience and perseverance and to withstand mockery and ridicule when choosing the right action. But, like other educators attempting to tell the story of Columbus in the 1860s, she was faced with a dilemma: This man of all virtue, "softened by strong religious feeling," also enslaved men. Bradford cited this action as "his one error." Every man has *some* error, she says, and slavery was common at the time. Circumstances inspired the behavior against which he seemed to have struggled but was driven to by necessity. She was quite sure that, if he had lived in a later, more enlightened time, he would not have suffered this blot upon his character. Midnineteenth-century writers for children, interested in education and the nobility of man, were attracted to heroes like Columbus, even when they were abolitionists. Of course, they had to point up the cruel behavior and condemn it as a great sin before moving on to the virtues.[47]

Over the century, the moral fable was used to teach many suitable lessons, sometimes subjecting the story of Columbus to contradictory interpretations. Two children's books, published within a year of each other, came to quite opposite conclusions. Sarah Knowles Bolton, in her *Famous Voyagers and Explorers* of 1893, thought of the natives and considered the career of Columbus "sadder . . . than any other mortal presents in profane history." Elbridge Streeter Brooks in his 1892 book, *The True Story of Christopher Columbus*, thought of the adventure and concluded that the story was "happier than any fairy tale, more marvelous than any wonder book."[48] The conclusions were equally true in their own ways.

The contradictory statements by Bolton and Brooks accurately represented the outcome of a century of writing on Columbus for children. Beginning with the early efforts to create a model character, an inspiration for youth, the books steadily introduced more and more of the dark side of the record. In a period of abolition, the enslavement of Indians was especially difficult to overlook. The two Columbuses sometimes inhabited different volumes as with Bolton and Brooks, sometimes sailed within the same pages as with Bradford. By the end of the century, however, both Columbuses were in the record, even within the literature most given to suppressing evil—stories for children. That we have remembered the heroic discoverer more than the cruel enslaver says more about our own blithe confidence in the past than it does of the deceptions of our authors.

Revisionist History

Vindicate Columbus!
Esteemed Friend: Many recent Biographies and Histories of Columbus and of his Discovery contain serious charges against his public and private life and character; that he deserted his first Wife and Family, that he was never married to his second wife, Beatrix Enriques, that his son Fernando was illegitimate, and that he was guilty of cruelty, oppression, avarice, falsehood, hypocracy. . . . These charges are capable of historical refutation.

Advertising card for "Old and New Lights on
Columbus" by Richard H. Clarke, 1893

By the time Irving's biography was published, Americans had been drawing the admiral in their own desired image for fifty years. His reputation had fluctuated widely. For Philip Freneau, Columbus was a dark and tragic figure. In other portraits, he was stripped of specificity, a symbol only. Robertson created a magnificent and intrepid explorer. Irving painted a detailed and virtuous Columbus, but he was not to have the last word.

A number of other American historians dealt with Columbus in the nineteenth century. W. H. Prescott, writing history "to be read as a pastime," considered Columbus in his *Ferdinand and Isabella* of 1837, presenting his character in the most positive terms. "Whatever the defects of Columbus' mental constitution, the finger of the historian will find it difficult to point to a single blemish in his moral character."

His conclusions remained positive, although the reader is aware of deceit and selfishness.[49]

George Bancroft, the most widely read American historian of the nineteenth century, could be expected to speak highly of Columbus as he traced "the steps by which a favoring Providence, calling our institutions into being, has conducted the country to its present happiness and glory." He treated Columbus only briefly in his multivolume history, but his rolling sentences ennobled the explorer.

Though yet longer baffled by the skepticism which knew not how to comprehend the clearness of his conceptions, or the mystic trances which sustained his inflexibility of purpose, or the unfailing greatness of his soul, he lost nothing of his devotedness to the sublime office to which he held himself elected from his infancy by the promises of God.

His style was well suited to the dramatic reverses of the admiral. "In May, 1498, Columbus, radiant with a glory that shed a lustre over his misfortunes and griefs, calling on the Holy Trinity with vows, and seeing paradise in his dreams, embarked on his third voyage to discover the main land, and to be sent back in chains." Bancroft considered the great discovery of Columbus to be the "triumph of a free mind."[50]

The zenith of praise for Columbus was probably written by Frenchman Roselly De Lorgues, adapted into English by J. J. Barry. These men argued for the saintliness of the mariner and supported his canonization by the Catholic church. This book is one long paean to the mariner. Barry declares that critics cannot deny his sublimity but are "forced to admire, after his patience and his energy, his unalterable virtue, and with his disinterestedness, his pardon of injuries and offences, and his magnanimity!" He remains "a prodigy of moral grandeur." Unfortunately, only the faithful can perceive this greatness. He "cannot be comprehended and appreciated but by Catholics; the hero of the Faith is not intelligible to incredulity." Barry asserts that God chose Columbus as a messenger of salvation. This is a man "whose moral grandeur surpasses the most celebrated types of antiquity, and who is not inferior to the noblest of those of the heroes formed by the Gospel." Columbus could work miracles, one of the "weighty reasons" Barry offers for considering him a saint. His "perfect virtue," his "entire purity of heart" cause De Lorgues and Barry to declare in concert "before God, who knows it, and before men, who do not know it, that CHRISTOPHER COLUMBUS WAS A SAINT."[51] The proposal for the canonization of Christopher Columbus was made to the pope in 1867. The Roman Catholic church has not, however, taken that action.[52]

After that high praise, the reputation of Christopher Columbus could go nowhere but down. *A History of the Character and Achievements of the So-called Christopher Columbus* by Aaron Goodrich, published in 1874, set out to debunk the explorer, aiming to place his character in a true light. Goodrich found hypocrisy, particularly in religious matters, and deceit as well as cowardice and cruelty to be the major traits of Columbus. He noted the distrust and aversion in all of his associates. Contemporary critics dismissed the petulant efforts of Goodrich as too biased and "too peevish," but his conclusions foreshadowed views that were later widely accepted.[53]

Hubert Howe Bancroft's *History of Central America* of 1882 presented the character in a franker manner than national pride, religious sympathy, or hero worship had formerly permitted. "As a mariner and discoverer Columbus had no superior; as a colonist and governor he proved himself a failure. Had he been less pretentious and grasping, his latter days would have been more peaceful. Discovery was his infatuation; but he lacked practical judgement, and he brought upon himself a series of calamities."[54]

Books of this period were significantly influenced by the revisionist work of American Henry Harrisse who, writing in French, reconsidered every source with more thoroughness and discrimination than had previously been shown. For most of his life, Harrisse dismissed the *Historie* of Ferdinand, the son of Columbus and the source of much of the biographical data, as a spurious work. His attacks aroused opposition, and much of the writing of the nineteenth century was in defense or in opposition to the veracity of the texts used, as well as to questions of birthplace, site of first landfall, and nationality.[55]

Henry Vignaud, writing about the turn of the century, continued the revisionist direction, doubting the statements that Columbus himself made about his life. He postulated that Columbus never intended to go to the Indies but sought only to discover new lands. Finding land much farther west than expected and concluding that he was in Asia, Vignaud proposed that Columbus falsified his journals and forged an early correspondence with Toscanelli, a Florentine physician whose map showed China and Japan to the west, to prove that Asia had always been his destination.[56]

The general public, encouraged by the positive work of Irving and the many works inspired by him, was distanced from this debate and continued to think highly of Columbus. He was elevated to serve the causes of progress and nobility, even as the historians argued about sources and tried to come to grips with what they saw as truth. While Columbus continued to ascend to a pinnacle of public adulation in 1892, the historians were evaluating his performance and passing judgment. The task of summing up the critical debate fell to Justin Winsor, a learned and prolific historian who directed the Boston Public Library and was later the librarian of Harvard College.[57]

Justin Winsor's book *Christopher Columbus and How He Received and Imparted the Spirit of Discovery,* published in 1891, assembled and critiqued the current thinking on Columbian questions for a learned audience at the four hundredth anniversary of first landfall. He evaluated the sources, steering through the conflicting accounts and the obfuscations of Columbus himself, seeking to rule on scholarly questions. Winsor dismissed many imaginative details that filled up a "scant outline with the colors of an unfaithful limner."[58]

Winsor believed that Irving's book on Columbus had done more harm than good. Irving had interfered with the understanding of the truth because his book was so charming as to be insidious. Irving's purpose had been to "create a hero." He glorified what was heroic, palliated what was unheroic, and minimized the doubtful aspects of Columbus' character. His book was, therefore, dangerously seductive to the popular sense, admitting the enormities of the Spaniards but excusing Columbus from them.[59]

Winsor suspected Columbus of intentions to enslave the natives from the beginning. The first words of description to the Europeans suggested a scheme for working the strange people to his benefit. Even on the first voyage, when the explorer allowed natives he had captured to escape, Winsor showed how Columbus watched the wondering crowds and noted that "his ruse of friendship had been well played." Columbus anticipated the fate of the natives, describing them as "well-fitted to be governed." During his second journey to the New World, Columbus wrote to the sovereigns, suggesting an exchange of Carib natives for livestock and requesting a reply. Using documents closely, Winsor quoted from the letter and recorded the marginal comments of the sovereigns. They noted, "He has done well," and, "His suggestions are good"; but they paused at the suggestion about the trade, suspending judgment and asking for further thoughts. Columbus received this message, but he had already been rounding up the offending Caribs. On the return voyage of the same little fleet that had brought the royal letter urging hesitation, he packed in more than five hundred unhappy natives to be sold in Seville as slaves. Winsor had nothing to say in his defense. "The act was a long step in the miserable degradation which Columbus put upon those poor creatures whose existence he had made known to the world."[60]

Winsor noted that Columbus had shown himself superior to the world in geographical knowledge but inferior in moral judgment. Las Casas had criticised Columbus in the light of religion and higher vision, revealing the "reeking passions of the enslaver." The moral perception of Las Casas cancelled the excuse frequently made for Columbus, that he was a man of his time. Winsor scornfully noted, "It may be indeed asking too much of weak humanity to be good in all things, and therein rests the pitiful plea for Columbus, the originator of American slavery." The policies of repartimientos and encomiendas, instituted by Columbus, bound the natives to the land, allowing every colonist absolute power over the natives entitled to him by his rank and position.[61]

When he summed up the life of Columbus, Winsor's judgments were ironic and harsh. No "child of any age" ever did less to improve his fellow man; yet few ever did more to open the way for improvements. "The age created him and the age left him. There is no more conspicuous example in history of a man showing the path and losing it." Columbus' domination of the history of two hemispheres required that he be judged by "an austere sense of occasions lost and of opportunities embraced." The truly great man is superior to his age and anticipates the future; Columbus was mired in the culture of his present. "It was indeed the misery of Columbus to miss the opportunity of being wiser than his fellows, the occasion always sought by a commanding spirit, and it was offered to him almost as to no other." Winsor believed that the passion for wealth tainted the impressive aspects of his character. After he had secured his privileges from the monarchs, the record of "falsities and indiscretions" began to demonstrate his greed. Columbus demanded gold—of his sovereigns and of the New World. He went to his death demanding more from King Ferdinand. The natives went to their deaths vainly trying to supply the coveted mineral, which they recognized as the white man's God.[62]

The explorer's demand that he be made viceroy over all discovered lands was "the serious mistake of his life." He thought the position would bring him honor; instead it poisoned his future. The honors that his first voyage brought him were compromised by his attempts to rule a colony, a job for which "no man ever evinced less capacity." Seeing in himself the fulfillment of scriptural prophecy, he abandoned his rational and scientific judgments, justifying his towering pride. Winsor laid him to rest thus:

We have seen a pitiable man meet a pitiable death. Hardly a name in profane history is more august than his. Hardly another character in the world's record has made so little of its opportunities. His discovery was a blunder; his blunder was a new world; the New World is his monument! Its discoverer might have been its father; he proved to be its despoiler. He might have given its young days such a benignity as the world likes to associate with a maker; he left it a legacy of devastation and crime. He might have been an unselfish promoter of geographical science; he proved a rabid seeker for gold and a viceroyalty. He might have won converts to the fold of Christ by the kindness of his spirit; he gained the execrations of the good angels. He might, like Las Casas, have rebuked the fiendishness of his contemporaries; he set them an example of perverted belief. The triumph of Barcelona led down to the ignominy of Valladolid, with every step in the degradation palpable and resultant.[63]

These stark words, fierce in their denunciation, were generated from the historian's study as he sifted through the evidence found in the old documents. Outside in the streets, the world prepared a celebration of gratitude for the four hundredth anniversary of the voyages of Christopher Columbus and for the great good and progress that had resulted from them. The speakers eulogized him, the paraders marched, the monuments were raised and dedicated, and the crowds cheered.

CHAPTER EIGHT

The Admiral Enthroned

COLUMBIA! to Columbus give thy hand!
And, as ye on a sea of glory stand,
The world will read anew the story grand
Of thee COLUMBIA, and Columbus, too—
The matchless epic of the Old and New—
The tale that grows more splendid with the years—
The pride and wonder of the hemispheres.
In vast magnificence it stands alone,
With thee—Columbus greeting—on thy throne.

Kinahan Cornwallis, 1899

Distress and Hunger shall here dry their tears,
    Her humblest sons no tyrant shall obey;
A world of peace and harvests, they afar
    Who bear Oppression's yoke shall call her blest,
The peaceful half of this unpeaceful star;
    Thy world, Christopher, this, behold thy West
Henceforward open; thou didst break the bar
    Withstanding vainly thy triumphant Quest.

Henry Iliowizi, 1892

Columbus was not a subject of daily discussion by the American populace during the nineteenth century. He was relegated to the schoolbooks and brought out when young classes performed their recitations. His claims and character were debated only by historians, and in some ways he had been forgotten. But it was time for him to be discovered again, this time as America's symbol of achievement and progress, the embodiment of four hundred years of success as a nation and the promise of many more to come.

His combination of faith and perseverance was particularly compelling for the United States, still suffering the stresses of its metamorphosis from an agricultural to an industrial economy. Like Columbus, individuals were steadily casting off into the unknown. Immigrants crossed the seas seeking new opportunities. Others used the nation's immense rail system to move west to new lands or to the cities to swell the manufacturing population. The industrial workers, unskilled and without voices, plied the machines that heaped great wealth into the hands of a very few. The farmers increased productivity, even as their prices fell, and the simple yeomen of the American ideal saw their debts rise. Americans were unsettled and apprehensive. Individuals in the land of freedom were having difficulty understanding the forces that seemed to control their lives. They needed ideals and goals.

Columbus was a man who had suffered and triumphed over adversity. His story, familiar from childhood, spoke to the need for idealism and stability. He was an immigrant himself, decidedly ethnic in origin, and his experience paralleled the contemporary American experience. He also provided perspective. The nation had come so far in four hundred years that the tensions of the day disappeared in comparison to the magnificent progress witnessed. These and other factors contributed to the indisputable fact that the nation fastened onto the four hundredth anniversary of the first landfall of Columbus in the New World as an opportunity to commemorate America's success and basic goodness.

Aside from these theoretical reasons for the commemoration of Columbus, there were practical ones as well. The nation had honored her one hundredth birthday with a centennial fair held in 1876. Philadelphia had prevailed over other cities in the competition to host the fair, and the exhibition had proved to be a great success, focusing money and energy on the nation's progress. The exposition was the largest to date; its sixty-acre size was half again as large as the preceding fairs at Paris and Vienna. Records were broken, including the number of exhibitors—sixty thousand—total receipts at more than three and a half million dollars, and the cost, in excess of seven million dollars. Hundreds of thousands of Americans and visitors, almost ten million in total, surveyed the productive capabilities of the nation and the natural resources available. Alexander Graham Bell publicly exhibited his telephone for the first time. The fair commanded the respect of Europeans and was considered a national triumph.[1]

The Philadelphia fair had been held to honor the past, but history was really only an excuse to demonstrate how the present was turning into the future. Immediately after the Philadelphia Centennial Exposition of 1876, people began to suggest that a Columbian fair be held.

In 1888, the *Chicago Times* ran a letter from Dr. A. W. Harlan, a Chicago dentist, who proposed an international fair in 1892. In the usual juxtaposition of past and present, he suggested celebrating the discovery of the New World by using the progress of the western continent as the theme. He argued that everyone supported world's fairs—if they did not occur too often—that Americans in 1892 would want to show off their progress, and that the fair should be held in Chicago. None of these arguments mentioned anything about the mariner. Philadelphia, Washington, St. Louis, and Cincinnati also proposed to host the fair, and Baltimore, Mexico City and a group in New England showed interest. No one seemed to question whether it was a good idea to have such an exposition, the only question was where.[2]

In 1889, the third Paris Nationale opened, outdoing any previous fairs. Visitors admired the extent of the displays, the elegance of the buildings, the artistic spirit apparent everywhere, the grounds and the landscaping, the imposing machines, and the Eiffel Tower, which was not only the symbol of the fair but became the symbol of Paris itself. Americans were somewhat taken aback when they realized how difficult it would be to surpass that exposition, but New York City, the center of the nation's financial and commercial interests, took up the challenge. New York's Mayor Hugh Grant called a meeting of several hundred of the city's prominent industrial, national, and trade leaders to meet at City Hall on 25 July 1889. He suggested, even while France's event was in full swing, that New York host such a fair. The response was enthusiastic. Committees were named, the Chamber of Commerce pledged its support, and the New York press joined in.

New York's move discouraged most other cities, but Chicago stayed in the fight. The *Chicago Tribune* maintained that the fair should be an all-American exposition and charged that New York was not an American city, being neither patriotic nor national. New York countered that Chicago lacked tradition and that, if the fair were held in Chicago, Europeans would not come. Chicago responded that visitors would not see the country if the fair was in New York and that going to the United States without seeing Chicago would be like "going to France without seeing Paris." Chicagoans, eager to assert the city's claim to international importance, eliminated the word fail from their vocabularies. The energy with which this upstart city on the inland sea battled her powerful, older sister for primal position showed the growing strength and vigor of the nation's west. Chicago waged a publicity campaign in favor of the fair, organizing and founding a corporation capitalized at five million dollars.

When the United States Congress assembled in December of 1889, a joint committee set up to consider the fair began to debate the site. Which city could best present the nation to the world? Which had sufficient financial resources to make the fair feasible? Which could host millions of foreign visitors? Debate continued well into February, and the public followed developments with great interest.

These activities brought Columbus into wide public attention, but he was not the subject of debate. His importance was assumed and accepted. On 24 February 1890, the House of Representatives considered the site of the Columbian exposition. Eight roll-call votes finally established Chicago as the host of the world's fair. Chicago had to pledge ten million dollars. "An Act to Provide for the Celebration of the four hundredth Anniversary of the Discovery of America by Christopher Columbus by holding an International Exhibition of Arts, Industries, Manufactures, and the Products of the Soil, Mine, and Sea, in the City of Chicago, in the State of Illinois" was passed. It could be said that Chicago won out by showing the same desperate perseverance as Columbus himself.[3]

Chicago Captures Columbus

Chicago by her inland sea—
The mouthpiece of these mighty States—
With nations gathered at her gates,—
Their choicest treasures with them there
To swell The World's Columbus Fair,—
Invites the world to honor thee.

Kinahan Cornwallis, 1899

Welcome, you men of older civilizations, to this young city whose most ancient landmark was built within the span of a present life.

Mayor Washburne, 1892

When the Chicago exposition opened in 1893, the extravagance of the conception was reflected in rhetoric Columbus might have used for Cathay. "The dreams of bygone centuries are realized. . . . Imagination would fail to conceive the splendor and riches, the power and the glory, here displayed." The fair aimed to honor the fruition of that voyage into the unknown waters of the mighty Atlantic four hundred years before, to commemorate the discovery of the New World, and to serve as a tribute to the "sublime faith of him who dared to follow the guiding star of his reason" across an unknown ocean, until it stood above a continent that had become the "Promised Land" to the oppressed of all nations. The guiding star and the promised land lent biblical credence to this familiar tale. Columbus was exalted for these purposes, but he was just the excuse for the fair. He was a mere object of veneration, a success symbol.

The real purpose of this event, which united "the inspiration of the Artist, the skill of the Sculptor, the genius of the Architect, joined with the cunning hand of intelligent labor," was to show off American progress. What was honored was the glory and magnificence of the immense display, the power and energy of great American machines, and the riches of the field and the earth beneath. The fruits of the chosen land were here displayed: artistic excellence, technological superiority, and natural resources. Finally, Chicago was represented as the city of all cities. The fair fittingly gathered together the wealth of the world in the "Garden City of the West, the Queen City of that continent."[4]

Journalists were fond of throwing around impressive statistics about the fair. Of the total thirty million-dollar cost, more than half went into the construction of twenty-eight stately edifices built of glass and a snowy white stucco, creating a "city in the clouds." The largest building, for manufactures and liberal arts, housed more than thirty acres under a single roof, the largest structure in the world. This cloud city sat on land modeled and reshaped with a large lake, dockage for private vessels, as well as water and sewage systems to meet the needs of twenty-five million visitors for the 184 days of its life.

The centennial exposition at Philadelphia in 1876 had been equal to any two worlds' fairs held until then. The Paris Exposition of 1889 was greater than the centennial. The Columbian exposition equaled more space and had more acres of buildings than both the Paris and Philadelphia fairs together.[5]

Two-thirds of the space was devoted to North American resources and products displaying American resourcefulness, both material and mental. The government building, a marvel of science, invention, useful arts, education, agriculture, and industry, provided an understanding of the genius of American institutions for those who could not visit Washington. The displays could develop patriotism in the dullest mind, epitomizing the nation's century-long struggle for ideal human freedom. Some of the wonders created to depict American genius and to work this patriotic magic were displays of patent office models, a live Indian school in operation, a model post office, and a mint striking exposition medals.[6]

The artworks at the Chicago Exposition were produced by native artists as opposed to Europeans. Beautiful and extravagant, the artworks were decorations rather than integral parts of the fair. Frederick MacMonnies produced the Columbian fountain, based on a symbolic design said to have been sketched by Columbus himself. This exuberant fountain featured the Barge of State, which depicted the apotheosis of modern liberty—Columbia seated on a triumphal barge rowed by art, science, industry, agriculture, and commerce, guided by time, heralded by fortune. These figures have also been interpreted as Columbus seated by providence, attended by constancy, tolerance, victory, and hope, with fame overhead blowing trumpets. The peristyle of the republic had as its center portion a triumphal arch reminiscent of the Arc de Triomphe in Paris, surmounted by a Quadriga representing the triumph of Columbus who stood in his chariot drawn by four horses that were led by two women.

An additional artwork was the noble statue of Columbus, a large, standing figure facing the rising sun. The statue was the work of Mary Trimble Lawrence, a student of Augustus St. Gaudens, who was chosen to furnish the statue in the place of her more famous teacher. Her Columbus is shown claiming the New World, wearing armor, with his face uplifted, bearing the standard of Castile and Aragon in one hand and his upraised sword in the other. Of this vigorous statue it was said, "Could the cold clay by some occult power be animated with life, and Columbus be allowed to gaze on the scene over which his eyes would fall, he would realize as he could from no other spot on the continent, the greatness of the country which four centuries ago he brought to the knowledge of his fellow men."[7] The real business of the fair, demonstrating the superiority of the United States, went on in the buildings. Columbus majestically surveyed it all.

A view of the two major monuments relating to the mariner at the World's Columbian Exposition at Chicago, 1893. Frederick MacMonnies' Columbian Fountain, adapted from a design said to have been drawn by Columbus himself, is in the foreground. Columbia, seated on a triumphal barge, is rowed by art, science, industry, agriculture, and commerce. She is guided by time and heralded by fortune. The Quadriga, on top of the Peristyle Arch, can be seen at the rear. Contact print from a Frances Benjamin Johnston negative. Courtesy The Library of Congress.

The Peristyle of the World's Columbian Exposition at Chicago, 1893, was centered by a triumphal arch reminiscent of Paris' Arc de Triomphe. Surmounting the arch was a sculptured crown or Quadriga representing the triumph of Columbus. He stands in a chariot drawn by four horses and led by two women. The contact print is from a negative by Frances Benjamin Johnston. Courtesy The Library of Congress.

The Columbian Exposition that displayed American power and progress to the world was the creation of business interests. Only they had the power and finances to put such an ambitious program into effect. Other commemorations, where Columbus was still exploited for special interests and purposes, were held in various cities of the world. At festivities in Madrid, cannons, military music, and bells rang out on streets richly decorated with triumphal arches and gay with colors. Processions of Spanish students wended their way to solemn religious services. In London, distinguished Englishmen joined Americans, Spaniards, Germans, and Frenchmen at the same board to sing the praises of Columbus. Celebrations were carried out in Chicago, Boston, Baltimore, and many other places; but no other place launched a series of events that could surpass those held in New York City.[8]

New York Honors Columbus

[The navigators of 1492] dreamed of wealth, and here it is beyond imagination's furthest limit. They longed for power, and here it is greater than that of any ancient empire. They sighed for liberty, and nowhere is liberty more securely established and the right of citizens more jealously guarded. They sought the spread of Christianity, and nowhere is the influence of Christ's Church greater. . . . All the longings and aspirations which inspired the discoverers . . . have found fullest expression in the history of this city and state.

Roswell Flower, Governor of New York, 1892

St. Mary's Star of the Sea Cadets march in the school parade of the Columbus festivities in New York City in 1892. Notice the schoolgirls sitting in flag formation ready to sing patriotic songs, as well as the crowds and the decorated buildings. Strohmeyer and Wyman distributed this image as a stereograph. Courtesy Library of Congress.

The First Artillery of the U.S. Army passes through the Pergola at Fifth Avenue and Twenty-Second Street in New York City, 1892. Note the decorations on nearby buildings as well. Originally a stereograph by Underwood and Underwood. Courtesy Library of Congress.

New York, which had missed out on having the World's Columbian Exposition, launched five days of celebration that outdid anything in memory. The public rose to this event in overwhelming numbers, and on the final day, one million visitors came into the city to witness this expression of the city's patriotism. Homage to the mariner was mixed with home-grown chauvinism. One observer noted that nowhere else could the progress of four hundred years be so brilliantly illustrated as in the grand commercial city, standing, in its glory, as a "living, bustling, instructive monument to the honor of the pioneer of modern civilization."[9]

The Columbian legend had become so rich and complex by then

The Columbus Arch on Fifth Avenue at Fifty-Eighth Street in New York City framed the vista for parades during the five days of commemoration in 1892. Originally a stereograph by Stohmeyer and Wyman. Courtesy Library of Congress.

that many constituencies desired to pay proper tribute. Five full days and an extra evening of activity were scheduled to honor the grandfather of the nation.

Artists were called in to dress the city. An honorary advisory committee, including such artistic powers as Richard Morris Hunt, Augustus St. Gaudens, William Merritt Chase, Stanford White, Albert Bierstadt, Louis C. Tiffany, John Lafarge, and others, produced a book encouraging decorations along the parade routes and throughout the city. Prizes were awarded for the best designs. The artists urged that whole blocks cooperate in single decorative schemes. Drawings suggested luxuriant swags and festoons, elaborate garlands and wreaths, poles with banners, and large cartouches with flags radiating out from both sides. The committee urged lighting up at night with lampions—small glasses containing an illuminating composition—on window sills and cornices.[10]

The public took this advice to heart, and for the days of the Columbian celebration, the city was bravely festive in its gala dress, with the national colors of Spain, Italy, and France complimented by expanses of red, white, and blue. The mansions of the rich were masses of colored banners, streamers, and flags. The places of trade all over the city were decorated, and virtually every window had its symbol. Fifth Avenue received the most elaborate treatment. At Twenty-second Street, a classic arbor or pergola spanned the avenue, wreathed with palms and green garlands and lit by Chinese lanterns. Decorations were thick for a full mile north, which was canopied with ropes of lanterns, flags, greenery, and banners. At Fifty-eighth Street, a triumphal Columbus arch of gorgeous design closed the vista.[11]

Religious Opportunity

The Jewish people certainly have cause to express gratitude for the hero who founded a haven of repose for our noble race. The very name of Columbus is significant of love, truth, and rest, for Columbus discovered America because he had faith in himself and in God, and because he discovered a country for wandering Israel as well as for others.

Rabbi, Temple Ahawath Chesed, 1892

Of the themes to be struck, religion came first. The basic idea was that Columbus was responsible for the freedom of religion available in the United States. The congregations of all denominations were encouraged to devote their religious observances to him, and an estimated five hundred such special services were held in New York City alone. On Saturday and Sunday, 8 and 9 October, all denominations joined in general rejoicing and thanksgiving. Columbus had long been linked with the Jews, because he originally sailed from Spain the day after Ferdinand and Isabella expelled the Spanish Jews. He was apparently claimed because his voyages eventually led to a safe haven. Efforts to prove that he himself was a Jew have been inconclusive, but he was honored for his part in establishing a nation where the wandering Jews could rest. Special services in the synagogues on Saturday included sermons on "The Importance of Columbus' Discovery for the Jews" and "The Achievements of Columbus for the Benefit of Mankind and the Jews in Particular." In the sermon at Temple Emanuel on Fifth Avenue, the rabbi stated that the Hebrews had ceased to long for Jerusalem and had come to regard America as the true land of

Under a canopy that turns a wilderness into a church are *Columbus and His Companions Attending the First Christian Religious Ceremonies in the New World*. This image, engraved for *Sartain's Magazine*, illustrates how the myth of early religious presence and practice has been projected back upon the first landing in descriptive and visual forms. Courtesy Library of Congress.

promise,[12] a situation now changed by the reestablishment of their traditional homeland. This oldest New York congregation performed an ancient ritual of traditional chants dating back to before the expulsion.

The Christian churches on Sunday, 9 October, were brilliant in patriotic decoration—festooned flags, banked flowers, electric lights—and elaborate musical programs. The services praised the mariner as the world's benefactor in connection with his religiosity. One minister interpreted all of American history as an "Illustration of Providence."[13] Others referred to the critical debate. The eloquent Rev. Mr. Faunce of the Fifth Avenue Baptist Church regretted the "dissolving processes of historical criticism" in which "remorseless investigation" had broken apart the Columbus of his childhood. He urged caution in accepting the reckless criticism of historians. Patriotism was a way of believing in the nation's destiny and future.[14] Criticisms of the honor of Columbus were raised and dismissed, but his faith and divine direction were not questioned.

School for Patriots

At this moment, in every part of the American Union, the children are taking up the wondrous tale of the discovery; and from Boston to Galveston, from the little log school-house in the wilderness to the towering academy in the city and the town, may be witnessed the unprecedented spectacle of a powerful nation captured by an army of Lilliputians, of embryo men and women, of topling boys and girls, and tiny elves scarce big enough to lisp the numbers of the national anthem. . . . Better than these we have nothing to exhibit. They, indeed, are our crown jewels; the truest, though the inevitable, offsprings of our civilization and development. . . . God bless the children and their mothers! God bless our country's flag!

Henry Watterson, 1892

Columbus day was a people's day. The leadership of the public school, the one institution which is close to all the people, brought the occasion home to every family. The consequence was a patriotic and thoughtful uprising of the people, such as America has not seen since the Civil War; a celebration less attended with noise and mere display, and more marked by seriousness and unanimity, than any other single day in the last quarter of a century.

Francis Bellamy, *The Youth's Companion*, 1892

The schools had long been the custodians of the Columbian legend, passing it on to each new generation of impressionable young people. In 1892, this responsibility was officially turned over to them. President Benjamin Harrison proclaimed 21 October 1892 the four hundredth anniversary of the "discovery of America," and he did so in June of that year, allowing time to prepare for the event. Harrison proclaimed a general holiday to be noted by public demonstrations and by suitable exercises. The people, he suggested, were to cease from toil and devote themselves to honoring the discoverer and appreciating the accomplishments of four centuries of American life. Why should the populace note this event? Because Columbus stood as the pioneer of progress and achievement. Harrison then seized upon the most hopeful and promising result of the spirit of enlightenment made possible by the activity of Columbus: universal free education. Harrison designated the schools as the centers of celebration. He ordered flags flown over buildings open to citizens for festivities. The patriotic duties of American citizenship were to be impressed upon the whole populace.[15]

This school motif was struck repeatedly. In 1934, when President Franklin Delano Roosevelt proclaimed 12 October of each year as Columbus Day, he again called on the populace to observe the day in schools, churches, and other suitable places. Appropriate ceremonies, "expressive of the public sentiment, befitting the anniversary of the discovery of America," were called for. Officials were to display the flag of the United States on all government buildings.[16]

The Youth's Companion, a national magazine for young people, created, on the initiative of the editor Francis Bellamy, a uniform program to be used in every school in America on 21 October 1892, simultaneously to be enacted on the fairgrounds. The *Companion* published the program, approved for use, urging readers to share it with teachers, superintendents, schoolboards, and newspapers in their towns and cities so that "not one School in America should be left out in this Celebration."

The schools were to assemble at 9 A.M., to be joined by a group of veterans half an hour later. They would surround the flagpole, read the president's proclamation, raise the flag, and give "Three Cheers for 'Old Glory.'" Giving the military salute, all were to join in the pledge of allegiance and sing "My Country, 'tis of Thee," which was to be followed by an acknowledgment of God through prayer or scripture. Then they sang an original Columbus Day song by Theron Brown, which spoke of the nation as a home for exiles where "Pale children of Hunger and Hatred and Wrong / Find life in thy freedom and joy in thy song." Next came an address prepared by the *Youth's Companion*, followed by an ode. After this set program could come "whatever additional Exercises, Patriotic Recitations, historic Representations, or Chorals may be desired." Programs with the set information were available from the magazine for one dollar per hundred so that the songs could be in the hands of all members of the audience.

A Young Columbus of 1892, from *The Youth's Companion*, vol. 65, 13 October 1892, p. 511, illustrates the model for brave and adventurous lads. The page featured games, riddles, dialogues, a story, an ABC, and poetry, all bringing Columbian material to a child's level. Courtesy, American Antiquarian Society.

The ode for Columbus Day was called "Columbia's Banner," a tribute to the flag by Edna Dean Proctor.

Uplift the starry Banner! The best age is begun!
We are the heirs of the mariners whose voyage that morn was done.
Measureless lands Columbus gave and rivers through zones that roll,
But his rarest, noblest bounty was a New World for the soul!

The address for Columbus Day, "The Meaning of the Four Centuries," was not attributed to an author. The talk used this celebration of liberty and enlightenment to praise the schools, the most important institutions for improving the past and the most trusted hope for the future. Universal free education was hailed as the cornerstone of the republic. The founding fathers recognized that the education of citizens was not the prerogative of church or of other private interests, listeners were told. Religious training belonged to the church, and technical and higher culture could be provided by private institutions. But the training of citizens "in the common knowledge and the common duties of citizenship belonged irrevocably to the State."

Columbus set this program into motion; to achieve real success he had to start with nothing. In the "virgin world" of the past, "human life hitherto . . . had been without significance. In the Old World for thousands of years civilized men had been trying experiments in social order. Their efforts had been found wanting. But here was an untouched soil that lay ready for a new experiment in civilization." The new order was created. "We see stalwart men and brave women, one moment on the shore, then disappearing in dim forests. We hear the axe. We see the never-ceasing wagon trains always toiling westward. We behold log cabins becoming villages, then cities. We watch the growth of institutions out of little beginnings—schools becoming an educational system; meeting-houses leading into organic Christianity; town-meetings growing to political movements; county discussions developing federal governments."[17] For the writer, this growth unquestionably equaled progress.

A later issue of the magazine reported a wide and significant response from the American people for the school celebration. More enthusiastic rhetoric noted that "America lifted up her public school system as the most characteristic product of her four centuries, and as one of the principal sources, under God, of her greatness." Public education would ensure the endurance of American principles, and as a pledge, the flag was raised "not over her forts and battle-grounds, but over her public schools." In this observation, which marked a lesson in patriotism, Columbus was honored, but America was celebrated.[18]

The schools had been charged to commemorate the day, and in New York in 1892, the school groups joined together to parade in honor of the admiral. About twelve thousand public school students marched in twenty regiments, each commanded by a principal. Some military groups marched with them, along with twenty-nine bands, each with thirty to fifty pieces. Some students marched in knickers, some in uniforms, some in their Sunday best with flowers in their lapels. All had drilled carefully and were of serious mien. All were determined "to do or die for the glory of Columbus."[19] It should be noted that few girls participated in this procession. The female students, who would presumably compromise their respectability by marching in the public streets, were allowed to participate in a more refined manner. Dressed in red, white, and blue, they were seated in flaglike blocks in bleachers along the parade route, where they sang patriotic songs and waved American flags to great effect.[20]

The public school division was followed by a group from Catholic schools and colleges that contained more than fifty-five hundred New York pupils. A large division of uniformed students from a variety of private schools and institutions came next. Such groups as the Hebrew Orphan Asylum with its minuscule drum major, the Barnard School Military Corps, the West End School, the Glittering Spears, the Italian and American Colonial School, and the Knights of Temperance of the Episcopal Church Temperance Society marched in formation. The Hebrew Sheltering Guardian Society Orphan Asylum wore grey suits with blue hats and carried American flags; the little boys could hardly keep them off the ground. The evening school of the General Society of Mechanics and Tradesmen wore quiet black suits and carried a banner that proclaimed the American message, "By hammer and hand all prosper." The Dante Alighieri Italian College of Astoria produced enough boys in sailor's costume to man a schooner. The Indian band from the school at Carlisle, Pennsylvania, accompanied the smoothest marching group with three hundred Indian boys moving precisely down the street. They were accompanied by fifty tall Indian girls wearing eyeglasses, who were considered to look "as cultured as the blue-blooded pupils of our most fashionable schools."[21]

Then followed the college division. These merry collegians rent the air with their songs and college yells. At least eight hundred from New York University marched to the music of a kazoo band wearing mortarboards. Between songs, they chanted "Who are we? Who are we? New-York U-ni-ver-si-tee." The College of Physicians and Surgeons had grinning white skeletons painted on their hats. The thousand students from Columbia College were led by a group of seventeen in tall white hats and snowy white sweaters, each of which was emblazoned with a large capital letter spelling out "COLUMBIA COLLEGE." As they passed the reviewing stand, the sweatered group saluted, doffing their hats and holding them to their breasts. The message painted on the tops of their hats was "WE ARE THE PEOPLE." Perhaps twenty-five thousand students of various sorts participated in this unusual procession, which lasted over two hours.[22] For all these groups, participation in this procession meant planning, drilling, expense, participation, and acclaim.

Many adults considered the school parade the zenith of the commemoration, for it added moral tone to the festivities. For Chauncey

DePew, the schoolchildren proved that America's intellectual and spiritual growth had been equal to its unparalleled material achievement. General Porter, in a strain of impassioned eloquence, saw the huge phalanx of schoolchildren, waving their flags proudly, as the way to teach patriotism. The minds of the students would be impressed that the flag was not only for holiday display but that this proud emblem brought "dignity, authority, power."[23] For schoolchildren, Columbus was a means of empowerment as well as indoctrination and social control.

The Sea Honors the Navigator

Ever speed on, O world-revealing Soul—
  Spirit of Exploration, sail anew—
Trace our broad freedom's soil from pole to pole,
Time's ocean-mist that veils her form uproll—
  Outline her shore of hope for universal view!

Henry O'Meara, "Columbus, The World Revealer," 1893

The seamanship and navigational skill of Columbus required a naval tribute, and on 11 October 1892, a parade of ships moved up the Hudson River. They were preceded by a broad line of twenty-one tugs, manned by white-uniformed volunteers and followed by a number of little boats and three large steamers holding the dignitaries. Then came the stately men-of-war of four nations—America, Spain, Italy, and France—which proceeded majestically up the Hudson River in three columns: twenty-seven foreign ships flanked by thirteen white-hulled American vessels. More people were afloat than had ever before been observed by human eye. Both shores of the Hudson River were filled with excited observers. The air was punctured by twenty-one gun salutes; fireboats spouted great streams of water into the air. When all the huge and fierce vessels were in place, a little Spanish cruiser, *Infanta Isabel*, sailed slowly up the river, proudly carrying the colors of Columbus and accepting the obeisance of the modern nations. Once again the mighty honored the lowly, recognizing the great things the intrepid commander had set in motion.[24]

Catholic Columbianism

As American Catholics we do not know of anyone who more deserves our grateful remembrance than the great and noble man—the pious, zealous, faithful Catholic, the enterprising navigator, and the large-hearted and generous sailor: Christopher Columbus.

Connecticut Catholic, 1878

A major theme of New York's commemoration was the importance of Columbus as a Catholic leader, an identity related to but superseding his identity as an Italian. Catholic groups were closely involved in all the events, and several peculiarily Catholic activities were scheduled during the week. These included an evening parade of United Catholic Societies on 11 October and a meeting of the Catholic Historical Society. In honoring Columbus, these groups were able to demonstrate their own impressive organization and numbers.

The Catholic Historical Society claimed the credit for instigating the commemoration. Organizers began with the idea of a simple eulogy, but plans for the event steadily escalated. A society committee waited upon His Grace, Archbishop Corrigan, to suggest their plans for the four hundredth anniversary. The archbishop communicated the ideas to prelates and distinguished laymen and to His Eminence, Cardinal Gibbons. Gibbons addressed an enthusiastic circular letter to the bishops of the country urging concerted action toward special religious services and civil celebrations as well. He suggested that united action would "enhance the glory of the celebration and invest the day with especial solemnity." Catholic groups adorned their cathedrals and churches splendidly, and many of them celebrated Solemn High Mass, enhanced by music and orations. Catholic participation in public processions and orations formed the backbone of events everywhere.[25]

The New York parade of Catholic organizations included four divisions set off with marching bands and all the trappings of a military parade. The first division featured twenty-seven different institutions of the Diocesan Union of Holy Name Societies; the second division, forty groups from Catholic Young Men's Societies. Division three was made up of members from forty New York groups of the Catholic Benevolent Legion along with members from four visiting councils. In the fourth division, thirty-five branches of the Catholic Knights of America were followed by ten branches of the Catholic Mutual Benefit Associations, followed by ten full parishes and members of visiting societies.[26] Since many marchers were immigrants and children of immigrants, this opportunity to unite the heritages of their past and future and to proclaim publicly their religion from such a position of strength was a potent experience.

This participation illustrated a well-organized American nationalism that could be called Columbianism. The movement was both militantly Catholic and proudly American, and it superseded ethnic backgrounds. Even as the Catholic parade progressed through the street the Catholic Historical Society met at Carnegie Hall. Archbishop Corrigan spoke briefly before excusing himself to go to the parade. He laid special claim to the celebration, noting that San Salvador, the site of first landfall, was under the jurisdiction of the diocese of New York.[27]

Columbus had sailed as the emissary of a Catholic queen. One of his major achievements had been to establish Catholic Christianity in the New World. The nineteenth-century American Catholics could read their own presence in America as the direct fulfillment of prophecy. Their prosperity and organization was the result of the Christian faith of Christopher Columbus, the answer to prayer.[28] They were also proud of their early missionary work with the natives. John Lee Carroll, former governor of Maryland, spoke of the severe trials of the early Jesuits, who, unlike others, were motivated by religion with no thought of personal gain. Their record on the Indian frontier was free from corruption, and he claimed that the Catholic missionary priest, bearing no arms but his rosary, was the only man who could influence the savage mind.[29]

This Columbianism was manifest in a whole genre of Catholic literature that used only Catholic elements to tell the familiar story. The important roles of Catholic priests, the miraculous powers of Columbian relics, the supernatural aspects of Columbus' guidance were stressed. The authors gave attention to the religious aims of Columbus: to gain gold for a Crusading Army, to liberate the Holy Land from Turks, to propagate the Gospel among heathens, and to live up to his sainted name, Christ-bearer. Religious hymns and prayers were included. One writer aimed to correct the Protestant failings of the otherwise admirable Washington Irving.[30]

These interpretations were generally told in such glowing terms of divine interference that it is refreshing to find evil powers lurking in one work. In Theodore Sydney Vaughn's extended poem, *Satan in Arms Against Columbus*, the demons dreaded a threatened invasion of their realm and desperately tried to bar the Church of Peter from reaching the New World. The picture of the demons luring heathens to lands that they then set adrift by sinking Atlantis is fresh and charming.

> Remember what it cost! remember how
> We labored to allure the fallen tribes,
> Forgetful of their God, to that fair land;
> And, far removed from people knowing God,
> To perfect more their separation, we,
> Beneath the great Atlantis digging, delved
> Until it sank beneath the mighty sea.[31]

Catholic Columbianism produced more practical lasting fruit in the organization of the Knights of Columbus. Founded on 2 October 1881 in New Haven by a young Irish priest, Father Michael McGivney, the group adopted the name four months later. The Knights organized for social, religious, and fraternal purposes, aiming to meet the needs of

Catholic men and their families. Father McGivney proposed to help his parishioners maintain their Catholic faith and to encourage close ties of fraternity, demonstrated through a mutual insurance system. Church officials assisted in creating the rituals that dramatized the values of charity, unity, fraternity, and, later, patriotism. Beginning with just six members, the group numbered over forty thousand by 1899.[32]

From its beginnings to World War I, the Knights aimed at asserting the "social legitimacy and patriotic loyalty" of Catholic immigrants. The Irish Father McGivney and his first members could have convened a Knights of St. Patrick, but anti-Irish sentiment might have doomed such a group. A previous attempt to organize the parishioners as the Ancient Order of Foresters had failed; the Robin Hood legend did not fit urban needs. Columbus was chosen as the figurehead because he represented the enormous Catholic contribution to the life of the nation rather than because he was Italian. By adopting Columbus, the Knights showed their pride in America's Catholic heritage. The name affirmed the discovery of America as a Catholic event. The Knights of Columbus adopted the first landing as a design for their seal.[33]

The association with Columbus was a brilliant stroke in creating a meaningful identity for the Catholic organization. In a now familiar juxtaposition, one Knight testified that the lessons taught by the life of Columbus were as "dear to the Catholic citizen as were those inspired and inculcated by the ideals and acts of George Washington."[34]

Catholic Columbianism was a major factor in celebrations in other cities. In New Haven, when the tenth anniversary of the Knights coincided with the four hundredth anniversary of the first landfall, six thousand Knights paraded with floats, thirty-six bands, and eleven drum corps. It took them forty-five minutes to pass the reviewing stand.[35] In Boston, the committee raised funds to procure a statue of Columbus, which was installed on the grounds of the Cathedral of Holy Cross. The large procession there was composed chiefly of Catholic societies and organizations.[36]

Before the Catholics took hold, no holiday honored Columbus. The organized Knights of Columbus began an effort in individual states to have him recognized. The Knights encouraged Columbian commemoration in many states, and in 1905, Governor Alvah Adams of Colorado issued a proclamation calling on the people to observe 12 October. Colorado was first to have a state holiday, in 1907, thanks to the effective interest of Angelo Noce, who was not actually a member of the Knights. Mayor Dunne of Chicago issued a proclamation in 1906. The

New York legislature passed a law in 1908 making Columbus Day a holiday, but it was vetoed by Governor Charles Evans Hughes, who was not convinced that it was needed and because of defects in phraseology. Hughes' veto aroused a vigorous protest. In an example of Catholic Columbianism, "Big Tim" Sullivan, a state senator who represented the Italian district in New York City, exerted himself to bring about passage of the bill. By the end of 1909, Illinois, Virginia, Connecticut, California, Massachusetts, Missouri, Michigan, New Jersey, New York, and Pennsylvania had named 12 October as a holiday.[37]

The People Celebrate

We may say reverently, as Christianity came for us through the son of a carpenter, so the invention which opened the way for christianizing the world was wrought out by a humble artisan.

Chauncey DePew, 1894

Across the sea yet still they come,
For work, for fortune, or a home
Whom motherlands have these denied.
Labor's sons still wandering wide;
Of every color, race & kin,
Columbia's favor still to win.

Columbia's Courtship, 1892

Participation in New York during the four hundredth anniversary celebration was intense. Among the entertainments gotten up during the week was the "Monster Festival Concert" under the auspices of the United German-American Singing Society at the Seventh Regiment Armory, where the prize cantata, "Columbus," composed for the occasion by B. Millamet was performed. A chorus of thirty-five hundred singers lifted the roof.[38]

The story of the American worker was part of the Columbian legend. Other nations had been demoralized by gold, but fortunately North America had very little. Columbus founded there a greater treasure: freedom for conscience. His genius gave to succeeding generations the opportunity for life and liberty. When groups came to practice religious freedom, they found they needed labor, temperance, and thrift to get along. Rigorous life styles built character to brave war, rescind slavery, and maintain the union. The United States continued to welcome the farmers and artisans of other nations, eager to escape from oppression or to better their lives through hard work. This kind of wealth enriched without enervating, stimulating invention, promoting progress, founding institutions of learning, building homes for the many, and increasing the happiness of all. All these blessings of wholesome life for the American worker followed the discovery of Columbus.[39]

It was fitting that the people should act out their appreciation for the gift given them. On the fifth day of the New York celebration on 12 October 1892, all business was suspended. The public was wakened by church bells and cannons. Every incoming boat disgorged a crowd of visitors. Seats to hold sixty-four thousand persons were erected along the six-mile route of the military parade, and almost all those were sold and occupied by nine in the morning. Every barrel, box, or other item that could be sat or stood upon was requisitioned into use. A million people sat all day on narrow pineboards, their backs against the knees of the people behind them. Another million sat or stood on the sidewalks or streets. Many in the crowds could not see a thing, yet there they all were.[40]

Deafening applause greeted each unit in the Columbian parade. The mounted governors of New Jersey, Pennsylvania, and Connecticut each rode at the head of their state troops. Mounted aides preceded large contingents of the army and all those who had sailed in on ships the preceding day, as well as ceremonial units visiting in town. These were followed by a huge contingent of Civil War veterans, representing fifty-six different posts of the Grand Army of the Republic. Next came twelve hundred uniformed letter carriers, followed by several fire companies with their hooks and ladders. Hundreds of firefighters were included. These representatives of the local and national governments were followed by ethnic groups.

Diverse ethnic groups of the city were welded together to honor Columbus. He was for all Americans, relieving the tensions that separated groups. Ethnic organizations were able to combine their ethnic and American identities under the banner of Columbus, the first immigrant. These groups marched in their uniforms, accompanied by their bands, displaying their numbers and their pride. Many companies of Italian military organizations were followed by German American societies, including the German American Shooting Society and the New York Turners. Some of the independent ethnic organizations were the Ancient Order of Foresters in America, the Deutsche Landvehr Verein, the Bohemian Organization, the Polish Military Organization, and the First Austrian Schützen Band. Military, social, and musical groups with members from Italy, Germany, Poland, Bohemia, Austria, and others marched with their bands blaring.[41] Participation in this parade amounted to a pledge of allegiance to the American flag.

Art, The Italian Connection

The Italian residents and citizens in the United States are conscious that the true monument of Columbus is this grand land, its institutions, its prosperity, its blessings, and its lessons of advancement for all humanity. Yet the Italians have desired to testify, at least to the present generation, their full and unfailing sense of their great and peculiar debt. They have procured, in contributions great and small, but uniformly large in spirit, the execution of this monument, and have erected and presented it in token of their affection and gratitude to this great and beloved country, the country in which they have found a permanent home, a more congenial form of government, and better and freer facilities generally to earn their livelihood.

General di Cesnola

By four in the afternoon, New York's military and ethnic parade had reached Eighth Avenue and Fifty-ninth Street. The procession paused to mark the major Italian contribution, the Columbus monument. Largest, best-placed, and most imposing of the American Columbian monuments, this statue was set on a high column at the entrance to Central Park. It was the gift of Italians and Americans of Italian descent. Addresses were presented by Benjamin Harrison, president of the United States, and Roswell P. Flower, governor of New York, before the monument was blessed by New York's Catholic Archbishop Corrigan. The Italian minister, consuls, and vice-consuls of the Italian societies and officers of the Italian cruiser *Bauson* were officially present. As Italian bands played and the artillery fired a salute, the monument was unveiled by Annie Barsotti, daughter of the monument committee's president.[42] Italian sculptor Gaitano Russo had created the eighty-four-foot monument in Italy and brought it by ship to America, yet another conscious symbol of the transportation of Italian culture to the New World.[43]

This sculpture was part of a much larger debate about public art provided by private sources. Some New York citizens had become concerned by the city's indiscriminate acceptance of public statuary and the installation of these works in prime locations. A group of these New Yorkers representing many artistic interests established the Fine Arts Federation to "ensure united action by the art societies and to foster and protect the artistic interest of the community."[44]

Park commissioner Paul Dana had earlier turned down two separate proposals for statues of Christopher Columbus: one from the group of Italian-Americans and one from a group of Spanish-Americans. Both requested the same space at the entrance to Central Park at Fifth Avenue and Fifty-ninth Street on the east side. The Italian-Americans were offered the prominent location at Eighth Avenue and Fifty-ninth Street on the west side, which they accepted and where they erected their sculpture. The Spanish-Americans were offered a site at the isolated end of Mt. Morris at 120th Street and Fifth Avenue. They refused this "second-class place" and never executed the project.[45]

The Italian sculpture at Columbus Circle served as a secular shrine for immigrants trying to find their place in the New World, a fact New Yorkers have commented on in discriminatory tones. After the Columbus monument was installed, the *New York Times* observed that the circle had become "a sort of mecca," where "troops" of the "swarthy sons of the Sunny South wander about the bit of marble, looking it over with the deepest interest."[46] This scornful tone was later outgrown, and the Columbus monument was adopted by the public at large while still serving as a hallowed Italian place.

The New York celebration had major leadership from two groups: the blueblooded aristocrats and the Catholic ethnics. The lasting monument that dominates Columbus Circle was erected by the latter group. Someone might wonder why the aristocrats did not unveil a permanent memorial that same day. In fact, they had hoped to dedicate a statue of their own, and plans had been underway for a decade. James Grant Wilson had seen a handsome marble effigy of Christopher Columbus in the Prado while visiting in Madrid. Fashioned by Spanish artist Jerónimo Suñol, the work was just what Wilson wanted in New York. He ordered a bronze replica for Central Park.

Wilson collected money from his friends. The wealthy and socially elite of New York with names like Vanderbilt, Astor, Belmont, Fish, Morgan, Gould, Schermerhorn, and Rhinelander subscribed at least one hundred dollars each toward the cost of fifteen thousand dollars.

The young king of Spain had promised to come unveil the artwork in the summer of 1892, but he died prematurely. The Duke of Veragua, who held the title descended through the line of Christopher Columbus himself, planned to unveil the work while in the United States for the Columbian festivities in 1892; but the statue was delayed in its journey from Spain by a steamship mishap. The duke was able to see the statue before he departed, but he could not stay to dedicate it.

And so the Suñol statue, similar but not identical to the original work, was dedicated in the Mall of Central Park in New York on Saturday, 12 May 1894, a little late. The New York Genealogical and Biographical Society sponsored the unveiling, and Chauncey Depew gave the address, hailing Columbus as "hero and benefactor" and saying that "Columbus was of that rare type of genius which belongs to no age, and rises above the errors, or superstitions, or ignorance of his period." Everyone praised Suñol's beautiful statue. The New York *Tribune,* snubbing the Columbus Circle work, noted that "New York has reason for satisfaction that at last she has what, to her shame as the chief city of the American continent, she long lacked, a creditable statue of Columbus." The heroic statue regards Shakespeare across the Central Park Mall to this day.[47]

Although Columbus has not been represented in such heroic size as the Statue of Liberty or with a shaft the dimensions of the Washington Monument, he has probably been carved and graven more often than anyone but Jesus Christ. As of 1892, twenty-nine statues and monuments were standing in the United States alone, most of them the result of Catholic Columbianism and Italian artists. Six more sculptures stood in Spain and seven in Italy. More rise every quarter century. The Philadelphia statue is an example of how the works came to be installed. At the Centennial Exposition of 1876, a statue of Columbus was exhibited by an Italian artist. Italian residents raised money to purchase the statue and presented it to the city. It now stands in Fairmount Park.[48]

Myth and Pageantry

Thou Searcher of the Ocean, thee to sing
Shall my devoted lyre awake each string!
Columbus! Hero! Would my song could tell
How great thy worth! No praise can overswell
The grandeur of thy deeds!

Samuel Jefferson, 1892

The theme to be illustrated in 1892 was the "Triumph of America," the idea that all history had conspired to climax with the glorious United States. New York's Columbian Night Pageant presented the history of the world, a vision of past ages and the giant strides of progress that have since taken place. Once again this demonstration was done in parade form, prefaced by a platoon of mounted police and a body of bicyclists five thousand strong. The story was told with banners and floats, illuminated by lanterns. The first floats featured prehistoric Americans, the Stone Age, the Toltecs, the Sun Worshippers. Next came the Victory of Genius, illustrated by Christopher Columbus and some of his fellow explorers, followed by King Ferdinand, Queen Isabella, and their court on horseback. A large model of the *Santa Maria* was drawn through the streets by sailors. Columbus was easily the center of attraction in this segment.

The next section skipped the settlement of the continent, featuring the Puritan Wedding of John Alden and Priscilla, Dutch colonists, and

Penn and the Quakers, each on a separate float. The focus moved to the nation with a float carrying beautiful daughters of war veterans of each of the forty-four states and George Washington with his staff, escorted by Frontier Scouts and by the Chiefs of Allied Tribes on horseback with groups of Indians. The next section dealt with the present, and the parade presented floats devoted to the Press, to Music, to Science, to Poetry and Romance, to the American Woman, to the Oceans, to Columbia's Ship of State, to the Battalion of Progress, and finally, as the climax, to Electra. The strange selection of themes probably revealed the tastes of available sponsors. But Christopher Columbus was the hero of the event, with electricity as the heroine.[49]

Light at night was featured in two evenings of fireworks. On the first, a Grand Cascade of silver fire fell more than two hundred feet from a tower of the Brooklyn Bridge. Even while the illumination was in progress, a telegraphic message written in letters of fire was sent by Morse Code from one tower to the other. The climax of the next evening was a recreation of the Niagara Falls in fire spanning the whole length of the Brooklyn Bridge, covering over five hundred thousand square feet with a solid waterfall of liquid fire.[50]

All these lush celebratory events extolled the mariner. Extravagant praise was the order of the day. But even through the adulation, some people were aware of the darker side of the story. The historical record included many negative accounts that contradicted the fulsome acclamations. Justin Winsor's critical book had detailed the human failings and the cruelties of Columbus, and these troublesome areas did not fail to emerge.

What of the Natives?

> You white men came to us as strangers, and we welcomed you as guests and as friends. You have gone on stealing from us, month after month, until you claim now to own the whole land. This beautiful land, which the good god of the skies,·gave to our fathers.
>
> Henry Peterson, *Columbus*, 1893

What of the native Americans during this massive commemoration? The Indian students from Carlisle, Pennsylvania, marched in the school procession, where they were praised for smooth marching and regal carriage. A model Indian school thus demonstrated the "civilization" of the natives. Characters in feathers and war paint rode horseback in parades or provided colorful backgrounds for a triumphant tableaux of the first landing. When mentioned at all, the natives were said to have benefited from the "discovery."

Baptist minister George Dana Boardman skirted the discovery problem by calling it a rediscovery. He believed that these American aborigines had come from the land of Eden, wherever that might be. Apparently, they had first discovered the New World. Boardman called Columbus the great re-discoverer of America.[51]

Educator Thomas Morgan wondered what would have happened if Columbus had returned to Spain and announced that he had found a new land and that a group of virtuous and attractive people lived there. These superior people, Columbus might have said, were endowed with the simplicity of nature so preferable to artificial refinement. Morgan praised the natives as communists who anticipated the teachings of modern socialism, and he regretted that Columbus and his followers took such pains to destroy the Indian civilization. Still, Morgan favored complete integration of the natives into white American culture, where they could become part of a richer, broader mainstream.[52]

Henry Peterson in his play *Columbus* of 1893 (quoted above), came closer to showing a sympathetic understanding of the native American position, but even his natives were subordinated to the white man's point of view.[53]

The Black Presence

Foreigners will naturally ask: Why are not the colored people, who constitute so large an element of the American population, and who have contributed so large a share to American greatness,—more visibly present and better represented in this World's Exposition?

[Ida B. Wells], 1893

If, therefore, the object of the Woman's Department of the Columbian Exposition is to present to the world the industrial and educational progress of the breadwinners—the wage women—how immeasurably incomplete will that work be without the exhibit of the thousands of the colored women of this country.

Hallie Q. Brown, 1892

If no distinctions were to be drawn in favor of the colored man, then it was only fair that none should be drawn against him. Yet the whole history of the exposition is a record of discrimination against the colored people.

F. L. Barnett, 1892

Black citizens were eager to participate in the World's Columbian Exposition at Chicago. They proposed to exhibit the progress of twenty-five years of freedom as opposed to 250 years of slavery as a tribute to the greatness and progressiveness, the "moral grandeur," of American institutions. They claimed they had performed half the labor of the nation and had produced a great deal of the wealth that allowed progress in education, art, science, industry, and invention. They were sure that any effort to present American greatness to the world would include their accomplishments. Here was the chance to show "not only what America has done for the Negro, but what the negro has done for himself. . . . But herein he was doomed to be disappointed."

The efforts of black citizens to be included in the fair were repeatedly rebuffed. President Benjamin Harrison named 208 commissioners and an equal number of alternates, none from the colored population. Efforts to have a representative named to the staff were declined. Suggestions that a Department of Colored Exhibits be organized were dismissed. An appeal to the Board of Lady Managers, which included a published prospectus of ideas and plans to exhibit the "evidence of thrift and intelligent labor" of black women's work, failed. The women's board had received petitions from two groups and ruled that the two factions made it impolitic to recognize either one. Individual letters of inquiry were sent to board members soliciting support for inclusion in the exhibits. Opponents to separate exhibits for black and white based their opposition on the principle that merit knows no color line. The black community was willing to be judged by merit but wanted representation on committees and boards to promote the work.

Some black people were eventually involved with the exposition. Hale G. Parker was named an alternate commissioner from Missouri; New York named Imogene Howard to the State Board of Lady Managers. In addition, the fair employed one male clerical worker and two short-term female workers. Any other employees were janitors, laborers, or porters. William J. Crawford applied for a position as a guard. When he was turned down, the doctor wrote on his application, "not on account of color, but because chest measurement not thirty six inches." When a disinterested doctor remeasured his thirty-six-and-a-half-inch chest and he resubmitted his application, it was ignored. The only official representation came when Frederick Douglass was chosen to represent the republic of Haiti.

F. L. Barnett documented and concluded that blatant racism was at work. Theoretically open to all American citizens, the exposition was literally, figuratively, and practically a totally white creation that the black American was not allowed to help build nor permitted any share of success.[54]

Speech, Speech!

Columbus is blamed for cruelty to his men. A commanding officer must sometimes be cruel in dealing with cut-throats, pirates, and mutineers.

Columbus, we are told, did not succeed in ruling his colony and in pre-
serving order. Possibly he was not cruel enough.

Herbert Baxter Adams, 1892

Orators strove mightily to find something new to say about the
mariner. Many succeeded. The orations were expected to be positive,
yet they also had to be based on respectable historical research, much
of which was negative. The resulting speeches contained some interesting modifications.

Many found in the deed justification for the man. Henry Warren
Childs in Minnesota admitted that Columbus had many faults, "yet
there still attaches to him, deathless as the mighty world he brought
to light, the sublime attribute of Discoverer of America."[55] This was
the approach of Herbert Baxter Adams: "There is a certain immortality
in a great deed, like that of Columbus, which makes the doer, even
though in many respects an ordinary man of his time, forever memorable." The deed, all agreed, was of the very greatest importance. No
single secular act could even approximate in grandeur the significance
of finding a New World on this earth. "The passage of Christopher
Columbus across the western sea, bearing the weight of Christendom
and European civilization, opened the way for the greatest migrations
in human history, for the steady march of enlightened nations toward
civil and religious liberty."[56]

One device used by several orators was to divide the heroic mariner
from the faulty human. The world did not honor the faulty human but
exalted the one glorified by the great exploit. The Columbus George
F. Talbot honored was the one to whom the world built monuments
and statues, not the one the historians disparaged. He honored the
Columbus of the great exploit, the Columbus whose faults were "con-
doned, expiated, washed away in the glory of a great deed for
science."[57]

Another standard tactic was to admit some of the faults of Columbus
while murmuring that he was only human and a man of his age. A
speaker could disarm critics by getting all the worst things out of the
way before ending triumphantly. George Dana Boardman, for instance,
admitted for starters that Columbus was ambitious, avaricious, cruel,
deceitful, despotic, and superstitious. (George F. Talbot described this
legal maneuvering as "confess and avoid.")[58] Boardman saw Columbus' worth in moral rather than geographical terms. Columbus was
wrong in his facts, but, though geographically mistaken, he was spir-
itually right. "If ever a man walked by faith, not by sight, that man
was Christopher Columbus." His theory was a fallacy, his discovery
was a blunder, but his faith was so sublime and dauntless that it enabled him to brave every discouragement.[59]

Some speakers still accorded to the admiral the virtues traditionally his. Herbert Baxter Adams intoned, "Something of the haughty spirit of Cortez and Pizarro was in this Columbus of ours. By all accounts he was noble and even kingly in his appearance. He could not be false to his royal nature."[60] Chauncey DePew detested the "spirit of critical historical inquiry which doubts everything." He did not care for the modern illusion-destroying spirit. He preferred to keep heroes who inspired patriotism.[61]

The speeches could be opposite in meaning and content. James Grant Wilson, president of the New York Genealogical and Biographical Society, spoke on "Memorials and Footprints of Columbus" on January 1888. He had made a reverential pilgrimage to Columbian shrines, and he was full of praise for the mariner. His name and fame were the proud possession of the whole civilized world. His act was more vast than any other in the world's history.[62] By contrast, William F. Poole, the librarian of the Newberry Library, spoke with a cool distance. The discovery was an accident, bound to happen soon, if not then. Columbus demonstrated little evidence of learning, of divine or supernatural influence, or of saintliness. He was just a person who had been injudiciously praised. After his first voyage, his life was a series of failures that abounded in shocking cruelty and brutality. Poole saw Columbus as a dreamer whose mind went to pieces in 1501. After that, he was an avaricious driveler.[63] Columbus was disparaged, even as he was praised.

Frederic R. Coudert, a lawyer speaking at the Catholic Historical Society, attempted to straddle the fence. Columbus had been praised and blamed, and Coudert expected that history would eventually judge him by neither extreme but by what he did and what he failed to do. His record of tenacity of purpose and unflinching devotion to a single idea was admirable, as was his courage in the face of peril. Still, measured by the standards of 1892, no accusations were too severe. The final question was whether he should be judged by the measure of his own time or that of his critics.[64]

And In Conclusion

How shall we praise him on this day of days,
Great son of fame who has no need of praise?

How shall we praise him? Open wide the doors
Of the fair temple whose broad base he laid.
Through its white halls a shadowy cavalcade
Of heroes moves o'er unresounding floors—
Men whose brawned arms upraised these columns high,

And reared the towers that vanish in the sky—
The strong who, having wrought, can never die.

Harriet Monroe, 1892

Harriet Monroe wrote this poem for the dedicatory ceremonies in Chicago. She delivered it on 21 October 1891, accompanied by a chorus of five thousand voices, before one hundred thousand people in the largest structure ever built by human hands, the building for Manufactures and Liberal Arts. Her poem does not name the "Great Son of Fame" she is honoring, but no one could have any question as to the identity of the absent hero. His name was hanging in the air over the entire globe.

Even Columbus, who thirsted for power and fame, might have been embarrassed by the outpouring of adulation evoked by his name in the nineteenth century. He would have been surprised to see these strange people, so different from those he last encountered here, singing his praises for virtues even he knew he did not possess. He would have marveled to see how his story had been reinvented for peculiar purposes. He would wonder at the multiplying effigies rising in his name when no one had bothered to record his likeness during his life. He might have failed to place his name upon the continents, but, four hundred years later, he had captured America's soul.

The enthusiasm for the admiral at the five hundredth anniversary of landfall is tempered by skepticism and laced with scorn. He will not be forgiven for his disregard of native peoples, and he will have to bear the full responsibility for the policies he instituted and the consequences from which he was exempted for so long. He will be blamed for squandering the opportunity of all time: the first meeting of two civilizations. When once he was considered too good for his time, he is now considered not nearly good enough.

Munroe's suggestion that the great one be honored by honoring the masses is as good as any. She favored opening the country to others coming from far lands and valuing the labor that had built the nation. Americans appreciated that spirit and continue to do so. In this way we can view Columbus neither as discoverer nor as despoiler, but as pioneer immigrant, as one who came first and opened the way for others.

One repeated theme of 1892 was that the great Columbus would never die but would live forever, honored and praised by each succeeding generation. The New World ignored him for the first two hundred years. On the three hundredth anniversary of his first landfall, decorous and dignified ceremonies marked the day. On the four hundredth anniversary, the business of the world halted to note his accomplishment. The five hundredth will show a new sensitivity and appreciation of the diversity of cultures. Some have suggested that Columbus will now begin to recede as an individual, with his voyage considered less of a personal achievement as we consider the larger forces of which he was a part. But Columbus is likely to stay with us for the history of our country; he is too useful to lose. All-purpose symbol that he is, he serves as a mirror for Americans, always ready to accept our praises and our blame. What we think of Columbus reflects what we think of ourselves.

1. The Admiral at Five Hundred (pp. 1–21)

1. James Oliver Robertson, *American Myth, American Reality* (New York: Hill & Wang, 1980), 32–33, 42.

2. Edward E. Hale, "The Results of Columbus's Discovery," *Proceedings of the American Antiquarian Society* 8 (April 1892–April 1893): 203–207.

3. Hans Koning, *Columbus: His Enterprise* (New York: Monthly Revue Press, 1976), 10–11, 119–20, 122.

4. Samuel Eliot Morison, *Admiral of the Ocean Sea: A Life of Christopher Columbus* (Boston: Little, Brown and Company, 1942), xv, xviii, xix.

5. Björn Landstrom, *Columbus, The Story of Don Christobal Colon,* (New York: The Macmillan Company, 1966), 191.

6. Alfred W. Crosby, *The Columbian Voyages, the Columbian Exchange, and Their Historians* (Washington, D.C.: American Historical Association, 1987), 24–25.

7. John J. Mazza, *The Discovery of America: The Columbus Day Pageant* (San Francisco: Privately printed, 1945).

8. Joseph Chiari, *Christopher Columbus: A Play,* (New York: Cordian Press, 1979), viii, 6–7.

9. Chiari, *Christopher Columbus,* 81–82.

10. Morison, *Admiral of the Ocean Sea,* 15–16.

11. William Robertson, *History of America,* vols. 8–10 of *The Works of William Robertson with a Sketch of his Life and Writings* (London: Thomas Tegg, 1824), 8:109.

12. Herbert Baxter Adams, "Columbus and His Discovery of America" in *Columbus: Modern Views of Columbus and his Time,* edited by Anne Paolucci and Henry Paolucci (Whitestone, N.Y.: Council on National Literatures, 1990), 37; Jeremy Belknap, *The History of New-Hampshire* (Philadelphia, 1784), 1, 2.

13. George A. Zabriskie, "Why We Are Called Americans," *New-York Historical Society Quarterly* 27 (October 1943): 85–86.

14. Robertson, *American Myth,* 7, 33.

2. The Historical Record (pp. 22–40)

1. Howard Mumford Jones, *O Strange New World* (New York: The Viking Press, 1952), 1–2.

2. Translated by and quoted in Samuel Eliot Morison, *Admiral of the Ocean Sea* (Boston: Little, Brown and Company, 1942), 231.

3. Benjamin Keen, ed. and trans., *The Life of the Admiral Christopher Columbus by His Son Ferdinand* (New Brunswick, N.J.: Rutgers University Press, 1959), xvi.

4. Justin Winsor, ed., *Narrative and Critical History of America* (Boston: Houghton, Mifflin and Company), 2:ii–iv, 67–68.

5. Jones, *O Strange New World*, 15–20.

6. Translated by Richard Eden in 1555, quoted in Samuel Eliot Morison, *Admiral of the Ocean Sea*, 382–83.

7. Richard Hakluyt, *The Principal Navigation, Voyages & Discoveries of the English Nation*, 2 vols. (Cambridge: Cambridge University Press, 1965), 703–704.

8. Samuel Purchas, *Hakluytus Posthumus or Purchas His Pilgrimes Contayning a History of the World in Sea Voyages and Lande Travells by Englishmen and others*, 20 vols. (London, 1625; New York: AMS Press Inc., 1965), 2:19–20, 31.

9. Cotton Mather, *Magnalia Christi Americana; or the ecclesiastical history of New-England; from its first planting, in the Year 1620, unto the Year of our Lord 1698*, 2 vols. (London, 1702; New York, Russell & Russell, 1852), 41, 53.

10. Thomas Prince, *A Chronological History of New-England, in the Form of Annals* (Boston: Kneeland & Green, 1736), 1:78.

11. William Stith, *The History of the First Discovery and Settlement of Virginia: Being an Essay towards A General History of this Colony* (Williamsburg, Virginia: William Parks, 1747), 3.

12. Lyon N. Richardson, *History of Early American Magazines, 1741–1789* (New York: Thomas Nelson and Sons, 1931), 123–29.

13. Ibid.

14. Sylvanus Americanus [Samuel Nevill], ed., "THE HISTORY OF THE Northern Continent of *America*," *The New American Magazine* (Woodbridge, New Jersey) 1 (January 1758):8.

15. Ibid., 10.

16. Ibid., 12.

17. Ibid., 15–16.

18. Abbé Raynal [Guillaume Thomas Francois], *A Philosophical and Political History of the Settlements and Trade of the Europeans in the East and West Indies*, trans. J. O. Justamond, F.R.S., 6 vols. (Dublin: John Exshaw, 1784). The second volume, Book VI, first published in 1770, covers the discovery of America and the conquest of Mexico as well as the settlements of the Spaniards in the New World. Henry Steele Commager and Elmo Giordanetti, *Was America a Mistake? An Eighteenth-Century Controversy* (New York: Harper Torchbooks, 1967), 122–24; R. A. Humphreys, *William Robertson and His "History of America,"* (London: The Hispanic & Luso-Brazilian Councils, 1954), 15–16.

19. Raynal, *Philosophical and Political History*, 2:409.

20. Ibid., 2:420.

21. Ibid., 2:425.

22. Ibid., 2:427.

23. William Robertson, *Works*, 8:iii, iv–vi, 61–181; Commager and Giordanetti, *Was America a Mistake?*, 139–40.

24. R. A. Humphreys, *William Robertson,* 22–23.

25. Ibid., 25.

26. Robertson, *Works* 8:63.

27. Ibid., 8:69.

28. Ibid., 8:73.

29. Ibid., 8:84.

30. Ibid., 8:86.

31. R. A. Humphreys, *William Robertson,* 25.

32. Robertson, *Works* 8:102–103.

33. Ibid., 8:120.

34. Ibid., 8:123.

35. Ibid., 8:132.

36. Ibid., 8:133.

37. Ibid., 8:160–61.

38. Claudia L. Bushman, *So Laudable an Undertaking: The Wilmington Library,* 1788 to 1988 (Wilmington: Delaware Heritage Press, 1989); Harold B. Hancock, *Delaware Two Hundred Years Ago: 1780–1800* (Wilmington, Delaware: The Middle Atlantic Press, 1987).

39. Spencer Bassett, *The Writings of "Colonel William Byrd of Westover in Virginia Esqr."* (New York: Doubleday, Page, 1901).

40. *Catalogue of the Books of the Columbian Peithologian Society Library* (New York: published by the Society, 1813).

3. Naming the Nation (pp. 41–59)

1. Albert H. Hoyt, "The Name 'Columbia,' " *The New England Historical and Genealogical Register* 40, no. 159 (July 1886):310.

2. Kenneth Silverman, *A Cultural History of the American Revolution* (New York: Thomas Y. Crowell Company, 1976), 214–17, 395, 494.

3. Julian D. Mason, Jr., ed., *The Poems of Phillis Wheatley* (Chapel Hill: The University of North Carolina Press, 1989), 87–90; Silverman, *A Cultural History,* 320, 284–85.

4. *Pietas et Gratulatio Collegii Cantabrigiensis apud Novanglos* (Boston, Massachusetts: J. Green & J. Russell, 1761), 106; quoted in Hoyt, "The Name 'Columbia,' " 310–11.

5. Ibid., 311.

6. Silverman, *A Cultural History,* 227, 320.

7. Martin Kallich, *British Poetry and the American Revolution, a Bibliographic Survey of Books and Pamphlets, Journals and Magazines, Newspapers, and Prints, 1755–1800,* 2 vols. (Troy, New York: The Whitston Publishing Company, 1988), 2, sec. 83:25, p. 1294.

8. Hoyt, "The Name 'Columbia,' " 312–13.

9. Cotton Mather, *Magnalia Cristi Americana; or the ecclesiastical history of New-England; from its first planting, in the Year 1620, unto the Year of our Lord 1698,* 2 vols. (London, 1702; New York: Russell & Russell, 1852), 41, 53.

10. Hoyt, "The Name 'Columbia,' " 312.

11. *Eulogy on Major General Joseph Warren by a Columbian* (Boston, 1781), is in the collection of the Huntington Library.

12. Fred Lewis Pattee, ed., *The Poems of Philip Freneau* (New York: Russell & Russell, Inc., 1963), 1:142–52; Silverman, *A Cultural History,* 320.

13. Philip Freneau, "A Voyage to Boston," in Frank Moore, ed., *Illustrated Ballad History of the American Revolution, 1765–1783* (New York: Johnson, Wilson & Company, 1876), 1:179–96, quotation p. 196.

14. Moore, ed., *Illustrated Ballad History*, 288, 295.

15. Frank Moore, ed., *Songs and Ballads of the American Revolution* (New York: D. Appleton & Co., 1856), 156–59.

16. Hoyt, "The Name 'Columbia,' " 312.

17. Moore, ed., *Songs and Ballads*, 385.

18. Ibid., 363–66.

19. Hoyt, "The Name 'Columbia,' " 312.

20. Mary Dexter Bates, "Columbia's Bards: A Study of American Verse from 1783 through 1799," (Ph. D. diss., Brown University, 1954), 85–86.

21. *Tom Paine's Jests* (Philadelphia, 1796), quoted in Mary Dexter Bates, "Columbia's Bards," 71–72.

22. "The Rising Glory of America," in Harry Hayden Clark, ed. *Poems of Freneau* (New York: Hafner Publishing Co., 1929), 3–4.

23. Clark, ed., *Poems of Freneau*, xiii–xxvi, 3–17; Lewis Leary, *That Rascal Freneau* (New Brunswick: Rutgers University Press, 1941), 34–36.

24. Edward G. Porter, "The Ship Columbia and the Discovery of Oregon," *The New England Magazine* (June 1892):370–71.

25. John Higham, "Indian Princess and Roman Goddess: The First Female Symbols of America," *Proceedings of the American Antiquarian Society* 100 (1990):part 1, pp. 45–79.

26. John Brougham, *Columbus El Filibustero!!, a new and audaciously Original historico-plagaristic, ante-national, pre-patriotic, and comic confusion of circumstances, running through two acts and four centuries* (New York: Samuel French, performed 1857), 13–15, 23–24.

27. Silverman, *A Cultural History*, 221, 403.

28. Charles E. Cuningham, *Timothy Dwight: 1752–1817, A Biography* (New York: Macmillan Company, 1942), 54; Leon Howard, *The Connecticut Wits* (Chicago: University of Chicago Press, 1943), 98–100; Samuel Bernstein, *Joel Barlow: A Connecticut Yankee in an Age of Revolution* (Cliff Island, Maine: The Ultima Thule Press, 1985), 40–41.

29. Timothy Dwight, *Columbia: A Song* (New Haven: Timothy Dwight College, 1940), n.p.; Caleb Bingham, *The American Preceptor, Being a New Selection of Lessons for Reading and Speaking, Designed for the Use of Schools* (Boston: Manning & Loring for Hall, 1794), preface, 44–5.

30. William J. McTaggart and William K. Bottorff, eds., *The Major Poems of Timothy Dwight* (Gainesville, Florida: Scholars' Facsimiles & Reprints, 1969) xi–xii, 3–4.

31. From *American Poems, 1793*, quoted in Mary Dexter Bates, "Columbia's Bards," 321.

32. Lewis Leary, ed., *The Complete Published Poems of Nathaniel Tucker Together with Columbinus: A Mask* (Delmar, N.Y.: Scholars Facsimiles and Reprints, 1973):127–28.

33. Elhanan Winchester, *An Oration on the Discovery of America Delivered in London October 12, 1792 Being Three Hundred Years From the Day on Which Columbus Landed in the New World* (London: Kemble and Arcutts, ca. 1792), 31–32.

34. "Prudence," *Columbian Magazine* 6, no. 1 (1791):54.

35. Bernstein, *Joel Barlow*, 139–40.

36. Another example of the linking of the names is described in Anne E. Bentley, "The Columbia-Washington Medal," *Proceedings of the Massachusetts Historical Society* 101 (1990):120–27. The ship *Columbia-Rediviva* and the sloop *Lady Washington* sailed from Boston on 30 September 1787, opening the triangular trade with Canton and the Pacific Northwest. The Columbia-Washington medal, showing the two ships, was to be distributed among natives for trade purposes and to commemorate the first "American Adventure on the Pacific Ocean." The *Columbia* returned to Boston on 9 August 1790, the first American vessel to have circumnavigated the globe.

37. Richard Snowden, *The Columbiad: Or, a Poem on the American War in Thirteen Cantoes* (Philadelphia: Jacob Johnson and Co., 1795), iii–iv.

38. Ibid., 43.

39. Jonathan Eliot, *Historical Sketches of the Ten Miles Square Forming the District of Columbia* (Washington, D.C.: J. Eliot, Jr., 1830), 320.

40. David C. Humphrey, *From King's College to Columbia 1746 to 1800* (New York: Columbia University Press, 1976), 270–72.

41. Charles Herbert Stockton, *The Historical Sketch of George Washington University, Washington, D.C.—Formerly Known as Columbian University and Columbian College. Read before the Society, April 20, 1915,* records of the Columbia Historical Society (Washington, D.C.: published by the society, 1916), 99–100, 103–7, 113–17.

42. Susanna Rowson, *Miscellaneous Poems* (Boston: Gilbert and Dean, 1804), 48, 50–51.

43. Dorothy C. Barck, "The Columbian Anacreontic Society of New York, 1795–1803," *The New-York Historical Society Quarterly Bulletin* 16, no. 4 (January 1933):123.

44. "LADY WASHINGTON'S LAMENTATION FOR THE DEATH OF HER HUSBAND," 1799 broadside from the collections of the Essex Institute, reproduced in Ola Elizabeth Winslow, *American Broadside Verse from Imprints of the 17th & 18th Centuries* (New Haven: Yale University Press, 1930), 60–61.

45. Silverman, *A Cultural History*, 486–87.

46. Anne Louise Heene, "American Opinion on American Cultural Nationalism as Reflected in American Periodicals, 1790–1830," (M.A. thesis, Columbia University, 1944), 32. These institutions were torn between allegiance to the new nation and models from the past. In 1813, the society was criticized for including old and imported paintings in its exhibitions when their avowed purpose was to create an American school.

47. Simon Willard, *The Columbian Union: Consisting of General and Particular Explanations of Government, and the Columbian Constitution* (Hudson, New York: printed for the author, 1814), 125, 484, quotations, pp. 126, 487.

48. Rowson, *Miscellaneous Poems*, 201.

49. [Jonathan Seymour], *Columbia's Naval Triumphs* (New York, 1813), 15, 41–42.

50. *Port Folio* 1 (June 1813):633–36; 2 (July 1813):94–95; quoted in Heene, "American Opinion," 31.

51. Rowson, *Miscellaneous Poems*, 178–79.

52. Vera Brodsky Lawrence, *Music for Patriots* (New York, 1975), 129, 204–9.

53. Ibid., 262.

54. Ibid., 142–45.

55. Ibid., 300–301.

4. Columbus in Poetry (pp. 60–80)

1. Leicester Bradner, "Columbus in Sixteenth-Century Poetry," in *Essays Honoring Lawrence C. Wroth* (Portland, Maine, 1951), 29.

2. *La Colombiade*, 1756, is the first reference to a Columbiad in the *Oxford English Dictionary*, 100:642.

3. Grace Gill-Mark, *Une Femme de Lettres au XVIIIe Siecle, Anne-Marie du Boccage* (Paris: Librairie Ancienne Honore Champion, 1927), 92.

4. Gill-Mark, *Une Femme de Lettres*, 160–66.

5. O. E. Bierstadt, "Columbus in Romance," *Magazine of American History* 28 (July to December 1892):275.

6. Philip M. Marsh, *Philip Freneau: Poet and Journalist* (Minneapolis: Dillon Press, 1967), iii; Leary, *That Rascal Freneau*, 19–20.

7. Bierstadt, "Columbus in Romance," 273.

8. Clark, ed., *Poems of Freneau*, 17–20; Leary, *That Rascal Freneau*, 44–45.

9. Adams, "Columbus and His Discovery of America," 70.

10. Philip Freneau, "Columbus to Ferdinand," in Pattee, ed., *The Poems of Philip Freneau*, 46–48; Philip Freneau, *Poems. Written Chiefly During the Late War* (Philadelphia: F. Bailey, 1786), 39–41. This poem has been edited somewhat in various versions.

11. Marsh, *Philip Freneau*, 34–35; Bates, "Columbia's Bards," 352–54.

12. Clark, ed., *Poems of Freneau*, 230–59; Leary, *That Rascal Freneau*, 46–48.

13. Philip Marsh, "Freneau and the Bones of Columbus," *Modern Language Notes* 60, no. 2 (February 1945): 121–24.

14. Joel Barlow to Buckminster, 19 March 1779, Henley-Smith Papers, Library of Congress, quoted Bernstein, *Joel Barlow*, 22; James Woodress, *A Yankee's Odyssey: The Life of Joel Barlow* (Philadelphia: J. B. Lippincott Company, 1958), 51; Silverman, *A Cultural History*, 403.

15. Silverman, *A Cultural History*, 519–24, 535–36.

16. Ibid., 519.

17. Bernstein, *Joel Barlow*, 185.

18. Joel Barlow, *The Columbiad, a Poem* (Philadelphia: Fry and Kammerer, 1807), x.

19. Woodress, *A Yankee's Odyssey*, 249–51.

20. *The Works of Joel Barlow*, facsimile reproductions with an introduction by William K. Bottorff and Arthur L. Ford (Gainesville, Florida: Scholars' Facsimiles & Reprints, 1970), 2:413.

21. Ibid., 417.

22. Ibid., 559.

23. Ibid., 697.

24. Ibid., 779–80.

25. Ibid., 357, compare 2:779.

26. Bates, "Columbia's Bards," 240–42.

27. Howard, *The Connecticut Wits*, 144–47.

28. Silverman, *A Cultural History*, 519.

5. The First Commemoration (pp. 81–97)

1. Silverman, *A Cultural History*, 579.

2. Ibid., 585–86.

3. Edward F. De Lancey, "Columbian Celebration of 1792, The First in the United States," an address read before the New-York Historical Society on Tuesday evening, 4 October 1892, *The Magazine of American History* 29 (January 1893):1.

4. "Constitution of The Society of Tammany or Columbian Order in the City of New York, established 1789," constitution revised and adopted 10 November 1817, Article II, collections of the New-York Historical Society.

5. Edwin P. Kilroe, *Saint Tammany and the Origin of the Society of Tammany or Columbian Order in the City of New York* (New York: M. B. Brown, 1913), 184.

6. De Lancey, "Columbian Celebration of 1792," 4.

7. Louis Leonard Tucker, *Clio's Consort: Jeremy Belknap and the Founding of the Massachusetts Historical Society* (Boston: The Massachusetts Historical Society, 1990), 76–81.

8. Kilroe, *Saint Tammany*, 132–35, 136.

9. De Lancey, "Columbian Celebration of 1792," 2; Kilroe, *Saint Tammany*, 136–37.

10. Kilroe, *Saint Tammany*, 185.

11. Ibid.

12. Ibid., 215.

13. *New York Journal and Patriotic Register*, Oct. 17, 1792, quoted in Kilroe, *Saint Tammany*, 215.

14. De Lancey, "Columbian Celebration of 1792," 6.

15. Ibid., 7–8.

16. Edwin P. Kilroe, *Saint Tammany*, 136–37.

17. Justin Winsor, *The Memorial History of Boston*, 4 vols. (Boston, Ticknor and Company, 1886), 4:27–29.

18. Kilroe, *Saint Tammany*, 184.

19. Ibid.

20. De Lancey, "Columbian Celebration of 1792," 8–10.

21. Charles T. Thompson, "Columbus Day One Hundred Years Ago," *The Chautauquan, A Monthly Magazine* 16 (October 1892–March 1893): 190.

22. Kilroe, *Saint Tammany*; Tucker, *Clio's Consort*, 59–98.

23. De Lancey, "Columbian Celebration of 1792," 4–5.

24. Ibid.

25. Ibid.

26. Jeremy Belknap, *A Discourse Intended to Commemorate the Discovery of America by Christopher Columbus; Delivered at the Request of the Historical Society in Massachusetts, on the 23d Day of October, 1792, Being the Completion of the Third Century Since that Memorable Event* (Boston: The Apollo Press, 1792), 56–58.

27. Tucker, *Clio's Consort*, 134–35; Edward E. Hale, "The Results of Columbus's Discovery," *Proceedings of the American Antiquarian Society*, new series, 8 (April 1892–April 1893): 190–212.

28. De Lancey, "Columbian Celebration of 1792," 5.

29. Belknap, *Discourse*, 25.

30. Ibid., 23, 25, 27.

31. Tucker, *Clio's Consort*, 40–43.

32. Jeremy Belknap, *American Biography, or An Historical Account of those Persons Who Have Been Distinguished in America*, (Boston: Isaiah Thomas and Ebenezer T. Andrews, 1794–1798), 123–4.

33. Solomon Stoddard to Joseph Dudley, 22 October 1703, quoted in John Demos, ed., *Remarkable Providences, 1600–1760* (New York: George Braziller, 1972), 312–13.

34. Belknap, *American Biography*, 127–28.

35. Thompson, "Columbus Day One Hundred Years Ago," 192.

36. Adams, "Columbus and His Discovery of America," 90–91.

37. John Marcus Dickey, *Christopher Columbus and His Monument, Columbia* (Chicago: Rand, McNally & Co., 1892), 75.

38. Ibid., 73–78.

39. De Lancey, "Columbian Celebration of 1792," 12.

40. Adams, "Columbus and His Discovery of America," 89–91.

41. Dickey, *Christopher Columbus and His Monument*, 75–78.

42. Adams, "Columbus and His Discovery of America," 92, 94n.

43. Dickey, *Christopher Columbus and His Monument*, 73.

44. De Lancey, "Columbian Celebration of 1792," 12–13.

45. Kilroe, *Saint Tammany*, 242.

46. De Lancey, "Columbian Celebration of 1792," 12–13.

47. Kilroe, *Saint Tammany*, 186.

48. Penmanship specimen in the collection of the Senate House Museum, Kingston, New York, reproduced in Kenneth C. Lindsay, *The Works of John Vanderlyn, from Tammany to the Capitol, the Catalog of an Exhibition* (Binghampton, New York: University Art Gallery, 1970), 142.

6. The Heroic Image (pp. 98–126)

1. [Christopher Smart, Oliver Goldsmith, Samuel Johnson], *The World Displayed; or, a Curious Collection of Voyages and Travels, Selected from the Writers of all Nations, In which the Conjectures and Interpolations of Several vain Editors and Translators are expunged, Every Relation is made concise and plain, and The Divisions of Countries and Kingdoms are clearly and distinctly noted* (London: J. Newbery, 1759), 1: xxx, 63, 88–89, 141–42.

2. *The American Primer Improved, For the more easy Attaining the True Reading of English, to Which is Added, The Assembly of Divines, and Mr. Cotton's Catechism* (Concord: N. Coverly, 1776); *The Columbian Primar, enlarged and improved: Or, an easy and Pleasant Guide to the Art of Reading, Adorn'd with cuts to which is added, The Assembly of Divines Catechism* (Boston: Thomas Fleet, 1799).

3. *The Columbian Reading Book or Historical Preceptor: A Collection of Authentic Histories, Anecdotes, Characters, &c. &c. Calculated to Incite in Young Minds, A Love of Virtue from its Intrinsic Beauty, and A Hatred of Vice, From its Disgusting Deformity . . .*, 2d edition (New Brunswick, N. J., Blauvelt for Carey, 1802), 19.

4. Monica Kiefer, *American Children Through Their Books, 1700–1835* (Philadelphia: University of Pennsylvania Press, 1948), 151; John A. Nietz, *Old Textbooks* (Pittsburgh: University of Pittsburgh Press, 1961), 234.

5. *The History of America, Abridged for the Use of Children of all Denominations, Adorned with cuts* (Philadelphia: Wrigley & Berriman for John Curtis, 1795), v, 10 quoted in Kiefer, *American Children*, 151.

6. *A Concise History of the United States, From the Discovery of America till 1795 with a Correct Map of the United States* (Philadelphia: John M'Culloch, 1795), 5–7.

7. Nietz, *Old Textbooks*, 234; Alice W. Spieseke, "The First Textbooks in American History and Their Compiler, John M'Culloch" Teachers College Contribution to Education, Columbia University, 1938, wherein the author traces all M'Culloch's sources.

8. Jedidiah Morse, *Geography Made Easy* (New Haven: Neigs, Bowen and Dana, 1784).

9. Harry W. Warfel, quoted in Charles Carpenter, *History of American Schoolbooks* (Philadelphia: University of Pennsylvania Press, 1963), 197.

10. Noah Webster, *An American Selection of Lessons in Reading and Speaking, Calculated to Improve the Minds and Refine the Taste of Youth, and also to Instruct Them in the Geography, History, and Politics of the United States* (Philadelphia: Young and M'Culloch, 1787), 103, 109.

11. Caleb Bingham, *The American Preceptor, Being a New Selection of Lessons for Reading and Speaking, Designed for the Use of Schools* (Boston: Manning & Loring for Hall, 1794), title page, preface, 39, 43.

12. *The Columbian Reader Containing a New and Choice Collection of Descriptive, Narrative, Argumentative, Pathetic, Humourous, and Entertaining Pieces, Together With Speeches, Orations, Addresses, & Harangues, to Which is Added, A New Collection of Dialogues Designed for the Use of Schools* (Otsego, New York: H. & E. Phinney, 1811), 44–45. The first use of the Columbian egg story is in Benzoni's *Historia del Mondo Nuove* of 1565, according to Morison, *Admiral of the Ocean Sea*, 361–62. The story had been told of others before Columbus.

13. *The Life of Christopher Columbus* (Philadelphia, 1837), v.

14. Ibid., 11–12.

15. Ibid., 32–33.

16. Susanna Rowson, *A Present for Young Ladies; Containing Poems, Dialogues, Addresses, . . .* (Boston: John West & Co., 1811), 130, 135.

17. Benjamin Tucker, *Sacred and Profane History Epitomized, with a Continuation of Modern History to the Present Time* (Richmond, Virginia: Jacob Johnson, 1806), 225, 231, 233.

18. Stanley T. Williams, *The Life of Washington Irving* (New York: Oxford University Press, 2 vols. 1935), 1:21.

19. Washington Irving, *The Life and Voyages of Christopher Columbus*, 2 vols. (New York: George P. Putnam, 1850), 1:xiii. For the edition by George P. Putnam of 1848–1849, Irving read and revised proof for the first time. This edition was recast, re-thought and redocumented and is probably closest to what the author wanted. Washington Irving, *Bibliography*, vol. 30 of *Complete Works of Washington Irving*, comp. Edwin T. Bowden (Boston: Twayne Publishers, 1989), 289.

20. Jeffrey Rubin-Dorsky, *Adrift in the Old World: The Psychological Pilgrimage of Washington Irving* (Chicago: University of Chicago Press, 1988), 221.

21. Wayne R, Kime and Andrew B. Myers, eds., *Journal and Notebooks of Washington Irving*, no. 4: 1826–1829, vol. 4 *Complete Works of Washington Irving* (Boston: Twayne Publishers, 1984), 10, 12–13, 24–26, 32–33, 58.

22. Williams, *Washington Irving*, 318.

23. Johanna Johnston, *The Heart That Would Not Hold: A Biography of Washington Irving* (New York, M. Evans and Co., 1971), 177ff.; Rubin-Dorsky, *Adrift*, 221.

24. Irving, *Life of Columbus*, 1:xv–xvi.

25. Kirkpatrick Sale, *The Conquest of Paradise* (New York: Alfred A. Knopf, 1990), 341–45, provides a critical appraisal of Washington Irving's book.

26. Ralph M. Aderman, Herbert L. Kleinfield, and Jenifer S. Banks, eds., *Letters of Washington Irving*, no. 2: 1823–1838, vol. 24 of *Complete Works of Washington Irving* (Boston, Twayne Publishers, 1979), 325–326; Morison, *Admiral of the Ocean Sea*, 9.

27. Williams, *Washington Irving*, 323–24.

28. Irving, *Life of Columbus*, 1:21.

29. Ibid., 1:27; 2:484, 485, 487.

30. Rubin-Dorsky, *Adrift*, xv–xvi.

31. Irving, *Life of Columbus*, 1:406, 418–19, 436; 2:109, 382–83.

32. Ibid., 1:21.

33. Ibid., 1:152, 155, 174–75.

34. Ibid., 1:266–69.

35. Ibid., 1:276.

36. Ibid., 1:55.

37. Ibid., 1:277.

38. Ibid., 1:346–47, 2:40–41.

39. Ibid., 2:198.

40. Ibid., 2:26–27.

41. Ibid., 2:187–229, quotation on p. 210.

42. Ibid., 1:116, 222; quotation on 2:294, 451.

43. Ibid., 2:490.

44. Ibid., 2:492.

45. Ibid., 2:425–27.

46. Ibid., 2:428, 434, 437.

47. Ibid., 2:446–47, 450–51.

48. Ibid., 1:222; 2:147–48, 338, 485.

49. Ibid., 2:260, 485, 487, 490.

50. Haskell Springer, *Washington Irving: A Reference Guide* (Boston, G. K. Hall & Co., 1976), 21–23. The references for individual reviews follow in order: *Kaleidoscope* 8 (12 February 1828):265–67; *London Weekly Review* 2 (16 February 1828):97–99, (23 February 1828):115–17; *New York Mirror* 5 (22 March 1828):295; *Southern Review* 3 (August 1828):1–31.

51. Charles Adams, *Memoir of Washington Irving* (Freeport, New York: Carlton and Lanahan, 1870), 157–58.

52. Springer, *Irving: Reference*. Specific reviews are from *Monthly Review*, n.s., 7 (April 1828):419–34; *London Magazine*, 2d ser., 10 (March 1828):281–325; *Athenaeum*, no. 7 (12 February 1828):102–103; no. 9 (22 February 1828):131–33; no. 10 (26 February 1828):150–51.

7. Glory and Gloom: Columbus after Irving (pp. 127–157)

1. Lydia H. Sigourney, *Poems* (Philadelphia: Key & Biddle, 1834), 71–72.

2. The Architect of the Capitol, *Art in the United States Capitol* (Washington, D.C.: United States Government Printing Office, 1978), 413–14.

3. *The WPA Guide to Washington, D.C.*, The Federal Writers' Project Guide to 1930s *Washington* (reprint, New York, Pantheon Books, 1983), 137.

4. *Art in the United States Capitol*, 343.

5. Ibid., 346–51.

6. Kirkpatrick Sale, *The Conquest of Paradise* (New York: Alfred A. Knopf, 1990), 344, 347, 379.

7. Charles B. Reynolds, *Washington the Nation's Capital* (New York: Foster & Reynolds, 1907), 32.

8. John B. Ellis, *The Sights and Secrets of the National Capital: A Work Descriptive of Washington City in all its Various Phases* (Chicago: Jones, Junkin & Co., 1869), 69.

9. Ibid., 70.

10. Marius Schoonmaker, *John Vanderlyn Artist 1775–1852* (Kingston, New York: The Senate House Association, Inc., 1950), 9–10; William Ingraham Kip, "John Vanderlyn His Work and His Character," *The Kingston [N.Y.] Daily Freeman*, Saturday, 13 June 1931, taken from the *Atlantic Monthly*, February 1867; Review of *"Biographical Sketch" of John Vanderlyn published by William Dunlap in his "History of the Arts of Design,"* (New York, 1838); Dickey, *Christopher Columbus and His Monument*, 310.

11. Schoonmaker, *John Vanderlyn*, v, 2.

12. Lillian Beresnack Miller, "John Vanderlyn and the Business of Art," *New York History* 32, no. 1 (January 1951): 33–44.

13. Schoonmaker, *John Vanderlyn*, v.

14. Sale, *The Conquest of Paradise*, 347.

15. *Landing of Columbus in the New World, in* 1492 (ca. 1846), 2, 3, 7; compare to Washington Irving, *The Life and Voyages of Christopher Columbus* (New York: G. & C. & H. Carvill, 1829), 73–75.

16. Allan Nevins, ed., *The Diary of Philip Hone, 1828–1852*, 2 vols. (New York: Dodd, Mead & Co., 1927), 776 (20 October 1846).

17. Néstor Ponce de León, *The Columbus Gallery: The "Discoverer of the New World" as represented in Portraits, Monuments, Statues, Medals and Paintings* (New York: N. Ponce de León, 1893), 153.

18. Kenneth C. Lindsay, *The Works of John Vanderlyn, From Tammany to the Capitol*, the catalog of an exhibition, Binghamton, New York: University Art Gallery, 1970, p. 74.

19. *Art in the United States Capitol*, 295.

20. Ibid., 304–11.

21. Ibid., 334.

22. Ibid., 338.

23. *The WPA Guide to Washington, D.C.*, 142; *Art in the United States Capitol*, 155, 158.

24. Dickey, *Christopher Columbus and His Monument*, 311.

25. *Art in the United States Capitol*, 353, 356, 361, 413.

26. Néstor Ponce de León, *The Columbus Gallery* (New York: N. Ponce de León, 1893), 125.

27. James Buchanan, quoted in Vivien Green Fryd, "Two Sculptures for the Capitol: Horatio Greenough's *Rescue* and Luigi Persico's *Discovery of America*," *American Art Journal* 19, no. 2 (1987): 20.

28. Fryd, "Two Sculptures for the Capitol," 17, 20, 21.

29. Ibid., 24.

30. Ibid., 17; *Art in the United States Capitol*, 353, 356, 361, 413.

31. John A. Nietz, *The Evolution of American Secondary School Textbooks* (Rutland, Vermont: Charles E. Tuttle Company, 1966), 241–42.

32. *Early American Textbooks, 1775–1900, A Catalog of the Titles Held by the Educational Research Library* (Washington, D.C.: U.S. Department of Education, 1985), xi.

33. Charles Augustus Goodrich, *The Child's History of the United States*, 31st ed. (Philadelphia: H. Cowperthwait & Co., 1855); quotation from *Early American Textbooks*, 1775–1900, 180.

34. Charles A. Goodrich, *A History of the United States of America; from The Discovery of the Continent by Christopher Columbus, to the Present Time* (Hartford: H. F. Sumner & Co., 1833), 16, 42–43.

35. Charles A. Goodrich, *Great Events in the History of North and South America; from the Alleged Discovery of the Continent by the Northmen, in the Tenth Century to the Present Time* (Hartford: House & Brown, 1851), 25.

36. Samuel G. Goodrich, *The First Book of History for Children and Youth* (New York: Collins and Hannay, 1831).

37. Peter Parley [Samuel Griswold Goodrich], *Tales About America and Australia* (London: Darton and Clark, (ca. 1842), 1–2, 10–11, 30, 51, 55, 71.

38. *The Stories of Great Men* (Boston, 1895), 10, 35–36.

39. Emma Willard, *History of the United States, or, Republic of America* (New York: A. S. Barnes & Co., 1848), 3; Nina Baym, "Women and the Republic: Emma Willard's Rhetoric of History," *American Quarterly* 43, no. 1 (March 1991):4–6.

40. Joachim Heinrich Campe, *Columbus, or The Discovery of America; as Related by a Father to his Children*, trans. Elizabeth Helme (Boston, 1826), iii–iv, vi. Several editions were published between 1826 and 1840.

41. Ibid., 87.

42. Ibid., 136–37, 141–42.

43. [Eliza Robbins], *Tales from American History* (New York: William Burgess, 1829), 11, 12.

44. Ibid., 32.

45. Ibid., 91.

46. Ibid., 108, 151–52.

47. Sarah E. Bradford, *The Story of Columbus, Simplified for the Young Folks* (New York, 1863), vi, vii.

48. Sarah Knowles Bolton, *Famous Voyagers and Explorers* (New York: Thomas Y. Crowell & Co. [1893]), 72; Elbridge Streeter Brooks, *The True Story of Christopher Columbus* (Boston: Lothrop, Lee and Shepard Co., 1892), 187.

49. Justin Winsor, *Christopher Columbus and How He Received and Imparted the Spirit of Discovery* (Boston: Houghton, Mifflin and Company, 1891), 58, 501.

50. George Bancroft, *History of the United States of America, From The Discovery of the Continent*, revised 1885 (reprint, Port Washington, N.Y.: Kennikat Press, Inc., 1967), 1:3, 8, 11, 13.

51. J. J. Barry, *The Life of Christopher Columbus, compiled from the French of Roselly De Lorgues* (Boston: P. Donahoe, 1869), 552, 565, 569, 573, 595.

52. Edward Everett Hale, *The Life of Christopher Columbus* (Chicago: G. L. Howe & Co., 1891), 285.

53. Aaron Goodrich, *A History of the Character and Achievements of the So-Called Christopher Columbus* (New York: D. Appleton and Company, 1874), v, vii, 351, 355, 367; Winsor, *Columbus*, 59, 60, 504.

54. Quoted in Dickey, *Christopher Columbus and His Monuments*, 80. Other studies treating Columbus in English in this period include Arthur Helps, *Christopher Columbus* (London: J. M. Dext & Sons, Ltd, 1910), which primarily treats the Spanish Conquest and its results; and Richard Henry Major, *Select Letters of Columbus* (London: Hakluyt Society, 1870).

55. Winsor, *Columbus*, 44–46, 59, 503.

56. Henry P. Biggar, "The New Columbus," *Annual Report of the American Historical Association for the Year* 1912 (Washington, D.C., 1914), 95–105; Morison, *Admiral of the Ocean Sea*, 55, 106.

57. Dumas Malone, ed., *Dictionary of American Biography* (New York: Charles Scribner's Sons, 1943), 20:403–404.

58. Winsor, *Columbus*, 84.

59. Ibid., 60.

60. Ibid., 220–21, 230, 281, 311, 506.

61. Ibid., 311–12, 314–15, 506–507.

62. Ibid., 499–500, 507–10.

63. Ibid., 510, 512.

8. The Admiral Enthroned (pp. 158–190)

1. Lenor R. Lohr, "Exhibitions and Fairs," *Encyclopaedia Britannica* (Chicago, Encyclopaedia Britannica, Inc., 1958), 8:965–67.

2. Reid Badger, *The Great American Fair: The World's Columbian Exposition and American Culture* (Chicago: Nelson Hall, 1979), 44–52.

3. Reid Badger, *The Great American Fair*, 44–52; Joseph Kirkland, "The World's Columbian Exposition, Its Cost and Resources," *The Chautauguan: A Monthly Magazine*, 16 (October 1892–March 1893):268–71.

4. *The Columbian Souvenir Album: A Memento of the World's Fair* (Boston: The Art Souvenir Company, 1892), introduction.

5. Kirkland, "The World's Columbian Exposition," 268–71.

6. Charles Worthington, "Our Government Exhibit at the World's Fair," and Richard Lee Fearn, "Exhibits of the Nations," *The Chautauquan, A Monthly Magazine* 16 (October 1892–March 1893): 393–98, 651–57.

7. William Eleroy Curtis, *Christopher Columbus: His Portraits and His Monuments* (Chicago: The W. H. Lowdermilk Co., 1893), 72; *Columbian Exposition Album Containing Views of the Grounds, Main and State Buildings, Statuary, Architectural Details, Interiors, Plaisance, Scenes, and Other Interesting Objects which have Place at the World's Columbian Exposition* (Chicago: Rand, McNally and Co., 1893), 12, 13, 14.

8. The Catholic Club of New York and the United States Catholic Historical Society, *Columbus Memorial Volume* (New York: Benziger Brothers, 1893), vii––viii.

9. Roswell Flower, "New York's Great Object Lesson," *Magazine of American History* 28 (November 1892), 5, 321, 326.

10. *Some Suggestions for the Exterior Decoration of Dwelling Houses, Clubs, and Hotels by the Committee on Art for the Columbian Celebration, New York, October 8, 9, 10, 11, 12, 13, 1892, Perry Belmont, Chairman, New York, 1892; Flower, "Object Lesson," 326.

11. Flower "Object Lesson," 326.

12. Ibid., 328.

13. *Official Souvenir Programme, New York Columbian Celebration, October 8th to 15th, 1892* (New York: Brentano's in Union Square, 1892), 5.

14. Flower, "Object Lesson," 329.

15. Henry B. Carrington, ed., *Columbian Selections: American Patriotism, For Home and School* (Philadelphia: J. B. Lippincott Company, 1892), 27–28.

16. Hilah Paulmier and Robert Haven Schauffler, *Columbus Day* (New York: Dodd, Mead & Company, 1938), 259–60.

17. *The Youth's Companion* 65 (8 September 1892): 446–47.

18. Ibid., 17 November 1892, 608.

19. Flower, "Object Lesson," 330.

20. Ibid., 334–35.

21. *Souvenir Programme*, 7–13; Flower, "Object Lesson," 331–33.

22. Flower, "Object Lesson," 333–35.

23. Ibid., 336–37, 345.

24. *Souvenir Programme*, 13–15; Flower, "Object Lesson," 337–39; *Illustrated Programme and Descriptive Souvenir of the International Naval Review, New York Bay, April 27th, 1893* (New York, Nevius & Kane, 1831).

25. *Columbus Memorial Volume*, x, xi. This commemorative subscription volume with heavy, deckle-edged pages, crimson crested binding, and engravings protected by onion-skin is in itself an example of Columbianism.

26. *Souvenir Programme*, 17–20.

27. Flower, "Object Lesson," 339–40; *Columbus Memorial Volume*, 7–8.

28. Jay P. Dolan, *The American Catholic Experience: A History from Colonial Times to the Present* (Garden City, New York: Doubleday and Co., Inc., 1985), 15–17; *Columbus Memorial Volume*, 4.

29. *Columbus Memorial Volume*, 15.

30. See Arthur George Knight, *The Life of Christopher Columbus* (New York: The Catholic Publication Society, 1877), vii, xi, 220–31; Thomas F. Coakley, *The Discovery of America, A Pageant*, illus. by J. Woodman Thompson (n.p., 1917), 5–7, 21, 55.

31. Theodore Sydney Vaughn, *Satan in Arms Against Columbus* (Chicago: J. S. Hyland & Company, 1892), 16, 20.

32. Dolan, *American Catholic Experience*, 257–58; Elmer von Feldt, "Knights of Columbus: Service in Peace and War," in *Catholics in America, 1776–1976*, ed. Robert Trisco (Washington, D.C.: National Conference of Catholic Bishops, 1976), 189–91; Christopher J. Kauffman, *Faith and Fraternalism: The History of the Knights of Columbus 1882–1982* (New York: Harper & Row, 1982), 1.

33. Kauffmann, *Faith and Fraternalism*, xii, xiii, 1, 16, 17, 28.

34. Maurice Francis Egan and John B. Kennedy, *The Knights of Columbus in Peace and War*, 2 vols. (New Haven: Knights of Columbus, 1920), 1:47.

35. Kauffmann, *Faith and Fraternalism*, 80.

36. *A Memorial of Christopher Columbus From the City of Boston in Honor of His Discovery of America* (Boston: City Council, 1893), 15, 17.

37. Egan and Kennedy, *Knights of Columbus*, 181–91; Paulmier and Schauffler, *Columbus Day*.

38. *Souvenir Programme*, 59.

39. Chauncey M. Depew, *Address at the Unveiling of the Statue of Columbus in Central Park, New York, May 12, 1894* (New York: Edwin C. Lockwood, n.d.), 8–12.

40. Flower "Object Lesson," 340–43.

41. *Souvenir Programme*, 24–39.

42. Ibid., 49.

43. William Eleroy Curtis, "The Columbus Monuments,"*The Chautauguan, A Monthly Magazine* 16 (October 1892–March 1893): 138–46.

44. Michele H. Bogart, *Public Sculpture and the Civic Ideal in New York City, 1890–1930* (Chicago: University of Chicago Press, 1989), 60–61.

45. Bogart, *Public Sculpture*, 61, 66, 334; "The Columbus Fountain: Spanish Americans Particular About Its Location," *New York Times*, 20 December 1892, 2; "The Columbus Fountain," *New York Times*, 22 December 1892, 8.

46. Bogart, *Public Sculpture*, 334n; "New Shrine for Italians," *New York Times*, 28 November 1892, 2.

47. *Presentation of Suñol's Bronze Statue of Christopher Columbus* (New York: De Vinne Press, 1894), 7, 11, 19, 25–30.

48. Curtis, "The Columbus Monuments," 138, 140.

49. *Souvenir Programme*, 49–52; Flower, "Object Lesson," 344.

50. *Souvenir Programme*, 53–55, 57.

51. George Dana Boardman, *The Discovery of America, An Address Delivered on Columbus Day, October 21st, 1892*, in the First Baptist Church (Philadelphia: Allen, Lane & Scott, 1892), 3–4.

52. Carrington, ed., *Columbian Selections*, 32–34.

53. Henry Peterson, *Columbus* (Cincinnati: Walter Peterson, 1893), 41.

54. F. L. Barnett, "The Reason Why," in *The Reason Why The Colored American is not in the World's Columbian Exposition*, [Ida B. Wells, compiler] (Chicago: n.p., [1893]), preface, 63–81.

55. Henry Warren Childs, "Columbian Address, Delivered before the Minnesota Historical Society, at the Capitol, in St. Paul, Oct. 21, 1892," *Collections of the Minnesota Historical Society* (St. Paul, Minn.: The Pioneer Press Company, 1894), 6:322.

56. Adams, *Columbus and His Discovery of America*, 8.

57. George F. Talbot, "The Character of Columbus," Columbian Quadricentennial, Portland, Maine., Thursday, Oct. 20, 1892, program, in *Collections and Proceedings of the Maine Historical Society*, 2d ser. (Portland: The Society, 1893), 4:22–23.

58. Talbot, "The Character of Columbus," 22–23; Boardman, *The Discovery of America*, 10.

59. Boardman, *The Discovery of America*, 9–11, 13.

60. Adams, *Columbus and His Discovery of America*, 29.

61. Flower, "Object Lesson," 336–37, 345.

62. James Grant Wilson, *Memorials and Footprints of Columbus, an Address to the New York Genealogical and Biographical Society, 13 January 1888* (New York: privately printed, 1888).

63. William F. Poole, *Columbus and the Finding of the New World* (Chicago: privately printed, 1892), 3, 5–6, 13, 15, 18–19.

64. *Columbus Memorial Volume*, 51–52.

UNIVERSITY PRESS OF NEW ENGLAND publishes books under its own imprint and is the publisher for Brandeis University Press, Brown University Press, University of Connecticut, Dartmouth College, Middlebury College Press, University of New Hampshire, University of Rhode Island, Tufts University, University of Vermont, and Wesleyan University Press.

Library of Congress Cataloging-in-Publication Data

Bushman, Claudia L.
    America discovers Columbus : how an Italian explorer became an American hero / Claudia L. Bushman.
        p.   cm.
    Includes bibliographical references and index.
    ISBN 0-87451-576-9
        1. Columbus, Christopher—Influence.   2. Columbus, Christopher—Anniversaries, etc.—History.   I. Title.
    E112.B95   1992
    970.01'5—dc20   91-50809